Environmental Management

Environmental Management

Economic and Social Dimensions

Based on Papers Prepared for the Second National
Symposium on Corporate Social Policy Convened
by the National Affiliation of Concerned Business
Students (NACBS) in Chicago, Illinois, October
1974

Edited by
George F. Rohrlich

Ballinger Publishing Company ● **Cambridge, Massachusetts**
A Subsidiary of J.B. Lippincott Company

Several papers in this volume have appeared in print in identical or substantially similar form in the following publications, whose publishers have graciously given permission for their inclusion in the present collection:

R. Lisle Baker's paper in *Environmental Affairs*, vol. IV, No. 3, Summer 1975;

Edwin T. Haefele's paper in *Managing the Water Environment*, edited by Neil A. Swainson, University of British Columbia Press, Vancouver, B.C. (in press);

Carl H. Madden's paper in *Virginia Quarterly*, Spring 1974 issue;

Henry M. Peskin's paper in *Social Indicators Research*, Vol. II, No. 2, October 1975, and in part in *The Distribution of Economic Well-Being*, edited by F.R. Juster, National Bureau Of Economic Research, New York (in press).

 This book is printed on recycled paper.

International Standard Book Number: 0–88410–421–4

Library of Congress Catalog Card Number: 76–2355

Printed in the United States of America

Library of Congress Cataloging in Publication Data

Main entry under title:

Environmental management.

"Edited version of selected papers . . . presented at the National Affiliation of Concerned Business Students' (NACBS) three-day 'second national symposium' conducted in October 1974."
Bibliography: p.
Includes index.
1. Environmental policy—Congresses. 2. Environmental protection—Congresses. 3. Externalities (Economics)—Congresses. I. Rohrlich, George Friedrich, 1914– II. National Affiliation of Concerned Business Students.
HC79.E5E56   301.31   76–2355
ISBN 0–88410–421–4

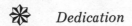 *Dedication*

THIS VOLUME IS DEDICATED

TO

PROFESSOR KARL WILLIAM KAPP

DEAN OF SOCIO-ECONOMIC ENVIRONMENTALISTS,

IN HONOR OF HIS 65TH BIRTHDAY, OCTOBER 27, 1975,

AND OF THE 25TH ANNIVERSARY OF HIS PIONEERING WORK,

"THE SOCIAL COSTS OF PRIVATE ENTERPRISE"

Contents

Chapter 5
Corporations as Resource-Allocators
—William L. Mobraaten   69

Chapter 6
Environmental Policies and Full Employment
—Mason Gaffney   81

List of Figures

List of Tables

Foreword

I am deeply appreciative of the fact that Professor George F. Rohrlich, in agreement with the NACBS, has thought of dedicating this volume to me on the occasion of the 25th anniversary of the publication of *The Social Costs of Private Enterprise*. It is a source of genuine satisfaction to me that concerned students of business are making the problems of environmental disruption, its social costs, and the related issues of corporate social policies an object of their discussions.

I am happy to comply with the editor's invitation to write a foreword to the present volume and I have felt free to offer a few observations on the substantive nature of the interaction of the economy and the environment as well as on possible ways and means of environmental control as these issues appear to me today after 25 years of rapid technological change and economic growth measured in terms of Gross National Product.

The degradation of the human environment by economic processes, and the resulting social costs in the wider sense of the term, challenge many concepts and theories which students of economics and business have developed for their interpretation. In fact, the theoretical and policy problems raised by the disruption of the environment cover the whole range of our past interpretation of the nature of economic processes (i.e., production, consumption, allocation of inputs, choice of technologies and location). Are these processes taking place in closed or semi-closed systems, as our models seem to suggest? Are they self-sustaining and essentially self-regulating systems which can be adequately interpreted in analogy to and with the aid of the equilibrium notions of classical mechanics? What are costs? Are entrepreneurial outlays adequate measures of the actual (real) costs? What are entrepreneurial returns? Do they cover the actual costs of production to society, and if not, how economical, i.e., how rational, are decisions guided by expected net entrepreneurial monetary gains? What confidence can we place in the market mechanism as a steering mechanism, not only for the allocation of scarce resources but also for the determination of the direction, speed, and qualitative content of economic growth and development? Far from being rhetorical questions, these are some of the fundamental and troublesome issues raised by the sudden eruption of the environmental issue into the foreground of public concerns. These issues will not disappear but may actually become more acute as we approach the limits of the assimilative capacities of different local and regional environmental media (air, water, the soil), and as we begin to experience in real terms the effects of the increasing scarcity of non-renewable and renewable resources. Depressions and stagnation may push these problems temporarily into the background, but they do not change their persistent nature. The environmental issue may still turn out to be the key question which will shape the future of the capitalist system and indeed of all economic systems.

The degradation of the physical (and social) environment has demonstrated that economic systems are open systems which are neither self-sustaining nor self-regulating. In fact, economic processes can be understood only as depending upon a continuous "exchange" of energy and matter between the economy and nature. In the course of these largely non-market exchanges, available or economically accessible energy/matter are transformed first into inputs and then into vendible outputs and partly into residuals which will be dispersed into the atmosphere, the water, and the soil, giving rise to qualitative and quantitative changes of both the environment and the economy itself. Inputs of accessible energy-matter are not inexhaustible, and the volume of pollutants cannot be increased indefinitely without reaching critical limits of the assimilative capacity of a specific local, regional, and even the global environment. Hence economic processes have the effect of continuously altering the conditions of the environment and of the economy. Under the impact of the market system and modern technology these changes of the environment and the economy may become cumulative with far-reaching negative consequences for the conditions of human health and life, and may even endanger the conditions of economic and social reproduction in the long run.

Viewed in this way, it should be clear that environmental disruption and social costs are not minor distortions or "external" side effects of economic processes, but are regular and inherent phenomena in modern industrial societies.

Environmental disruption and social costs challenge not only conventional concepts and theories but the whole pattern and structure of unregulated and accelerated growth and, by the same token, our current attempts and policies to stabilize the economy by traditional fiscal and monetary anti-cyclical policies. It is sometimes believed that the greatest dangers to the environment arise in times of rapid economic growth. We are now realizing that anti-depression policies designed to combat unemployment and inflation by stimulating investment, production, and consumption are being pursued without regard to their effects on the environment. In fact, there exists a real danger that environmental objectives will be considered as of secondary importance and may be neglected altogether in periods of depression. What makes these traditional anti-depression policies particularly problematical is the fact that anti-cyclical policies and public investment programs could be directed toward the development and introduction of alternative technologies, with a lower ecological impact (for example, through an appropriate promotion of research and development; or they could provide the infra-structure required to reduce the generation of residuals and the rate of extraction and utilization of available resources (for instance, by increasing the recovery and reuse of residual materials and, last but not least, by increasing the assimilative capacity of the environment by the construction of reservoirs to regularize and stabilize river flow, the reaerization of lakes, and the systematic construction of plants for the treatment and neutralization of chemical and biological wastes prior to their emission into rivers, lakes, etc.). There are good reasons for using, and in fact an urgent need to use, anti-depression policies aiming at economic stabilization and higher employment for the protection of the environment, either indirectly by fiscal policies or directly under public auspices, or both. As a matter of fact, such a combination of anti-depression policies with an environmental investment programme has been in operation—on a limited scale, it is true—in Sweden during the 1972 recession.*

The question may well be asked why progress in the field of environmental protection has been slow and why many policies and instruments of environmental control have not been successful. I believe the answer to this question can be found partly at the ideo-

*Lennhart Lundquist, "Sweden's Environmental Policy," *Ambio* 1 (1972):100.

logical-theoretical and institutional level, and partly in the political sphere of resolving conflicting interests. I do not think that conventional concepts, theories, and models are based upon an adequate understanding of the fundamental nature of the problem. For instance, conventional welfare economics, the concept and theories of "externalities," embedded as they are in general welfare economics, and the equilibrium approach to the analysis of the economy as an essentially closed system, cannot come to terms with the fact that economic processes depend upon an exchange of energy-matter between the economy and nature, and that these non-market interrelations give rise to changes of the environment and the economy with cumulative deleterious effects for both. Nor is it sufficient to base environmental policies upon the principle of internalizing social and environmental costs into entrepreneurial outlays in accordance with the "polluter pays" principle. Neither punishments nor rewards in the form of effluent charges, taxes, penalties, subsidies, etc., or for that matter the establishment of private or public property rights and the sale of permits to pollute, can be considered as adequate instruments of control. Their effects cannot be gauged beforehand, and their redistributive consequences are problematical and largely indeterminate. The interests of future generations are not represented at all in market operations and market values. Cost-benefit analyses as criteria of what is essential, desirable, and possible are hardly adapted to the determination of priorities.

In addition to these inadequacies at the theoretical level which, in my estimation, reflect an incomplete understanding of the substantive nature of the problem and an ideological attachment to existing theoretical frameworks, there is the political fact that environmental problems and the formulation of environmental policies raise important social conflicts. Powerful groups with vested interests in existing institutional arrangements and present technologies are able to exert strong pressures on public decision-making and regulatory agencies charged with the implementation of environmental policies. Neither administrative decisions nor regulatory agencies are immune to pressures and resistances by interest groups which may even inhibit and delay the successful search for truthful information by engaging in selective research, selective release of information and counterinformation, and denials and counter denials.*

Furthermore, scarcity of resources and the limits of the assimilative capacity of the environment place definite constraints on economic processes and particularly on economic growth. These constraints

---

*Ralph C. D'Arge and James Wilen, "Government Control of Externalities or the Prey Eats the Predator," *Journal of Economic Issues* 8 (1974):360–365.

challenge existing institutional arrangements, the efficiency of the market mechanism as a regulator of economic processes, and the whole pattern of unregulated economic growth and development. Nevertheless, it is not impossible to mitigate environmental disruption and social costs by appropriate, direct measures such as prohibitions of the use and disposal of noxious materials, the development of low ecological impact technologies and investments aiming at increasing the natural environment's capacity to assimilate residuals, and the development of new ways of recovering and reusing chemical and biological waste materials. The formulation of adequate environmental control policies and environmental planning calls above all for a clear concept of what is essential, desirable, and possible in the form of environmental quality standards or norms. This is anything but an easy matter and raises many complex questions of evaluation and public decision-making (which cannot be explored in greater detail in this context). Suffice it to say that the establishment of environmental quality standards raises problems of social conflicts, the resolution of which has to be found in the political arena, independent of the individual's revealed preferences, his willingness and hence capacity to pay, or a corporate ability to compensate ("bribe") those whose interests may be adversely affected by investment decisions. Effective decisions concerning the quality and protection of a common asset such as the human environment, upon which depends the whole process of social and economic reproduction, calls for explicit societal evaluations. To base such evaluations upon the utilitarian moral principle of maximizing individual "pleasure" or criteria of Pareto optimality would be equivalent to grant a veto power to individuals or minority groups and, for all practical purposes, would seem to imply a value-loaded (i.e., not value-free) ideological defense, and presumption in favor of the status quo. Societal valuations and public choices need to be based upon more objective and concrete criteria than the maximization of pleasure. Such criteria could be, for instance, the minimization of human suffering through a guarantee of the satisfaction of basic human needs.* This was my thesis in *The Social Costs of Private Enterprise* in 1950. The discussion of environmental management and environmental planning stimulated by the growing disruption of the environment which has brought the issue into the forefront of theoretical and policy analysis has not, in my estimation, produced anything

*For a more detailed analysis of the meaning and practical implications of this rule, see K. William Kapp, "Environment and Technology: New Frontiers for the Social and Natural Sciences," Paper presented at the International Congress of Scientists on the Human Environment, Kyoto, November 16–26, 1975 (forthcoming).

which might invalidate my original thesis. Problems of societal evaluation, social (use) values, and basic human needs remain fundamental issues in general; they are of particular relevance within the context of environmental decision-making, and deserve greater attention by economic, business, and social theory than they have received so far.

K. William Kapp
Basle, Switzerland
October 1975

Preface

The present volume, *Environmental Management—Economic and Social Dimensions*, is the edited version of selected papers from sessions on environmental management presented at the National Affiliation of Concerned Business Students' (NACBS) three-day Second National Symposium conducted in October 1974. The program on environmental management was planned and chaired by Hazel Henderson.

Originally a student organization, today the NACBS is a cooperative effort among business executives, business school faculty, and graduate business students. Incorporated as a nonprofit educational foundation in 1971, the organization's main objectives have been to promote research on the role of the corporation in society and to contribute to development of business school curricula relating to the business and society interface.

A companion volume, *Protecting Consumer Interests* edited by Robert Katz, is based on papers given on this subject in concurrent sessions at the Symposium and focuses on the most cogent aspects and emerging issues in consumerism.

Joining *The Unstable Ground: Corporate Social Policy in a Dynamic Society* (Sethi, ed.), a book published in 1974 based on the NACBS' First National Symposium, these volumes represent constructive viewpoints of university scholars, business executives, labor leaders, public interest advocates, and students concerned about the role of business in dealing with contemporary social problems.

Donald MacNaughton, Chairman of the Prudential Life Insurance Company has said:

Abundant evidence exists and keeps growing that the interface between government and business is the critical linkpin that will determine our nation's socioeconomic future.

Since we have a representative form of government reflecting the aspirations of a broad and diverse society, the NACBS believes that a reasonable inference from MacNaughton's observation is to view the business and society linkage as the critical determinant of our nation's socioeconomic future.

The pivotal importance of the field has attracted dedicated young professionals interested in the survival of a private sector and the health of society—in America and globally. Guided through its formative period by Kirk Hanson, who served as a co-chairperson for the Second National Symposium, NACBS' activities and programs have become widely recognized for their contributions to the field of business and society. Douglas J. Westervelt served as the organization's President and Executive Director during 1974–1975.

Recognizing the critical need to prepare today's MBA student for coping with the rapidly broadening social dimensions of management, 38 corporations currently sponsor the NACBS and make its independent activities possible. They are:

American Can Company
American Telephone and Telegraph Company
Arthur Andersen and Company
Atlantic Richfield Company
Bank of America
Bethlehem Steel Corporation
Borg Warner Corporation
Chase Manhattan Bank
Chrysler Corporation
CPC International, Inc.
Cummins Engine Company, Inc.
Dow Chemical Company
Equitable Life Assurance Society
Exxon Corporation
Ford Motor Company
General Electric Company
General Mills, Inc.
John Hancock Mutual Life Insurance
H. J. Heinz Company
Hoffmann-LaRoche, Inc.
Honeywell, Inc.
McDonald's Corporation
McGraw-Hill, Inc.

3M Company
Montgomery Ward Company
Newsweek, Inc.
Olin Corporation
J. C. Penney Company, Inc.
PepsiCo, Inc.
Prudential Insurance Company
Quaker Oats Company
Scott Paper Company
Shell Oil Company
Standard Oil Company of California
Standard Oil Company (Indiana)
Syntex, Inc.
United California Bank
Universal Oil Products

Special acknowledgment is due S. Prakash Sethi and Hazel Henderson, who, as co-chairpersons for the Second National Symposium, were responsible for arranging the consumerism and environmental tracts of the program and have contributed substantially to the NACBS in many other ways.

McDonald's Corporation provided funds to cover a portion of the cost of the Symposium, and a grant from the General Electric Foundation made possible the attendance of 40 students representing 27 leading graduate business schools. Their contributions are greatly appreciated.

Kirk Hanson
President and Executive Director
National Affiliation of Concerned
Business Students

Acknowledgments

Anyone who willingly takes on the chores of editing a book that consists of numerous contributions from many different authors must be convinced of the merits of his self-set task. To be sure, he hopes that the reading public will bear out his judgment and that ultimately, therefore, there may be a profit in the venture—or, at any rate, a net gain of sorts even if his own share of the toil is gladly given as a labor of love.

But at the time of the book's launching, at least in the present case, he senses most of all a substantial increase in his net indebtedness. Fortunately, it is, in the main, of the nonpecuniary kind.

First and foremost, I feel indebted to Hazel Henderson, this human dynamo, for her original inspiration and her continuing interest and moral support. I wish to express my warm thanks here in writing.

Next I want to thank the many contributors for their ready cooperation. Several had to obtain releases from publishers since (portions of) their papers have appeared elsewhere. To these publishers, likewise, we owe thanks. Their names are listed on the copyright page.

The officers of the NACBS, notably Kirk Hanson, the present President, and Douglas Westervelt, his predecessor in office, helped in any way possible, and with exemplary promptness.

The patient and understanding attitude of Geoffrey Gunn, Vice-President of the Ballinger Publishing Company, helped immensely all along. All this help is duly appreciated.

I feel an especial gratitude to Professor K. William Kapp for agreeing to write the Foreword, even though our request reached him in the midst of events staged in his honor on the occasion of his emeritation from Basle University and practically on the eve of his departure for Japan in connection with, inter alia, his participation in the International Congress of Scientists on the Human Environment, in Kyoto.

Temple University has provided me with manifold supports. Its libraries were a tremendous resource; and Robert Giesecke, the Business Librarian, unlocked access to various sources in imaginative ways. The School of Business Administration, notably through the resources of its Bureau for Economic and Business Research, afforded logistic support; none more helpful than that of Grace Tappert, who had the lion's share in organizing the manuscript, supervising, in part preparing, and checking the typescript. Janis Laurie, my student-assistant, helped with her ever-reliable typing.

The last bit was typed here, in San Juan, by my capable bilingual secretary-typist, Zenaida Ramirez de Arellano.

Leah Jackson did the copy-editing expertly and with lightning speed. The index was prepared by Elsa Dorfman.

To all of these splendid associates go my heartfelt thanks. Their work has been as good as is humanly possible; the flaws are mine.

George F. Rohrlich
San Juan, Puerto Rico
November 1975

Environmental Management

Introduction

George F. Rohrlich

PROMETHEUS TRIUMPHANT—AND AT BAY

Having stolen the fire from the Gods, according to the classic myth, Prometheus—man—has made the most of it.

And now we stand in fear and trepidation, as we confront the awesome consequences and possibilities of what we used to view as our evergrowing sovereign power over God's creation. Or, to shift our imagery to Biblical lore, having plucked all the marvelously varied fruits from the Tree of Knowledge, we have begun to wonder if the Tree of Life, within the gates of Paradise, instead of moving closer within our reach is forever receding so that not only life eternal but the gift of life as such may slip away from us. Mankind, at the height of its triumph, paradoxically, finds itself stymied and at bay. For, as has so aptly been observed, our most triumphant successes threaten to backfire. Many a "solution" has become the "problem" [1].

PREMISES AND ISSUES

What has happened is that over quite a period of time (yet imperceptibly to most of us) man—for all the continuing struggle to earn his daily bread by teeming millions—"no longer lives almost overwhelmed by the scale of his natural environment. It is the environment that is beginning to be overwhelmed by man" [2].

---

*George F. Rohrlich is Professor of Economics and Social Policy at the Temple University School of Business Administration.

The foregoing phrase was coined in anticipation of the Stockholm Conference on the Human Environment, which took place in June 1972 and brought together representatives from nearly all the nations of the world. Some of the best work of that Conference was done in its preparatory phase. Certain introductory observations by Maurice F. Strong, the Conference's Secretary-General, are well worth recalling. Referring to the task of environmental management, he dubbed it an issue which

> is moving out of the "motherhood" stage to the point where it is now being seen as one of the most pervasive, profound and revolutionary issues that man has ever faced. It requires us to confront such fundamental issues as the possible limitations to growth, the purposes of growth, the control of technology, the utilization of the world's resources and distribution of its opportunities. It points up the need for new attitudes and values, a re-direction of man's scientific and technological drives, a more balanced distribution of the world's industrial capacity, the widest possible dissemination of new environmentally sound technologies and changes in the organizations and institutions of society. And of special importance is the compelling new imperative it provides to the priority task of accelerating the development of the majority of mankind whose principal environmental concerns derive from their very poverty and underdevelopment [3].

In spelling out the components of the problem with which the conference would have to deal, the following premises were identified:

1. Man interacts with the natural environment through a complex system of relationships embracing the entire planet in which causes and effects are often separated by dimensions of space and time that transcend conventional geographical, national, and institutional boundaries. His life and well-being largely depend on a healthy equilibrium in this system of relationships.

2. Man's activities, based on the power which science and technology make available to him, now take place on a scale which makes them principal determinants of his own future. These activities have produced unprecedented levels of wealth for a significant minority of the world's people, but they also have produced serious physical, economic, and social imbalances; they have given man not only the technological potential to bring vastly improved conditions of life to all but also unprecedented potential for destruction.

3. Because man's future life and well-being depend increasingly on the choices he makes concerning his activities, he requires much better means of assessing their possible consequences.

4. On a global basis, the combination of man's increasing numbers and intensification of his activities is placing growing pressures on renewable and non-renewable resources, and these pressures cannot continue indefinitely without placing the future of all mankind in serious jeopardy.

5. Our physical interdependence makes a greater degree of economic and social interdependence essential for man's future. This reinforces the case for a more equitable utilization of the world's resources and distribution of its opportunities. It also points to the need for a more balanced development of the world's productive capacity and significant redirection of its industrial and scientific capabilities, including the acceleration of economic progress in the developing countries.

6. This calls for new dimensions of cooperative behavior on all levels—local, regional, and global—and more extensive participation in decisions by those who will be affected by them.

7. Developing countries, while increasingly affected by many of the same environmental concerns as the more industrialized countries, also face environmental problems deriving from poverty and their own lack of development, and from development they regard as unsuited to their needs. On the national level, these concerns can best be met by incorporation of environmental objectives into planning and implementation of the development process, and internationally, through increasing resources available to developing countries.

8. This will require re-examination of society's priorities, changes in attitudes and values, and in the policies and organization of the institutions of society. The ultimate goal must be to achieve a dynamic equilibrium between man and the natural environment which will allow the full development and expression of the highest potential of man [4].

Projecting these insights and assessments onto the realm of economic development and growth, the preparatory roundup concluded that

> what is needed as countries develop is a broader concept of economic growth in which some activities are adapted and re-oriented to place lesser burdens on the natural system and more emphasis on a greater satisfaction of non-material needs and values. Such a shift in priorities from the quantified goals which countries must pursue in the early stages of development surely would add richness, depth, and variety to the very purpose of economic growth—and thus exert a dynamic rather than a static influence on society [5].

Finally, but by no means least important, the fateful intergenerational question was raised in just a short but powerful query: "Dare we overlook the concept of a planet held in trust for future generations?" [6].

TOPICS, TREATMENT AND ATTITUDES

Needless to say, the NACBS Conference, on which this volume is based, could not hope to cover all this vast ground. Nor did it attempt to—though the opening statement by Hazel Henderson, the co-chairperson for the environmental sessions, covered many aspects, both in scope and depth. An excerpt from her thoughtful remarks is exemplary:

Today our industrial and technological mastery have allowed us to reach unprecedented population levels, but at the expense of creating an equally unprecedented degree of social complexity and interdependence. This complexity is now beyond the understanding of most human brains even when aided by the most advanced computer modelling capabilities and is, therefore, increasingly vulnerable to error, as evidenced by the mounting social and environmental costs and unanticipated consequences of techno-logical diffusion and interaction. Worse, our technology has permitted us to insulate ourselves from the natural systems which still ultimately sustain us, so that feedback from nature, which used to be immediate and incon-trovertible, is now dangerously delayed and incomplete. In fact, such feed-back, in the form of environmental disruption and social pathology, is often misread and leads to the application of yet another series of techno-logical fixes which further complicate social decision-making and add more variables to the Gordian Knot, so that we require almost "a breakthrough a day to keep the crisis at bay," in the words of economist E. F. Schu-macher, author of *Small is Beautiful.*

Willis Harman, in a recent article in *The Futurist*, has enumerated some of our new crises due to the very success of our technology and industrial development. They include overpopulation and the problems of the aged as problems created by our success at prolonging our life span; unemploy-ment due to our success at the replacement of manual and routine labor by machines; the dehumanization of work due to our success at designing efficient production systems; increasing air, noise, and land pollution due to our advances in transportation; information overload as a result of our communications developments and the increasing gap between the world's have and have-not nations and the problems of rising expectations, as the result of the success of the developed nations in expanding their wealth.

Jonas Salk, developer of polio vaccine, sees our current crisis in similar terms in his new book, *The Survival of the Wisest*. He points out that while humans were in their growing phase, increasing their numbers and techno-logical mastery, they behaved like other similar species in nature, multiply-ing as fast as possible and widening their own ecological niche by out-competing other species and gaining access to more resources. As their population growth begins to reach the exponential rate, it exhibits the familiar behavior of the S-curve: growth slows and the curve either slowly levels off, saturates, or crashes precipitously. As the curve reaches the "watershed" phase, Salk points out that all of the behavior that was re-warded in the first growth phase begins to be punished with failure. It is as if, like Alice, we have gone through the looking glass. Instead of growing, we must learn to maintain ourselves; instead of competing we must learn to cooperate with other species, our environment, and each other; instead of maximizing as individuals and subunits, we must learn the conditions necessary to optimize the larger social and ecosystem in which we are imbedded. This requires expanding our perception so as to understand that the new ball game for all of us as individuals and corporations is nothing less than that of maintaining the ballpark itself.

Some of Henderson's introductory remarks are taken up and further developed in the paper which she subsequently prepared for inclusion in this volume as the opening chapter of Part 1.

Most of the paper writers, however, covered but a small part of the wide-ranging panorama of problems. Even so, each writer's problem area seems overwhelmingly intricate. This is true, even where—as in most cases—the writer attempts principally or exclusively to explicate the problem, rather than purporting to solve it. Where answers are ventured, they are offered as targets for criticism based on deeper or newer insight, or simply on more complete or correct information, if and when it is available. As the preliminary UN report referred to earlier points out, "Of paramount importance is the transferring of existing knowledge to those who must apply it" [7]. But knowledge begins with a proper understanding of the problem. And in the last resort, at least in a democracy, it is the citizens as voters and, among them, those who in one capacity or another help mold the opinions of others, who form the link between (up-to-date) knowledge and its (timely) application.

Hence, in the following papers both the authors and the editor have aimed at presenting subject matters, as far as possible, in language which, while it permits the competent exposition of innately difficult subjects, refrains from using the professional lingo of any one discipline. Interdisciplinary understanding and broadening the horizon of students who specialize in different skills is, after all, the principal purpose of the conference sponsor, the NACBS.

Aside from avoiding disciplinary parochialism, we have striven conscientiously toward linking perceptions that are expressive of the variety of views to be found in our pluralist society, and at least in some respects representative of different roles played in our mixed economy. There has been no attempt to veil the paper writers' philosophical position or bias, or to edit out any sweeping formulations. The very fact that there were scholars—budding and accomplished, business executives—some on the make and some who have arrived, and spokespersons for labor and the public interest who collaborated in formulating the issues, and engaged each other in exploring the problems and possible solutions, bespeaks the absence of any preconceived ideological molds. Thus, there were no barriers to either voicing or comprehending both viewpoints and constraints that derive from one's station in society.

The fact that some answers, even though partial or conditional, could be offered which proved sufficiently acceptable to such a mixed forum to be listened to, debated on their merits, and, we hope, permitted to "sink in," is bound to promote understanding and cross-fertilization of thoughts across ecomomic, occupational, and other societal divides. In this respect, viz., in its commitment to a joint and constructive approach to problem-solving, NACBS may be unique among the university-bred, organized social critics and reformers of our day.

Our hope is that this condensation of the lively outpouring of problem assessments and progress reports across disciplinary lines and across economic, social, and political roles and sentiments that took place at the Conference will be reflected in this published record. And that—somehow, it might get us nearer to finding sound and acceptable solutions to some of the perplexing and alarming states of jeopardy in which our economic and social order and our very survival are caught up.

NOTES TO THE INTRODUCTION

1. "The Solution Becomes the Problem" is the subtitle to a book by Paul W. Barkley and David W. Seckler, *Economic Growth and Environmental Decay.* (New York: Harcourt Brace, 1972).

2. United Nations Conference on the Human Environment, Press Release UNCHE/ 102, 21 April, 1972, p. 7.

3. *Ibid.*, p. 3.

4. *Ibid.*, pp. 6–7.

5. *Ibid.*, pp. 8–9.

6. *Ibid.*, p. 9.

7. *Ibid.*, p. 14.

Part 1

The Limits of Market Economics

A twin bicentennial is upon us: that of the American Revolution, which proclaimed as the new nation's prime commitment the assurance of life, liberty, and the pursuit of happiness as "unalienable rights" to all its citizens; and the other, the publication of Adam Smith's "Inquiry into the Nature and Causes of the Wealth of Nations," in which was set forth the notion that "every individual . . . [though] he intends only his own gain . . .is . . . led by an invisible hand . . . [in such a way that] by pursuing his own interest he frequently promotes that of society more effectively than when he really intends to promote it" [1].

Were one to put in just a few words the basic convictions of generations of protagonists of the free market system—viewing the private-enterprise economy in the most constructive and supportive way possible—its characterization would probably contain a combination of the two foregoing pronouncements as the system's ends and means, respectively.

On the other hand, the number of critics and the points of criticism have spread far and wide in the last hundred years or more, with a crescendo in the past several decades, and have reached the proportions of an avalanche in the more recent past. This tide of criticism of market economics continues to grow in momentum, sparked in many instances by environmental concerns—growing fear lest the untrammeled play of market forces place in jeopardy both our natural and our social habitats.

What time could be more appropriate than this twin bicentennial juncture, to sample some of these critiques, especially as they raise or touch on issues of environmental management?

Hazel Henderson launches a broad-gauged frontal attack, as hard-hitting as it is erudite. Its ample documentation provides valuable leads for those who wish to pursue the various sources of criticism which she has so skillfully woven together.

Sam Love dwells on the separateness or apartness of business—or any primarily production-oriented enterprise system (even a non-capitalist one)—from the all-enveloping ecosystem. He points to the frequent incompatibilities that ensue, most glaringly at the interfaces between them.

This raises the spectre of correctives or alternatives: principles of organization and philosophies that promise to promote other than merely proprietary or corporate ends, to wit: the common good, the public interest. Love cites as a concrete precedent one that is a going concern rather than a plan—a current practice of one of the corporate giants. But his long-range hope is for a social transformation in that radical and seemingly utopian changes, even if not willingly adopted, will ultimately force themselves upon society.

Madden puts the stress on the positive—as the title of his essay would lead the reader to expect—and on the adaptive capacity of our present system.

Far from ignoring challenges and problems that confront business in a shrinking world that fears exhaustion of its resources and even wholesale destruction but, at the same time, calls persistently for "more" of everything "good," Madden foresees fundamental and far-reaching changes in business philosophy and organization.

The levers of this transformation, as Madden sees them, will be, in the first place, our growing scientific insights that will change not only our modes of thinking but will force us to change our ways. Concomitantly, or perhaps as a result, drastic value changes appear in the offing which, in their turn, are bound to engender a new social outlook.

Rather than fearing the new scenarios, as many businessmen do today, Madden emphatically welcomes them as pacemakers toward a viable "humanistic capitalism."

NOTES TO PART 1

1. Adam Smith, *The Wealth of Nations*, ed. Edwin Cannan (New York: Random House, 1937), Book IV, Ch. II, p. 423.

✳ *Chapter 1*

Limitations of Traditional Economics in Making Resource Decisions

*Hazel Henderson**

Today the discipline of economics and its practice as the basic tool used in allocating resources is being challenged on many fronts, by scientists from other disciplines and by an increasingly skeptical public. The current mismanagement of our economy calls into question the basic concepts of neo-classical economics and later Keynesian variations. Briefly, I shall review the bankruptcy of economics, now clearly a subsystem discipline, which has been expanded in a vain attempt to embrace phenomena which its concepts are inadequate to explain. By and large, most economists have tended to ignore those social and environmental variables that do not fit into their theoretical models, such as questions concerning the distribution of wealth and income which is too often accepted as a given, or ways in which the concept of the free market and the all-knowing, ever-rational consumer are distorted by the wielding of institutional power, by the manipulation of information, by the speed-up of technological change, and by those human needs that lie beyond the marketplace. Economics and its modern tools, such as cost/benefit analysis, have now begun to obscure social and moral choices and prevent a vital, new, national debate about what is valuable. Today, business cycles themselves are created by economists, rather than the market, as they alternately inflate and deflate the economy. Such aggregate demand management cannot address the structural problems of our complex, mature economy, where only vestiges of such free markets remain [1].

*Hazel Henderson is Co-Director of the Princeton Center for Alternative Futures, Inc.

There are, of course, some economists—notably, Kenneth Boulding, Kenneth Galbraith, Gunnar Myrdal, Barbara Ward, Robert Heilbroner, Adolph Lowe, Gardner Means and Nicholas Georgescu-Roegen, and others—who have kept such questions alive. However, the anomalies that economists cannot address are now painfully visible, whether in global inflation, pollution, or the unwanted side effects of economic development, such as social disruption, cancerous urbanization, soaring infrastructure costs, unemployment and maldistribution of income and wealth. Indeed, many third-world nations now question the advisability of trying to imitate the capital-intensive development strategy of the West, as typified by Walt W. Rostow in *The Stages of Economic Growth* [2]. Many are now looking to China as a more viable model, because its labor-intensive system uses the human resources that are abundant in all countries, as well as the fact that it does not require the surrender of national autonomy, which often becomes the price of foreign capital. The Chinese stress that they do not maximize "efficiency," in Western terms, but rather see it as one goal to be optimized in relation to others, such as decentralized population, domestic production, discouragement of elitism, and equalizing income distribution [3]. Obviously this kind of economy, which substitutes exhortation for incentives and utilizes the energy of its own people in mutual, non-mechanized service to each other, is a pragmatic response to the lack of capital to seed economic growth any other way; but it must also result in a resource-conserving, and therefore more environmentally benign, economy than a capital-intensive one.

TOWARD NEW NATIONAL DEVELOPMENT GOALS AND METHODS, AND DIVERSE ROLES OF ECONOMICS

Much of the new questioning of the goals of economic development has fallen into the rehashing of the communism-versus-capitalism dialectics of the last century. The Chinese denounce capitalism as the root of environmental problems. The U.S.S.R., after initially taking the same position, has now acknowledged its own environmental problems and collaborates with the U.S.A. on the bilateral committee set up to explore solutions to these mutual problems. Many economists reject a-priori environmental arguments against capitalism and point to government-directed investments in many centrally planned economies, such as power generation, steel and auto production, and many extractive industries which create problems in the same way as in capitalist settings [4]. Furthermore, many less-developed countries, without noticeably capitalist leanings, proclaim their willingness to capitalize their relatively clean environments in their understandable drive for economic growth. However, the now-famous Founex Report prepared by experts from developing countries for the 1972 U.N. Environment Conference raised the newer issues. "In the past, there has been a tendency to equate the development goal with the more narrowly conceived objective of economic growth as measured by rises in Gross National Product. It is usually recognized today that high rates of growth do not guarantee the easing of urgent social and human problems. Indeed, in many countries high growth rates have been accompanied by increasing unemployment, rising disparities in income, both between groups and between regions, and the deterioration of social and cultural conditions" [5]. In their 1974 book, *Economic Growth and Social Equity in Developing Countries*, economists Irma Adelman and Cynthia Taft Morris reached essentially the same conclusion [6].

All these new issues challenge prevailing economic policies in most industrial countries and highlight the fact that economics is not a science, but rather a normative discipline. How economists address these issues will determine its future usefulness, and whether the current drift toward irrelevant reductionism in the vain quest for "scientific objectivity" can be reversed, so as to permit integration of the new variables—be they the behavior of oil sheiks, multi-nationals, or ecosystems—into their models.

Let us focus on the priorities by which a nation determines the allocation of its resources. These are a product of many factors: its myths and traditions, its cultural assumptions of "value," its stock of knowledge, its assessments of risks, costs, and benefits within various contexts of space and time, the availability of land, material, and human resources, as well as the mix of public and private decision mechanisms by which its citizens needs and priorities are shaped, articulated, and implemented with sufficient general satisfaction to contain dissent at manageable proportions. Under such a general description of most nations' systems for allocating resources are subsumed the relative value-weightings between individual autonomy and societal goals, and the various centralized and decentralized configurations of power they produce. Many industrial nations in the West have opted for a greater degree of reliance on market mechanisms of allocation, on the assumption that they optimize individual autonomy while approximating shared societal goals. Other industrial nations have followed the lead of the U.S.S.R. and prefer centralized political mechanisms for resource allocation, on the assumption that overall social goals are optimized which simultaneously approximate individual needs. However, the two largest, most advanced models of these two differing value-systems, the U.S.A. and the U.S.S.R., are beginning to appear very similar, in several of their major contours: for example, in their dedication to ecologically unassessed growth, technological determinism, and their increased dominance by bureaucracies, whether officially designated as "public" or "private."

ENVIRONMENTAL AND OTHER IMPACTS OF DIFFERENT APPROACHES

A brief comparison of the environmental merits of these two major resource-allocating systems is necessary, because there is an increasing conviction among resource economists and thermodynamicists that environmental degradation is an index of an economy's inefficiency in utilizing resources; many social critics in market-oriented economies contend that overall efficiency and general welfare can be improved by shifting resources from the private to the public sectors of an economy. J. Kenneth Galbraith, in his 1958 book, *The Affluent Society*, focused widespread attention on the public amenity problems developing in the U.S.A. [7] through over-reliance on market mechanisms to allocate resources. We now see in many other "over-developed" countries, how over-heated consumption by an affluent stratum produces the excessive resource consumption, depletion, waste, obsolescence, and pollution which Galbraith had desscribed. He pinpointed the role of advertising in such over-heating of consumption to be that of continually expanding the private-sector production of goods on the demand for which the major reliance for employment had come to rest. Other critics in the 1960s offered solutions to this purchasing-power dilemma, such as Robert Theobald [8], Milton Friedman [9], and James Tobin [10], who proposed new distribution devices to guarantee minimum incomes to satisfy basic unmet needs, and to prevent these distortions in production patterns. Theobald accurately predicted that advanced, technological economies would be socially unstable and inflationary because consumption must be continually increased, while capital-intensive production would require less and less labor input. Many service industries have grown to take up some of the slack. Yet, today, unemployment and simultaneous inflation are our two most serious problems, thus invalidating one of the economists' traditional concepts known as the Phillips Curve, which postulates a (no-longer operative) trade-off between these two curses of mature, industrial economies The issue of whether a technologically advanced economy produces both structural unemployment and structural inflation has finally surfaced, after its successful submergence by Keynesians and their policies of general stimulation through tax cuts, easing credit, incentives for capital investment, and retraining programs for "unemployables" in the hope that if skills were increased, jobs would somehow materialize. More of the same was proposed in President Ford's FY '76 budget where, in spite of the biggest budget deficit in our history of $52 billion (not to mention the huge overrun,) double-digit inflation was accepted, along with unemployment rates expected to hover around 8 percent, as inevitable facts of life for the next two years.

Such anomalies must now be vigorously debated, especially since capital itself is now in short supply and many of our most pressing needs lie in the public sector. Market-oriented economies cannot deal effectively with these needs until potential consumers of these public goods and services aggregate themselves politically, and develop sufficient power to shift public funds into underpinning these new "markets" for mass-transit, education, health care, parks, and water-treatment facilities, as well as long term-investments to research and develop non-polluting, renewable energy sources, such as solar and wind power [11]. It is not to be overlooked that when massive public works projects are proposed to cure our recession, all these public sector goods services and investments create vital rather than make-work jobs. Not only does over-reliance on private production and consumption of material goods unnecessarily waste resources but it cannot be relied upon as a major source of employment in an advanced economy without other strategies to distribute purchasing power. In addition, Kenneth Boulding has pointed out that economic welfare constitutes *using*, rather than *using up* resources: the enjoyment of the stock of wealth, rather than the throughput of production, consumption, and waste [12]. Market economies, with their emphasis on private property rights, encourage such accelerated throughput because they assume that ownership confers the right to use up, rather than merely use, resources.

However, the more centrally planned economies seem to exhibit similar ranges of environmental problems, not caused by market decisions, but by bureaucratic ignorance or deliberate central decision-making that sacrifices the environment to economic goals. In addition, socialist economies have other problems uniquely their own, particularly in finding incentives more thrilling than "plan-fulfillment" to substitute for the individual profit motive and reduce the need for costly unpopular bureaucratic regulation. Indeed, in Eastern Europe and the U.S.S.R. we now see the age-old human motive of profit slipping in again through the back door, whether as individual productivity rewards, workers' councils, or in the form of royalties in deals with Western corporations [13]. Advanced technological societies, programmed by whatever set of economic assumptions, all suffer from bureaucratic giantism, technological determinism, human alienation, and environmental degradation. Marxian socialist and Western-style utopias all rely heavily on technological abundance, seemingly unconstrained by resource-depletion.

THE THREATENING CUMULATION OF SOCIAL ILLS

The new convergence in advanced economies of problems of inflation, pollution, and resource depletion, together with human alienation, unemployment, and maldistribution of income and wealth, is forcing new assessments of our almost subconscious labor-oriented theories of value. Such an anthropocentric emphasis on our own human inputs to value is understandable. All economic activity is human, and it is to be expected that economic policy discussions in democratic societies stress labor's input to the production process relative to the objective role of land, resources, and capital in determining value. Indeed, in the early stages of the industrial revolution, the role of these objective factors was limited, compared with the vast amounts of human toil required to produce commodities. Marx went so far as to attribute virtually all value in commodities to the labor factor [14]. Although as technology advanced, economists have assigned increasing weight to land and capital as factors of production, their orientation toward labor inputs to value is illustrated by the persistent use of concepts such as "man-hours" and "labor productivity," even though this latter term most often refers to additional *capital* placed at the disposal of the worker.

This emphasis on labor inputs to value, even in advanced, capital-intensive economies, became politically necessary to mask the fact that jobs were becoming a distribution device of major proportions [15]. For example, in their current plight, many industries use as a rationale for federal assistance, not their primary function as supplying needed goods, but that of providing jobs. If we were to acknowledge that in many highly automated industries capital creates wealth unattended by anything more human than a humanly programmed computer we would also have to deal squarely with the need to create institutions for distributing wealth, so that the increasing welter of goods can be consumed by those who still have unsatiated needs for them. This, in turn, would undermine many current assumptions in market economies concerning property rights, and that only work or contributions to production entitle to the right of an equivalent income and to consume (except in cases of age or disability). Furthermore, our emphasis on labor input still shortchanges nature's contribution to production at a time when natural resources are becoming scarcer in relation to human populations. Therefore, we must not only reverse our former notions of "efficiency" but also abandon attempts to neatly quantify the relative inputs to production provided by labor, land, capital, and knowledge, and to recognize the increasingly social nature of production in advanced economies [16].

STEADY-STATE ECONOMICS AHEAD

Since the planet's resources are finite and its processes are bound by the laws of physics, the First Law of Conservation, which states that matter can neither be created nor destroyed, and the Second Law, the entropy law of gradual disordering and decay, the basic requirements of economies operating as subsystems within it must eventually be "steady-state" economies, with constantly maintained stocks of people and physical resources. If economic growth of material wealth must be constrained at some moment in time, however distant, then human development must find another dimension. Luckily, knowledge development and, hopefully, wisdom are unfettered by the dismal laws of physics and are still wide open for evolutionary progress. A steady-state economy can no longer rely on employment in the production of energy and resource-intensive goods as its major distributive device, but must gear its production and distribution strategies to a sustained yield system based on renewable resources. Its theories of value must embrace the subjective, changing goals of people, the role of information and human knowledge, and the limits of the physical resources of the planet and its daily energy income from the sun. The new issues raised by the Club of Rome [17] concerning the ecological and psychological limits to growth will require a change of paradigm in economics, as we re-examine such concepts as "profit," "productivity," "efficiency," "utility," "maximizing," and "progress." None of these concepts has any meaning unless the frame of reference is made clear, and boundaries in space, and time horizons are clearly specified. We must know the answers to such questions as "profit for whom?," "efficiency at what system level?," "maximizing in what time frame?," for such terms to be precise, and to avoid the multiple crises of suboptimization that their fuzzy, confused use by economists, politicians, and businessmen has unwittingly created.

In its dedication to scantily defined "progress," we now see that the Keynesian enterprise of pumping up whole economies to ameliorate structural pockets of unemployment and mask distributional inequities has become too costly in raising rates of both inflation and resource depletion. The easy assumptions that an ever-expanding pie would provide increasing portions to the poor no longer offers the comforting rationale whereby the world's affluent justify inequities as essential to the formation of new capital for investment. Economists and businessmen with intellectual and financial investments in the growth syndrome can no longer defend it on the grounds that it is the only way to improving the lot of the poor and providing the "resources" to clean up the environment. There is now too much evidence that growth often does not trickle down to the poor in the prescribed manner, and using our current form of flawed, excessively polluting production to create the "resources" to clean up its results leaves us with a trade-off. Similarly, the claim that the poor will be denied hopes for increasing private consumption, to which they must aspire if private-sector prerogatives are to be preserved, are new red-herring issues to obscure the need for reassessment of the *nature* and *direction* of growth. The new growth debate is uncovering all the value assumptions it has relied on, forcing us to examine whether growth of consumption in the private sector, however harmful its neighborhood effects, is the only form of growth. Of course, we are obliged to admit that it is not, and that growth could be channeled into the many public service areas of our economy mentioned previously: mass transit, health care, education and research into new energy-conversion system and recycling, with minimal environmental impact. But such a consciously controlled readjustment would require internalizing the social costs of private production and consumption, diverting private resources through taxation, putting priorities on investment and allocating credit, measures which businessmen and many capital-owning citizens still vehemently oppose [18].

Indeed, we must ask whether in an age of increasing complexity, without vastly more information between buyers and sellers, the simple aggregation of micro-decisions in the market adds up to anything more than the macro-chaos described by biologist Garrett Hardin in his now-famous parable *The Tragedy of the Commons* [19]. In such problems of commonly owned "free goods" as air, water, and oceans, where everybody's business becomes nobody's business, lie some of the knottiest theoretical questions of how we are to make social choices in areas where market choices fail. However seemingly abstract, the debate over social choice theory is at the

heart of structuring orderly societies which optimize the general
welfare without individual repression. Kenneth Arrow's "general
impossibility theorem" states flatly that individual preferences cannot logically be ordered into social choices [20]. Arrow's dismal
prognosis for democracy was rebutted by economist Gordon Tullock
[21] as well as political scientist Edwin T. Haefele [22], who contends that Arrow's conditions can be met by representative governments with two-party systems. Herman Daly addressed the dilemma
in his 1974 book, *Toward A Steady State Economy* [23], and states
that for a society to achieve a political economy of biophysical equilibrium and non-material, moral growth will require radical institutional changes and a paradigm shift in economic theory. Daly
suggests that three institutions are needed for a steady-state economy
with constant stocks of people and capital maintained at a low rate
of throughput; aimed at providing macro-stability while allowing
for micro-variability, to combine the macro-static with the micro-
dynamic. Daly endorses Boulding's earlier plan for issuing each individual at birth a license to have as many children as correspond to
the rate of replacement fertility. The licenses could then be bought
and sold on the free market. Secondly, he argues for transferable
resource-depletion quotas, based on estimates of reserves and the
state of technology, to be auctioned off annually by government,
and thirdly, a distributive institution limiting the degree of inequality
in wealth and income.

ENTROPY—THE KEY FACTOR?

Somber proposals such as Daly's may be considered impractical, or
regarded as "social engineering," and yet the concepts of the
"steady-state economists" are beginning to gain a hearing. Most favor
theories of value based on entropy, such as Boulding, who states in
his essay, "The Economics of the Coming Spaceship Earth," that the
economic process consists of segregating entropy, where increasingly
improbably structures of low relative entropy are created at the
expense of higher entropy level wastes somewhere else. Nicholas
Georgescu-Roegen, in his book, *The Entropy Law and the Economic
Process* [24], traces entropy theories of economics back to German
physicist G. Helm, who in 1887 argued that money constitutes the
economic equivalent of low entropy. Georgescu-Roegen pierces the
fallacy that economic processes are analogous to the mechanical
Newtonian processes of locomotion. Because economic processes
also produce qualitative changes, usually associated with higher
entropy levels, he believes that they also elude "arithmomorphic

schematization" and, therefore, economics with its "arithmomania" ignores them. Basically, the problem is that although resources (matter) may be recycled, it can only be done with inputs of energy, and energy-use not only creates inevitable loss (generally heat) but it cannot be recycled. For instance, in most advanced countries, services are becoming major constituents of their economies, including communications (which often replace the need for more energy-intensive transportation), movies, TV, insurance, health care, education and research, whether performed in the public or private sectors. Even though these services are less entropic than heavy industries, we cannot forget that they rest on a base of extraction and production which pollutes and depletes resources, although they share the chameleon quality of appearing to be environmentally benign at the point of delivery. Even pollution control and recycling services, such as electrostatic precipitators and wastewater treatment processes, use a good deal of energy and resources in their operation and manufacture. In fact, Georgescu-Roegen states flatly that all economic processes use up a greater amount of low entropy than is represented by the low entropy resulting in the finished product, and that in entropy terms most recycling is equally fruitless. This is why he and the other steady-state economists stress that the real payoffs are in *durability*, which reduces this unnecessary flow of production-consumption-waste-recycling to the lowest level achievable. Therefore, we need very careful simulations of entire economic processes from extraction to refining, to manufacture, to consumption, to waste, to recycling, in order to assess their relative efficiencies in resource utilization and concomitant pollution and depletion rates.

Georgescu-Roegen's entropy theory of value cites natural chemical processes, rainfall, and solar radiation as separate, additional factors of production. These are usually subsumed under the factor of land, as free gifts of nature [25]. Since some would view this as double-counting, he adds that land, far from being inert, as in Ricardo's definition, is an agent of production in that it contains the chemical processes, catches the rainfall and the solar radiation, which is the only income or source of energy available for the performance of all planetary processes from photosynthesis (the basic and most vital) to our economic activities. The energy "capital" stored in the earth's crust as fossil fuels is a rapidly depleting stock of fossilized solar energy collected in the past by photosynthesis which is non-renewable. The chief difference in the process of agriculture as opposed to the process of industry is that traditional agriculture must rely on utilizing the unchanging rate of flow of solar energy, while industry can mine the stocks of stored energy in the earth's crust, at least while they last, at rates subject to its own determination. Georgescu-Roegen's book analyzes many current input-output models of economic processes in light of his entropy theories, and cites the omission in all such dynamic models of the representation of production of *processes*, rather than merely the production of commodities, as well as voicing other critiques [26]. His theory further challenges the assumption the increase in "labor productivity" resulting from capital input is only limited by economic costs of additional mechanization and depreciation, rather than any ultimate limits of how much matter/energy nature can put at man's disposal. Such inadequacies of economics give credence to self-defeating strategies, such as that proposed by Henry Kissinger, to place a floor under oil prices to make it "profitable" to develop shale, tar sands, and coal liquifaction, in spite of their dismal payoff in real net energy terms.

REDEFINING PROFIT

A shift toward entropy theories of value would require that "profit" be redefined to mean only the creation of real wealth, rather than referring to private or public gain which excessively discounts the future, or is won at the expense of social or environmental exploitation. Similarly, we would recognize that the concept of maximizing profit or utility is imprecise until qualified by a time dimension. Such realistic profits would include improvements in energy-conversion ratios and better resource management, and recycling geared to using the solar energy income available in nature's processes rather than further depleting energy "capital" in the earth's crust. As more externalities are included in the price of products, we may find that many consumer items' profitability will evaporate and these goods will disappear from the market. As I noted in "The Decline of Jonesism" (*The Futurist*, October 1974), this is already happening. Manufacturers such as Alcoa discontinue production of aluminum foil. Other goods requiring large inputs of energy/matter, such as high-powered cars, are being replaced by smaller models, and, there is a new boom in bicycles.

WHAT IS 'PRODUCTIVE'?

Or take the question of the unalloyed desirability of capital investment itself, which is used to justify much inequality of distribution. Under what circumstances are capital investments socially and environmentally destructive; and since we must and will continue our economic activities, how can we reduce their resource-depletion rates and restrain the often arbitrary and irrational investments of increasingly scarce capital? Economists, hypnotized by their elegant equilibrium model of free market supply and demand, cannot readily handle the possibilities of absolute scarcity on the supply side. We must also question the concept of "productivity," another value-laden term, which economists seek to "maximize" by raising the level of capital invested in the worker himself or the machines he uses. Raising agricultural productivity, for example, by mechanization and application of fertilizers and pesticides can often produce social costs, such as the income inequities engendered by the "green revolution," and environmental costs in breeding resistant pests, runoffs of fertilizer-polluted water, destroying more stable and resilient forms of agriculture, and rapid soil depletion. There are also some limits to investments in machinery and automation beyond which workers rebel at the increasing robotization of their jobs and begin sabotaging the production process, as has occurred recently in plants in the U.S.A. Many useful and profitable functions cannot use much capital investment, such as private tutoring, or producing works of art or custom, handcrafted goods; and they provide workers with psychic pleasure often envied by workers in capital-intensive industries. Economist E. F. Schumacher, in his book, *Small is Beautiful*, [27] points out the culture-bound nature of economics in his chapter on Buddhist economics, which, based on the concept of "right livelihood," would define labor as an *output* of production rather than an input, and valuable for its own sake. Schumacher also stresses the need for intermediate, labor-intensive technology to meet developing countries' requirements for rural employment, decentralization, and political stability, substituting for the Western economists' dedication to market-value the concept of use-value.

HUMAN VALUES THAT
TRANSCEND ECONOMICS

All this suggests the extent to which economic theories have fallen behind the welter of changes wrought by technological innovation. All these new issues lead to a re-examination of human cultural notions of "value." For example, we in the U.S.A. tend to over-value and over-reward competitive activities, which can only exist within an equivalent field of cooperation and social cohesion. At the same time, we under-value all these cooperative activities which hold the society together, such as child nurture and the vast array of services lovingly performed in the voluntary sector, and for the provision of which women bear an unfair burden of the opportunity costs [28].

Similarly, we and other Western countries tend to over-value material wealth, while dismissing psychic wealth. As Walter Weisskopf points out in his 1971 book, *Alienation and Economics* [29], the real dimensions of scarcity are not economic, but existential; that is, time, life, and energy, which for man are the ultimately scarce resources because of human fineteness, aging, and mortality. These factors and needs are similar to those identified by psychologists Fromm and Maslow: love, self-actualization, peace of mind, companionship, and time for contemplation and leisure, which can never be satisfied by purely economic means, although economic activity satisfies the lower-order survival needs that permit greater emergence of these non-economic motivations [30]. Likewise, in the U.S.A. we over-value private consumption and property rights while under-valuing public consumption and amenity rights, with which they often conflict. In short, we seem to collect data in the first place in ways that conform to our culture-bound assumptions of "value."

ECONOMICS TO BE RECAST IN THE PUBLIC INTEREST

Therefore, in the last analysis, we must zero in on the normative nature of economics and how economists' often subconscious value-assumptions weight their analyses. I have tried to enumerate many specific instances of this phenomenon in "Ecologists versus Economists" (*Harvard Business Review*, July-August 1973). Economies also attempts to deal with humans' subjective perceptions of value as well as the objective realities concerning the actual values of the complex matter/energy exchanges which maintain the viability of our global habitat. Kenneth Boulding [31] and Barbara Ward [32] were among the first to perceive that Spaceship Earth and its natural cycles powered by the sun contain information on the values of these matter and energy exchanges in the biosphere, and that economics must repair to the physical and biological sciences to obtain these essential baseline data for the accuracy of its own models. Unfortunately, human perceptions of value, i.e., prices, with which economists deal, are notoriously inaccurate because they are based on (a) our subjective, imperfect observations of the objective world and our resulting unrealistic expectations of the availability of its resources, and (b) our subjective evaluation of what is important to us, or "valuable." If our assessments of value are either arbitrary or erroneous, as they usually are, then our primary tool for studying their relative exchange values, viz., economics, must be similarly flawed. Indeed, if prices reflected accurately the true survival values of humans, then why would tobacco be expensive while air is not only cheap but free? The arbitrary nature of human expectations is familiar to all who have studied the behavior of stock exchange prices. In addition, there are often serious lag times between the reports of scientists on, for example, increasing eutrophication rates or acid-rainfall, and the incorporation of such data into economists' reports to bankers and investors or policy-makers, on how they may affect prices.

However, prices continue to have much useful potential for allocating resources in all situations where buyers and sellers still meet each other with equal power, and have faster information on true costs, so that lags in response and price correction are reduced. As Gunnar Myrdal has stated, "We can begin to fill that empty box in our diagrams marked 'externalities,' so as to calculate as far as possible the social costs of production so that they too can be accurately reflected in prices. In this way more accurate pricing can still function as an alternative to bureaucracy" [33]. In the same vein, Myrdal contends that organized citizens and consumers can function as a countervailing check on the power of public and private institutions [34], as evidenced in the U.S.A. by the rise of the movements for consumer and environmental protection and the direct confrontation of corporations by boycotts, the use of proxy machinery, and the politicizing of company annual meetings and institutional investment policies. Many externalities can be calculated or reasonably approximated so as to bring us closer to determining true value added, rather than immediate but evanescent gains won only at the expense of social and environmental exploitation.

Some more comprehensive calculations of what market economies call "profit" and state-directed economies call "economic growth", would vastly improve all resource allocation decisions. But in market economies particularly, the quantification of these externalities has been short-changed or overlooked because the majority of economists are employed by private interest groups or the empire-building public agencies that often cater to them, for the purpose of preparing biased and sometimes blatantly fraudulent cost/benefit analyses in advocacy of their profit-making or bureaucratic-aggrandizing projects. Even academic economists in both capitalist and socialist economies tend to be influenced by the prevailing political pressures and cultural assumptions of their societies. Therefore many economic analyses suffer from unacknowledged biases and overestimates of immediate benefits while underestimating more elusive social and environmental costs, whose impact may be born by the society in

general or a group within it, another nation, or succeeding generations. The Public Interest Economics Center of Washington, D.C., of
which I am a founder, attempts to address the need to enrich the
public debate and decision process by critiquing the often frankly
promotional cost/benefit analyses used to support both public and
private projects [35]. Costs and benefits are usually averaged out per
capita, which conceals who will bear the costs, in perhaps neighborhood despoilation or loss of jobs, and who will reap the benefits: the
contracts, bond issue business, profits, and new jobs. The Public
Interest Economics Center has a roster of some 500 volunteer economists willing to perform such economic analyses for groups who
could not otherwise afford economic expertise to buttress their
cases, either in courts or legislatures, such as citizens groups working
for environmental protection, social justice, or other volunteer
causes. The Center has pioneered this new branch of "public interest
economics" in the same way that similar movements have been established in law and the sciences, as well as in the accounting profession,
which recently set up its own National Association of Accountants
in the Public Interest [36].

In some cases, the mere collection of data and their dissemination
in the most effective channels can create pressure for change. New
York's Council on Economic Priorities, founded by Alice Tepper
Marlin, has broadened the traditional concepts of security analysis to
cover the social and environmental performance of corporations.
[37]. The Council's reports and in-depth studies count among sub-
scribers a growing number of brokerage houses, banks, mutual funds
and other institutional investors, as well as socially concerned stockholders and citizens. It publishes comparative information on the
social impact of corporation in various industries in the area of environment, minority rights, military contracting, consumer protection,
political influence, and foreign investments. The growing political
power of these multi-national corporations, which now threatens national sovereignty and world monetary stability, confirms the need
for this type of analysis. In addition, there are now enough U.S. investors to provide a market for these reports, as stockholders see the
desirability of having portfolios that do not contradict their personal
values. In response to these new stockholder pressures on their
members' clients, the American Institute of Certified Public Accountants is attempting to develop social auditing methods for corporations. One fruitful avenue growing out of their own experience
would seem to be that of expanding the familiar concept of "goodwill," which however unquantifiable, is routinely capitalized on

company balance sheets. It should also be possible to refine calculations of short- and long-term profit so as to elucidate the time dimensions which always qualify maximizing behavior.

TOWARD ECOSYSTEM CONCEPTS
AND MORE EFFECTIVE GUAGES
AND CONTROLS

Much new and useful work on modelling externalities is now in progress, by such economists as Wassily Leontief, and those working at Resources for the Future, including Allen V. Kneese, Charles Cichetti, and John Krutilla. Hirofumi Uzawa of Tokyo University advocates an annual deduction from Gross National Product (GNP) analogous to the capital consumption adjustment that now distinguishes Gross National Product from Net National Product [38]. The new deduction allows for the depletion of natural resources: the consumption of the irreplaceable original capital of the planet. On the assumption that industrialized nations are exhausting resources more rapidly than nature can renew them, each year Uzawa's deductions will increase. In the U.S.A., Thomas Juster sets forth a more realistic set of criteria for restructuring our own GNP, which include in the assets: knowledge, skills and talents, physical environment, and socio-political assets; his work apppears in the 50th Annual Report of the National Bureau of Economic Research. Resource economists, including Allen V. Kneese, argue for effluent and emission taxes as the most efficient way to control pollution through the market mechanism. Yet transaction costs also occur, and effluent taxes are more likely to be decided by the political power of corporate lobbying than the objective market. In addition, such taxes cannot address the problem of keeping toxic substances out of the environment which can only be accomplished by prohibition, nor can they prevent irreversible changes which are environmentally unsound. Similarly, the subsidy method also discounts true social costs of pollution, particularly the new pollution-control bonds, which are tax-exempt to encourage corporate spending on environmental improvement but are proving to be little more than another tax loophole [39].

But if economics is to develop ever more precise tools to assess the trade-offs in resource-allocations, it will need to incorporate a large portion of the new data being developed by the physical sciences, concerning those actual values in the macro-biosystem of nature's chemical exchange work, which maintains global equilibrium conditions for humans. Herman Daly makes an interesting analogy between economies and ecosystems: young ecosystems tend, like young economies, to maximize production. Mature ecosystems, like mature economies, are characterized by high maintenance efficiencies. From such insights came Daly's proposal for yearly depletion quotas to be auctioned off by government, which he claims are superior as a basic strategy for resource utilization efficiency than effluent taxes, which he sees as a fine-tuning tactic which only addresses itself to pollution control, rather than the primary issue of depletion.

Howard T. Odum, author of *Environment Power and Society* [40], has pioneered energy modelling, a quantitative method of tracking nature's flows of energy and matter, which is fast becoming more predictive than economics. Odum's system converts kilocalories into dollars so that economists can see and account for such work performed by natural systems in their traditional cost-benefit analyses: for example, in converting carbon dioxide from combustion back into oxygen or converting industrial wastes and sewage into fuel and fertilizers. As inflation renders money an even less precise measuring rod of true efficiency, Odum's method of measuring efficiencies of production and extraction processes in the terms of "net energy" is gaining wide acceptance. Odum views inflation as the symptom of a society with a declining energy and resource base, forced to extract energy and raw materials from more inaccessible and degraded deposits. Since it takes more and more energy to do this, more real wealth must be diverted from the purchase of goods and services. But the money supply is increased as if all this activity were productive, so the diminishing returns to all this energy-getting capital investment are expressed in the degradation of the currency, i.e., rising prices.

Energy-modelling is being conducted in scores of countries and by imaginative engineers, thermodynamicists, and physicists, such as Stephen Berry and Thomas V. Long at the University of Chicago, Bruce Hannon at the University of Illinois, and Malcolm Slesser at the University of Strathclyde, Scotland [41]. In spite of many unresolved problems of taxonomy and differences of method, it appears to be quite superior to economics in plotting resource utilization and management processes. In 1974, the International Federation of Institutes for Advanced Study in Stockholm convened energy-modellers from all over the world to map out their research agenda and agree on their terms. Other conceptual problems still faced are outlined in my "Energetics' Short-comings" (*Co-Evolution Quarterly*, Winter 1974) [42]. Yet, it may be the best new analytical tool at hand for the present.

However, analytical tools and reductionist methods all suffer from what Alfred North Whitehead referred to as "the fallacy of misplaced concreteness [43]. They cannot reveal truth that exists in other dimensions. Welfare formulas for humans cannot be derived from energetics any more than they have been successfully formulated by economists. Moral behavior cannot be derived from data, but only from our own expanded perceptions of our true interdependent situation as a species marooned together on this small planet and our own striving for wisdom and ethical principles.

NOTES TO CHAPTER 1

1. Adolph Lowe, *On Economic Knowledge* (New York: Harper Torchbooks, 1965), p. 65.

2. W.W. Rostow, *The Stages of Economic Growth: A Non-Communist Manifesto* (Cambridge, England, 1960).

3. Frank Riessman, "The Politics of Human Service: China and the United States," *Social Policy* (March-April 1972), p. 37.

4. See, for example, Marshall Goldman, "Ecological Facelifting in the U.S.S.R.," in *Political Economy of Environment* (Mouton, The Hague, 1971).

5. *Development and Environment Report*, U.N. Conference on the Human Environment, Founex, Switzerland, 1971.

6. Irma Adelman and Cynthia Taft Morris, *Economic Growth and Social Equity* (Stanford: Stanford University Press, 1973).

7. John Kenneth Galbraith, *The Affluent Society* (Boston: Houghton Mifflin, 1958).

8. See, for example, Robert Theobold, *Free Men and Free Markets* (New York: Anchor Doubleday, 1965). Also *The Guaranteed Income* (New York: Anchor Doubleday, 1967).

9. Milton Friedman, "The Case for the Negative Income Tax," *Congressional Record*, House, 90th Congress, 1st Sess., Document 172, 1967.

10. James Tobin, "The Case for an Income Guarantee," *The Public Interest* (Summer 1966), p. 34.

11. Hazel Henderson, "Toward Managing Social Conflict," *Harvard Business Review* (May–June 1971).

12. Kenneth Boulding, "The Economics of the Coming Spaceship Earth," in *Beyond Economics* (Ann Arbor: Ann Arbor Paperbacks, University of Michigan Press, 1970), pp. 275–287.

13. See, for example, Samuel Pisar's *Coexistence and Commerce, A Guide to Business Transaction Between Western Corporations and Eastern Bloc Countries* (New York: McGraw Hill, 1970).

14. Karl Marx, *Das Kapital* (Chapter VII, "The Production of Absolute Surplus Value") (Chicago: Gateway Paperback, 1970), pp. 143–189.

15. Hazel Henderson, "Ecologists versus Economists," *Harvard Business Review* (July–August 1973), p. 34.

16. *Ibid.*, p. 36.

17. See, for example, Meadows et al., *Limits to Growth* (New York: Universe Books, 1974). Also Mesarovic and Pestel, *Mankind at the Turning Point* (New York: Dutton/Readers Digest Press, 1974).

18. "Redefining Economic Growth," Conference on Environmental Quality and Social Justice, ed. James Noel Smith. (Washington: Conservation Foundation, 1974), pp. 135–139.

19. G. Hardin, "The Tragedy of the Commons," *Science* (December 13, 1968), p. 1243.

20. Kenneth J. Arrow, *Social Choice and Individual Values*, 2nd ed. (New York: John Wiley, 1963).

21. Gordon Tullock, "The General Irrelevance of the General Impossibility Theorem," *Quarterly Journal of Economics* (May 1967), p. 256.

22. Edwin T. Haefele, *Representative Government and Environmental Management* (Baltimore: Johns Hopkins Press, 1973), pp. 15–62.

23. Herman E. Daly, ed., *Toward a Steady-State Economy* (San Francisco: W. H. Freeman, 1973).

24. Nicholas Georgescu-Roegen, *The Entropy Law and the Economic Process* (Cambridge: Harvard University Press, 1971).

25. "The General Equation of Value," *ibid.*, pp. 283–291.

26. "Entropy and Development," *ibid.*, pp. 293–306.

27. E. F. Schumacher, *Small is Beautiful* (New York: Harper Torchbooks, 1974).

28. Hazel Henderson, "Information and the New Movement for Citizen Participation," *Annals of the American Academy of Political and Social Science* (March 1974), pp. 34–43.

29. Walter Weisskopf, *Alienation and Economics* (New York: Dutton, 1971).

30. See, for example, Abraham Maslow, *Toward a Psychology of Being* (New York: Van Nostrand, 1968).

31. Kenneth Boulding, *Beyond Economics, op. cit.*

32. Barbara Ward, *Spaceship Earth* (New York: Columbia University Press, 1966.)

33. Gunnar Myrdal, "Economics of an Improved Environment." Lecture given in Stockholm at the U.N. Conference on the Human Environment, June 8, 1972.

34. Gunnar Myrdal, *Beyond the Welfare State* (New York: Bantam Books, 1960), pp. 72–87.

35. Public Interest Economics Center, 1714 Massachusetts Ave., N.W., Washington, D.C.

36. National Association of Accountants in the Public Interest, 233 Sansome St., Room 400, San Francisco, California 94104.

37. Council on Economic Priorities, 84 Fifth Ave., New York, N.Y. 10011.

38. Robert Lekachman, "Humanizing GNP," *Social Policy* (September/October 1971), p. 39.

39. Hazel Henderson, "The Limits of Traditional Economics: New Models for Managing a Steady-State Economy," *Financial Analysts Journal* (May–June 1973).

40. Howard T. Odum, *Environment Power and Society* (New York: Wiley Interscience, 1972).

41. For more information about the new field of energy modeling, contact the International Federation of Institutes for Advanced Study, Sturegaten 11, Stockholm, Sweden, which has held two conferences on this subject.

42. Hazel Henderson, "Energetics' Shortcomings," *Co-Evolution Quarterly* (Winter 1974).

43. Alfred North Whitehead, *Process and Reality: An Essay in Cosmology* (New York: Macmillan, 1929), p. 11.

❋ *Chapter 2*

Business: Apart from or Part of the Ecosystem?

*Sam Love**

As I see it, we are in one of those rare historical moments when the past no longer serves. Virtually every institution in society is under unprecedented stress. Whether our institutions will adapt to these pressures or become fragmented and need to be reconstituted remains an open question. Given the magnitude of the problems emerging, I'm to the point of wishing us luck.

I could be ticking off the problems, but we all know them. The critical question is what do we do about them.

My own feeling is, that we no longer have the luxury of the Ralph Nader approach of attacking the symptoms one by one. It is time to identify and confront patterns and causal forces of the underlying sicknesses. Once we understand these forces, we must face a choice between mobilizing the social commitment necessary to restructure society to control them or watching disorder increasingly tug harder at the social fabric.

BUSINESS IN A WORLD OF CHANGED PERCEPTIONS

The days of business as unusual are counted. Like other institutions, the corporation is not insulated from the interplay of forces around us. In fact, increasingly it is becoming the focal point of the pressures for change. One indication of the magnitude of sentiment among activists, who are primarily responsible for many corporate headaches, is revealed in a recent poll by the Opinion Research Corporation. They found that 43 percent of the social activists they surveyed

*Sam Love is a writer and environmental activist.

believe that the bad features of the business system outweigh the good and that major changes are needed.

A particularly interesting statistic is that, of all activists interviewed, environmentalists expressed the strongest disaffection with corporations. For example, only 9 percent of the sample interviewed believe that free enterprise offers us the best way to achieve a higher standard of living.

I don't think it is any accident that such strong sentiments exist about corporations. Business is under siege because, in our commercial society, the logic underpinning the corporate system shapes the productive relationships. I also don't think it is an accident that environmentalists are in the vanguard of challenging corporations. Environmental concerns emerge from concern for the human impact on the physical world, and corporations—as much as any other institution—determine that.

But environmentalists' unique perspective as watchdogs for the physical world doesn't do much to endear them to any group concerned about accelerating production. At the present time, neither capitalists nor socialists would feel comfortable if their son or daughter married an environmentalist.

This unfortunate situation has arisen because events have cast environmentalists in a negative role. "Stop this, fight that, delay that" have become watchwords of the movement. Environmental activists are now industry's loyal opposition.

Increasingly though, environmentally sensitive people will start playing another role. They have a unique contribution to make to the future. Their understanding of natural systems and how the real world works provides them the ability to explode the social fantasies about reality which operate in executive suites.

This ecological understanding has led most environmental activists to adopt a philosophy I've heard best summarized by a lady clerk in a general store in rural North Carolina. After shopping for nails, a hat, food, and pants, I remarked to her that she had anything a fella could ever *want*. "No," she replied, "but I've got anything you'll ever *need*."

Behind that philosophy stands an ecological understanding that differs from the view of reality shared by corporate executives. Let me share with you the different realities perceived by environmentalists and corporate officials. By studying the natural world, ecologists have identified basic principles by which it functions. Through self-regulating mechanisms, natural systems have evolved the capacity to maintain a stable course at an optimum level for extended periods of time. This dynamic stability is a function of the interaction of many concepts, including the cyclical flow of material, diversity, decentralization, subsystem integration, limiting constraints, and cooperation. To place the present corporate system in proper perspective, each of these concepts merits further examination.

CYCLICAL FLOW VERSUS LINEAR PRODUCTION PATTERNS

Unlike nature's ingenious engineering systems which channel minerals, gases, and fluids through continuous cycles, the corporate system tends to organize the flow of material linearly. In this system it is more profitable to create products which can be used and then discarded than to create items which last for long periods of time. As far as business is concerned, matter begins its journey through the corporate system at the bottom of a mine and reaches a dead end at the refuse pile.

As a result of this linear thinking, the amount of solid waste generated annually in the United States is staggering. It includes 30 million tons of paper, 4 million tons of plastics, 100 million tires, 30 billion bottles, 60 million cans, 7 million discarded automobiles, and countless millions of other items.

This waste of resources is unnecessary. If the corporate system cycled and reused materials, as does a natural system, considerable overall economic and ecological benefits would be possible. Recovery and reuse conserve natural resources, eliminate disposal and collection problems, and substitute "waste" for virgin materials in the production system, thereby decreasing energy use in the industrial process and reducing the emission of air and water pollutants. For instance, according to the Environmental Protection Agency, recycling 1,000 tons of steel requires 74 percent less energy and 51 percent less water in production than does the same amount of virgin materials. Similar savings could be made by recycling or reusing glass and paper. Yet, in spite of these obvious environmental savings, industry refuses to stop operating in a linear fashion. Throwaway products are more profitable, and the use of cycled materials is declining relative to total material consumption.

INTEGRATION VERSUS SUBSYSTEMIC 'SOLUTIONS'

Ecosystems are composed of a complex array of subsystems which function together to maintain stability. In nature, waste from one process becomes a nutrient for another. Pollution results when human activity does not fit into this natural "web" of complementary subsystems.

Our synthetic, disposable environment is the ultimate form of this non-integration. Social solutions yield ecological problems. For example, the problem of keeping food fresh has been solved, in part, by packaging. Indestructible, non-biodegradable packaging of aluminum, plastic, and steel may make for a long shelf life, but when these items are thrown into the great "away"—a place for which they were not designed—they become an ecological disaster.

Automobile manufacturers solved the problem of engine knock by putting lead in high octane gasoline. But when their answers exploded in the combustion chamber and came out the exhaust pipe into the air of our cities, they left something to be desired—airborne lead has been linked with human brain damage. And as proof that they never learn, automobile engineers are now "solving" the internal combustion engine's air pollution problem with catalytic converters which reduce the three air pollutants named in the Clean Air Act, but which release two new substances that may be even more dangerous—platinum and sulfuric acid.

Some may wonder if the re-integration of technology and its byproducts into natural systems is possible. Although such re-integration will not be easily accomplished in a society that maximizes efficiency through the division of labor, it is imperative that specialization no longer be a goal of economic institutions.

DECENTRALIZATION AND DIVERSITY VERSUS CONCENTRATION AND HOMOGENIZATION

While nature may gain systemic stability through decentralization and diversification, capitalism and industrial technologies encourage imbalance by promoting concentration and homogenization. The concentration of wealth in our society reveals how well these forces work. A study by Robert Lampman of the University of Wisconsin points out that 1.6 percent of the American population owns 82.2 percent of all stock, 100 percent of state and local bonds, 38.2 percent of federal bonds, and 88.5 percent of all other bonds. Although these data were compiled in the 1950s, more recent materials support Lampman's analysis and reveal the static nature of large fortunes.

Industrial capital is not the only facet of American life that is concentrated. According to the 1969 Census of Agriculture, an increasingly small number of people own America's farms. In 1935, there were 6.8 million farms in the United States and by 1969, the number had fallen to 2.7 million. Of the farms remaining in 1969, the Department of Agriculture reports that 7 percent of them generated about 50 percent of all farm product sales, and 20 percent provided about 75 percent of the sales.

All of these statistics point to the fact that the small farmer has been overcome by agribusiness corporations which are interested solely in profit rather than sound, ecological management of the land. Land that once supported hundreds of families is now transformed into an "agribusiness production facility" that employs only a handful of workers and specializes in one or two crops. Such simplification of crops produces a monoculture that is more vulnerable to ecological collapse than a system of diversified crops. The precariousness of monocropping and breeding primarily for high yield is exemplified by the corn blight that swept across the United States in 1970, destroying at least 15 percent of that year's harvest.

The economics that breed concentration in agriculture also operate to encourage it in other areas of the society. The advent of nuclear power has made it possible to build facilities that generate three times as much electricity as contemporary units. And because nuclear power requires huge initial capital outlays and uses relatively cheap fuel, such plants are economically attractive to power companies which base their revenue on the size of their capital base. One such nuclear plant has the production capacity of three older fossil fuel-powered generators. Even if no major accidents occur, minor problems and refueling will necessitate the periodic shutdown of atom-powered units. Thus, the construction of a large nuclear facility instead of three smaller plants triples the shutdown impact of a single plant. This construction reduces the system's overall stability.

LIMITS VERSUS UNBOUNDED GROWTH

Ecologists recognize that ecosystems function within confined limits. These limits enable the system to maintain stability over time. The system must compensate when it exceeds these limits, and, in some cases, such as population crashes, the readjustment can be painful.

Even though the earth does not grow in direct relation to an expanding Gross National Product, followers of Adam Smith remain addicted to the idea of unbridled growth. Such growth is inherent in the Smithian system because it defines interest in such a way as to continually expand the system.

Corporate managers, who direct the never-ending task of expansion, must produce a surplus (profit) to stay in the good graces of their stockholders. Under the corporate system, part of this profit is paid to stockholders and investors. The remainder is reinvested to further expand the operation so that, with each reinvestment, the institution grows. Thus, the surplus becomes part of an expanding base which provides an ever-increasing foundation for more growth. Among students of corporate finance, Adolph Berle was first to point out that corporations grew largely through internal generation of capital. More than 60 percent of the capital needed for expansion comes from corporate revenues and the remainder from outside the corporation. This concept of growth conflicts with naturally occurring processes in which ecosystems continually attempt to reach and maintain an optimal "steady state."

Continued growth produces goods that have to be sold. Promotion is so essential to marketing that corporations sink $20 billion every year into advertising. But even with massive advertising campaigns, markets become saturated and other techniques such as planned obsolescence are necessary to create more markets. In addition to glutting the domestic market, sales increases can be obtained by promoting new foreign markets, especially in "undeveloped" countries. Many parts of the world are being exposed for the first time to the gadgetry owned by most Americans, creating new demands for more refrigerators, radios, televisions, cars, motorcycles, and air conditioners, and placing massive new demands on the earth's already-overburdened resource pool.

COOPERATION VERSUS COMPETITION

The debate as to whether organisms cooperate or compete in nature is one of ecology's hottest controversies. After the publication of Darwin's *Origin of the Species*, a protracted public debate emerged over the benefits of competition versus cooperation. Pëtr Kropotkin, a turn-of-the-century biologist by profession, and anarchist by persuasion, authored *Mutual Aid* to describe the biological and social benefits of cooperation. His classic work argues that nature's tendency, although not always realized, is toward cooperation or, as he termed it, mutual aid.

Although the controversy is far from settled, ecologists generally recognize that natural systems make extensive use of cooperation, but, that as population density increases or other limiting constraints are reached, individuals in a species are forced to compete with one another for survival. Thus, ecologists argue that competition tends to reduce the number of competitors. A strikingly similar principle can be observed in society as corporations compete with one another until only the largest ones remain to dominate the market.

Corporate managers pay lip service to the competitive ethic, but whenever possible, they move their enterprises toward cooperation with other businesses. Several times in American history, corporations have pursued concentration to the point that only a few large ones remained. Although these corporate giants appear to be competing with one another, they are actually cooperating with one another—fixing prices, allocating markets, fighting labor, controlling resource distribution, and squelching innovation. Society should take advantage of this natural and corporate tendency and institutionalize cooperation so that the public benefits from cooperation rather than being victimized by it.

In *Looking Backward*, a 19th century Utopian classic by Edward Bellamy, the book's protagonist learns such a lesson when he journeys to the year 2000 and looks back at 1888 (the year of the book's publication). Amazed at the social change which has occurred over the decades, he asks his host to explain how the new society had abolished strife. The host explains:

Selfishness was their [19th century people] only science and in industrial production, selfishness is suicide. Competition, which is the instinct of selfishness, is another word for dissipation of energy, while combination is the secret of efficient production.

These underlying logical premises of unbounded growth, competition, linear flow, centralization, homogenization, and nonintegration have reached their historic limits in the modern urbdustrial (urban/industrial) culture with its vast array of seemingly unsolvable problems. These cultural tenets have produced a mega-network feeding in fossil fuels, agricultural products, water, materials, and other inputs, and removing wastes. The intricate interdependence and scale of the network generate inherent instability of such magnitudes that these new mammoth social units now hover precariously on the brink of a collapse.

THE COBWEB ECONOMY AND
ITS VULNERABILITY

This new society's infrastructure can be comprehended by imagining something like New York City as the center of a giant network with tubes spreading out and intermingling over thousands of miles to form a pattern strikingly similar to a cobweb. Its functioning depends on oil flowing in from the Middle East, vegetables being flown and trucked in from California, natural gas piped in from Texas, electricity being brought in from Canada, wastes moving out by barge, and other processes too numerous to mention. In this *cobweb economy*, one strand cannot be jiggled without affecting the others. Its design is also such that small disruptions can cascade through the system to trigger seemingly unrelated results with an impact far greater than the original disruption.

Given such a situation no one example can fully convey the dynamics of what is under consideration. Take nuclear power: presently we have 98 reactors either operating or under construction. They represent more than $40 billion in private investment. Some utility systems are already one-third dependent on nuclear power for electrical energy. One credible bomb threat to the Atomic Energy Commission about a bomb in one of its reactors somewhere could result in the temporary shutdown of all operating reactors. Or one significant accident with its billions of dollars of property damage and large-scale evacuations of population could result in a nuclear moratorium. Such a shutdown, coming at a time when we are heavily dependent on nuclear power for electricity, could produce havoc. The impact on the financial community alone would be staggering. Even if the government attempts to bail out the utility systems by indemnifying them for their investments in the radioactive white elephants, the sheer amounts of money that would already be involved in a shutdown could only be generated by printing dollars.

Or think of the Arab oil boycott and the energy crisis. Regardless of who caused it, it precipitated a series of events yielding near panic in the suburbs, layoffs in factories, and a truckers' strike that threatened cities with a food shortage.

POSSIBLE REMEDIES AND A PRECEDENT

Recognizing the inherent instability makes it easier to understand what must be done. First, we must accept a logical framework which perceives that specialization, concentration, linear organization, unlimited growth and competition are harmful for both social and ecological reasons. Once this is perceived, society can formulate new goals and institutions based on the principles of human or natural scale, integration, diversity, decentralization, cyclical flow, and cooperation.

An illustration of how some of these principles can be applied to physical networks to gain stability can be seen with the telephone company. For all of its faults, it does apply some of these in its systems design. Technological capability has reached the point where one of its four-inch cables, the L–5, can carry 108,000 simultaneous conversations or a new microwave system can carry 15,000. The company recognizes that the cable's capacity is so large that it could handle nearly all of the traffic on a major route at one time, yet all of its calls are not routed through the cable. As an official policy, message loads are always routed through at least three routes, so that a break in the main cable would not completely shut down the entire system. Thus by applying the principle of diversity, the company un-hitches networks and gains stability. It does not use the L–5 to its full economic potential, but the company places enough value on systemic stability to make the necessary commercial sacrifice.

The phone company may be able to get away with the economic sacrifice because it is a natural monopoly. Still, other institutions, if they value their future, would do well to put more value on stability and less on short-term economic gain.

UTOPIA WITH A MESSAGE

Societally, many of these principles have been advocated by social movements at other times in history. Past efforts deserve to be studied, not for society to reach back to yesteryear, blow the dust off old banners and march off into the future, but so that we may learn from them.

If the past is any indication, people will clamor at some point for a rigid Utopian model—a concrete vision of a new age. A vision of decentralized, cooperative communities living in natural and social harmony could satisfy them; but, even though satisfying society's hunger for an organizing model in these confusing times is important, it is not the most important contribution of these ideas. What is offered here is a *Utopian process*, not a rigid Utopian diagram. By articulating principles which produce stability in ecological systems, guidelines for day-to-day decision-making are provided.

This Utopian process also offers an answer to the cry for law and order which has liberals doing incredible political gymnastics. People don't want law and order, which requires the imposition of force onto a sick social organism. What they really want is stability, and that can only come from within. It must emerge from the roots.

Many will view the chances for success of those committed to these ideals as hopeless because of the enormity of the task. But as the events in the real world increasingly puncture social fantasies, the task will become easier. For even if we are not willing to organize society to conform with the principles by which the real world functions, reality will painfully push us headlong into the new age.

Chapter 3

The Greening of Economics*

*Carl H. Madden***

In his 1970 best-seller, Charles A. Reich, a Yale University law professor, wrote about *The Greening of America.* In a romantic interpretation of the "youth culture" of the 1960s, Reich called on the youth to lead a revolution of consciousness, unlike any revolution of the past, to start with the individual and with his culture, and to change the political structure only as its final act. He described the youth culture as Consciousness III, likely to supplant Consciousness I—the traditional outlook of the American farmer, small businessman, and worker—and Consciousness II—the culture of large organizations, both public and private. In a burst of feeling, Reich ended his book with this sentence: "For one who thought the world was irretrievably encased in metal and plastic and sterile stone, it [the revolution of consciousness] seems a veritable greening of America."

My topic concerns the revolution in thought, the scientific revolution, through which we are living. It is not dependent on the "youth culture" of the 1960s for its power to affect the major institutions of society. As the scientific revolution affects economics, it might be described as "The Greening of Economics," because it seems likely to infuse economics in the broadest sense with ideas relating to the environment we live in.

*Appreciation is expressed to the publishers of the *Virginia Quarterly Review*, in which this paper has already been published, for permission to include it in the present volume.
**Carl H. Madden is Chief Economist in the Chamber of Commerce of the United States.

THE SCIENTIFIC REVOLUTION

First, consider some main ideas of the scientific revolution and their impact. According to the astronomer Harlow Shapley, the 10 most far-reaching achievements of 20th century science are: (1) knowledge of the chemistry of life's origin; (2) cosmic evolution—from neutrons to man and beyond; (3) relativity theories—special and general; (4) the corpuscular sciences—the subatomic world; (5) automation and computers (cybernetics); (6) space exploration; (7) galaxies, quasars, the expanding universe; (8) medical triumphs—conquering major diseases; (9) molecular biology—viruses and DNA; and (10) exploration of the mind.

Although most people don't know it, a similar list of achievements in the social sciences in the 20th century could be developed. It would surely include national income analysis, probability theory and sampling, general systems analysis, community structure analysis, and other achievements: To suggest that social science has made no important contributions or can make none to policy is merely to reveal one's ignorance of social science.

The point of listing these achievements is to remind us that they change the picture, the image, of the universe, of the earth, of man and his role in creation radically from the earlier picture of the time of Copernicus and Newton. The word *picture* is important. It is important because all of us act in response to our own image of reality, of what things are really like. The 20th century scientific revolution changes the dominant world view, the dominant image of reality as profoundly as did the Renaissance.

To be vivid but oversimplify, we now believe that we live in a universe at least 14 billion years old, composed of uncounted hundreds of millions of island universes, or galaxies, which are all moving away from one another at speeds proportional to their distances apart, up to some moving away from our galaxy at close to the speed of light, that is, close to 186,000 miles per second.

Within an ordinary spiral-armed galaxy of about 100 billion stars, that stretches 100,000 light years from edge to edge and whose center is about 10,000 light years thick, we find our quite ordinary sun in one of the spiral arms, located about 30,000 light years from the center, and slowly circling the center as the galaxy rotates every 200 million years. Our sun is about 4.5 billion years old, quite an ordinary age. Our earth, also about 4.5 billion years old, is only an interesting detail of this sun's planetary system.

The scale of these things is interesting. If the sun were the size of a basketball, then the earth would be located about 100 feet away, the size of a wheat kernel, and the farthest planet, Pluto, about a mile away the size of a millet seed. The nearest star to the sun would be about 4,000 miles away. Between is empty space.

We now believe, from much evidence, that life arose on our earth eons ago out of demonstrably natural conditions. Although man or his erect relatives have lived on earth only 2 to 4 million years, the dinosaurs reigned for 200 million years. It all developed through a process by which our sun, like countless others—100 billion others just in our galaxy alone—showers energy on us as it converts mass into energy in obedience to the laws of nuclear chemistry and relativity physics.

It took mankind 2 to 4 million years to reach a population of 1 billion. If we consider just the history of mankind's existence during the past 50,000 years, and divide them into lifetimes of 62 years each, we live in the 800th lifetime. Of these 800 lifetimes, mankind has spend 650 in caves. Writing has been possible in only the last 70 lifetimes. Only during the last 6 has printing been available. We have been able to measure time precisely only in the last 4. The electric motor came along only in the last 2.

In our generation, or at least since 1900, we face the revolution of 20th century science. Most of us are, by and large, ignorant of this revolution. If one compares his own knowledge today with the sum of knowledge, then each of us is probably far more ignorant relative to that total than educated people of a few generations ago.

Although it took 2 or more millions of years for mankind to reach 1 billion in population (1850), it took only 112 years more to reach an estimated population of 3 billion (1962); it will take, at present growth rates, only 30 years to reach 5 billion (2000).

The history of mankind, when relating population ceilings to stages of technology, has seen three major periods: food-gathering, farming, and industrial. The world population ceiling for man as food gatherer, reaching through 600,000 years of the Old Stone Age or Paleolithic period, was about 20 million, based on two square miles per person needed in the limited areas suitable for gathering and hunting. The second stage, beginning about 6000 B.C., brought the agricultural revolution, which raised the population ceiling of the world to 1 billion. The highest estimate of a population ceiling for the third stage, that of industrial technology, has been made by geochemist Harrison Brown, and stands at 50 billion. Brown, assuming worldwide industrialization, nuclear and solar power, and all technology now foreseen, concludes that 50 billion people could live on earth in a vast, worldwide megalopolis, eating food supplied mainly by algae farms and yeast factories, and using technology employing vast amounts of energy to process mostly air, water, and, in huge amounts, ordinary rock—granite. World population growth, if projected ahead at present rates, would bump into the Brown ceiling in only 150 years.

THE IMPACT OF SCIENCE ON CULTURE

A few moments' reflection on only an oversimple account of the impact of science shows it hits hardest at people's *beliefs about reality*. Most of us should have learned by now—though we haven't—that negative predictions about scientific achievements, achievements that do not violate universal principles—are usually false. Thus, eminent scientists themselves have claimed that radar was impossible, that space flight was impossible, that knowledge of the chemical composition of stars was impossible, and so on. Science has a powerful method that produces knowledge, and knowledge changes people's beliefs. In fact, it is the scientific revolution that is changing people's beliefs about what is valuable, and such changes involve us in economics.

It seems necessary to be concrete about the impact of science on belief, to give details about the way science changes our image of reality and of man's role—mankind's role, if you will—because by and large, people are woefully ignorant of science, so that they cannot think for themselves about generalities, generalities do not penetrate their consciousness. But now, for some generalities.

The impact of the scientific revolution is to change people's values in the sense of increasing their concern about "the quality of life," that is, about the quality of the culture they live in. The term *culture* is important to understand. It was coined by anthropologists in the 19th century as they began to study the artificial (nonbiological) extensions of human beings that allow them to survive. The anthropologists saw that people's tools, but also their beliefs, their poems, their songs, their myths, their religions—all the things and devices people use to enhance, protect, or express themselves—are designed to help groups survive. But with changing conditions, people's culture must change. Anthropologists study "culture crises" among human groups. When a culture is challenged by change, there are few alternatives. Either the group's population is checked and the culture is fragmented, or else a new culture is invented. Social change, as the anthropologist sees it, is inherent in the basic fabric of civilization. But culture "crises" are special cases.

Our "culture crisis" is associated with the breakdown of the existing industrial world view in the face of new knowledge. As Peter

Drucker has pointed out, we get our world view from René Descartes, the French philosopher and mathematician. He gave us the basic axiom of our thought: *that the whole is merely the result of its parts.* This is the way the ordinary man thinks about reality, it is "common sense" for us. And Descartes also gave us, by his analytical gometry, a universal language and method for exploring this axiom.

However, all the knowledge, the art, the culture of the 20th century is inconsistent with the Cartesian axiom. It is this clash of world views, as between the industrial world view and the new knowledge, that creates a crisis of culture. Our dominant world view, very different from the Middle Ages, has prevailed for 300 years since Descartes, and involves: (1) development and application of the scientific method; (2) wedding of scientific and technological advance; (3) intense application of the division of labor; (4) increasing scientific and educational specialization; (5) a positivistic theory of knowledge—only that is true which is operationally useful; and (6) the dominance in social policy of economic considerations, in private life of acquisitive materialism, and in work of the ethic of Puritanism.

The world view of the past 300 years has been remarkably successful, but its beginning breakdown can be seen in the paradox that its *successes* create many of our major problems. Its logic is beginning to encounter the paradoxes of extreme positions. For example: (1) affluence and the pile-up of goods lead to environmental decay, mounting pollution, materials and energy shortages, and a widening gap between rich and poor countries; (2) technological advances in "defense" lead to the threat of worldwide destruction; (3) rising standards of living lead to world overpopulation; (4) advances in communication and transportation lead to greater urbanization and increasing risk of societal breakdown from action by very small groups; (5) industrial engineering efficiency leads to the de-humanization of work; and so on.

SCIENCE REDEFINES CAPITALISM

The scientific revolution is redefining capitalism. The process is well under way and nowhere near its end. Not many theoretical economists have caught up with this development, since it involves the "invasion" of economics by other subject matter. By and large, economists have tended to ignore those social and economic realities that do not fit their theoretical models.

It is important to realize, however, that economic theory, as portrayed in the classical concepts of the free market, does not even consider, for example, the idea of evolution. The modern revolution in science demonstrates most powerfully that evolution is universal, from neutron to the universe itself, but economic theory is silent concerning the entire matter. This means that economics does not pay enough attention to the evolution of economic processes, of economic stages, nor does it even try to envisage future stages of economic advance.

What's more, economic theory has very poor means to deal with questions of resource depletion or environmental damage. Environmental damage can be interpreted under the concept of "externalities" introduced by Alfred Marshall in 1890 and discussed further by his contemporary at Cambridge University, A.C. Pigou. But the concept of *externalities*; that is, the idea that the social cost of environmental damage is not a cost of the firm and, so, is "external" remained theoretical until K. William Kapp's *The Social Costs of Private Enterprise* in 1950 documented important social costs of industry.

As for resource depletion, the economist does not yet have an adequate means of even discussing the question. Thus, one may review elementary college texts certainly up to 1970 and find only at best passing references to the subject.

Also, economists have not pursued the insight of the great Chicago theorist and philosopher Frank Knight, one of the most astute American economists. Knight was the interpreter par excellence of the market; however, he observed that people were almost entirely the creation of the social environment in which they live. Knight took a positivistic approach to economics and ruled out social influences of the market itself from study by economists.

Finally, another significant positivist, Lionel Robbins, argued persuasively to contemporaries that "positive" economics should be separated from "normative" economics. Robbins argued therefore that economists should eschew *value judgments*, concerning themselves only with the implications of actions. Thus, today many economists find it easy to pursue politics and political leadership as citizens, but they eschew value judgments, as they say, *qua economists*.

In contrast to economists, the basic theme of many of our most learned observers is that a radical intellectual revolution is in progress, propelled by new knowledge, in which the public is revising old values, and in which traditional economics alone is no longer an adequate guide to rational resource management. It is through the public response to this debate that capitalism is being redefined.

In short, capitalism is being redefined but mainly not by economists. The new concern about the quality of life is based rather on the wide dissemination of scientific knowledge itself, knowledge which causes a profound change in the prevailing world view, in people's image of reality and of man's place in nature. The industrial world view, to oversimplify again, sees processes, organisms, institutions as only the result of their parts. To understand something, one analyzes it; that is, he breaks it apart into its components. Business, for example, extols "the analytical mind." Second, the industrial world view sees man as separate from and apart from nature, a Prometheus who defies the gods and steals the fire from Mt. Olympus, a son of God who has dominion over the earth and the creature of the earth. And third, the industrial world view rules out of its consideration the inter-relatedness of all things; the corporation, for example, was invented to isolate a single purpose and to maximize the means of pursuing it.

By contrast, the new world view, enforced on us by new knowledge, sees reality quite differently and as marked by *holism*, *naturalism*, and *immanentism*. *Holism* refers to the pattern or configuration of processes, organisms, and institutions. It asserts that the whole of a thing is separate from its parts, may even define its parts. *Naturalism* implies that humankind is a part of nature, inseparable in its fate from the fate of nature itself. And the idea of *immanentism* is the idea of becoming, of evolution, of the irreversibility of time, of the ongoing relatedness of events.

These ideas redefine capitalism in important ways, some now being developed and others to come. These new shifts in value, stemming from new knowledge, are challenging concepts of what is *rational*. Since corporate management of economic resources derives its political and social legitimacy from the presumably rational allocation of resources, disputes over the nature of rationality itself are bound to affect corporate strategies, management, markets, and products.

A powerful example is the role played by entropy in economics. Its role can be illustrated by a simple explanation. If one considers what Reverend Thomas Malthus argued, that population would outstrip the means of subsistence, he can see that Malthus overlooked the increase in productivity. Malthus saw the relationship of the output of food to inputs of resources—he saw what economists today call "the production function," that is, the necessary functional relationship between output and inputs, the idea that output *depends on* inputs. What he did not see is that we could *shift* the production function, by increases in productivity, to gain *more* output from given inputs. But this is what the industrial societies have done in the last century and a half.

Now, we are discovering that waste and pollution are necessarily associated with output; that output is impossible without waste and pollution; indeed, that waste and pollution grow faster than output. If an economic good is something scarce and useful, one can define a negative economic good—by parallelism—as something plentiful and positively useless. We might call it a "nood," short for negative economic good. If a stockpile of goods is wealth, then a stockpile of noods could be called "crud."

In the age we are moving into, we need to learn how to shift the crud function; that is, to get a given amount of output with less waste and pollution. A moment's thought on this point shows that we have now encountered a task as profoundly important and disruptive to prevailing beliefs as the discovery of the role of productivity.

To some in positions of business or political leadership, the new shift in values appears as an enormous threat. Just as writers such as Reich reflect the language and suspicions of paranoia, so these "defenders of political or economic virtue" see about them a "conspiracy" of the scholar, the preacher, the youth, and the journalist, because these are the people reporting the "bad news": for example, that chemical fertilizer runs off into rivers, or that strip mining creates acid in streams, or that energy reserves of fossil fuels are being depleted, and the like. However, it should be manifest that science and technology, which have largely created our present living standards, are engaged in no conspiracy but are only pursuing with greater effectiveness an understanding of how processes interrelate on earth.

A NEW SOCIAL CHARTER

People are calling for a new social contract. The terms of the contract affect all the major institutions of our society, and since business and the corporation play so large a role in the society, the call for an improved quality of life affects business particularly.

Environment and Growth

Concern about the environment has led to questioning economic growth itself. Many scholars argue that at present rates of population growth, resource consumption, environmental degradation, and industrial development, the means of support for a world of more and more people living in industrial societies like ours will lag markedly within 100 years, creating conditions for a population catastrophe. There is, furthermore, concern that world scarcities of materials and energy lie ahead in the medium-term future, that troubled years lie ahead.

It should be clear: "growth versus no growth" is a non-issue. No one who has thought about the matter advocates no growth or offers any feasible plan to stop economic growth. The concern is with the size and distribution of the social and environmental costs of growth, and with our inability to take into account both social costs and benefits of various economic activities. This concern has already changed the nature of capitalism in quite significant ways. It has killed the SST, created the "environmental impact" statement, created "technology assessment," changed the organizational structure of public utilities, made the auto industry a highly regulated institution, and forced major industries such as steel to spend as much as 15 percent of their capital budget on unrequited pollution abatement.

All these measures reject the strict profit calculus. The SST was thrown out because people did not trust calculations of its environmental impact. Indeed, the "environmental impact" statement, required in government programs and soon, no doubt, of industry, is aimed exactly to force objective looks at the question. "Technology assessment," now law, requires study in advance of secondary and tertiary effects of technology; it means that laissez faire by corporations in introducing new technology is breathing its last. Public utilities, all too familiar with all this, now have environmental staffs to make location decisions for plants, rather than basing them on engineering economics. And does anyone doubt that the auto industry is now regulated?

The Social Responsibility of Corporations

The corporation, indeed, is about to become a social as well as an economic organization. The drive to create a "social audit" is clear evidence. Donald A. McNaughton, Chairman of Prudential, states the key issue most clearly. He points out, "It was not God but the people who granted us [the corporation] permission to function." In the 19th century, people wanted goods. Corporations produced them, and they invented *systems* to measure productivity. Now people want both goods, services, and quality of life. Corporations are being called on to become social organizations. Says McNaughton, it well behooves corporations to invent new forms of *social* measurement. And this is going on, through development of *social indicators, environmental indicators*, and the like.

What people seem to want in a new social charter is that major institutions reform themselves consistent with new knowledge. Health *systems*, educational *systems*, auto accident insurance *systems*, water systems, urban *systems*, can now be better understood as configurations and patterns. We are on the verge of vast new knowledge, aided by computers, of how these complex systems work, what they do, what their unintended as well as their intended effects are. We know more about the *system* for distributing wealth and income, and many others.

TOWARD HUMANISTIC CAPITALISM

The new revolution of knowledge, only dimly portrayed here, is better aware than before of the sources of wealth. It sees our machine civilization in a precarious position, threatened by catastrophe of war or breakdown from its own problems. The position is especially precarious because machine civilization is about to exhaust the richer ores of the earth. If machine civilization should deteriorate, the materials to pull ourselves up again would be lacking.

Thus, not only is our opportunity to manage the environment unprecedented but we are living through a phase of history that cannot be repeated. The source of our wealth that cannot be depleted but that offers promise of growth is not in the proliferation of consumer goods but in the growth of knowledge and of services to others.

The scientific revolution therefore raises the question about a theory of economics and of society that are sustainable over long time periods. The theory of economics would not be consumption-oriented but would be resource-oriented and environment-oriented. And the theory of such an economy is forced on us by the current energy crisis. Suddenly, we find large corporations urging us to take walks, to cut highway speeds, to conserve fuel. One might idly ask why, if these were such rational ideas, we only heard them lately, which is to say, what is the meaning of "the rational allocation of resources" these days? Is it consumption or conservation?

Such a sustainable society, one might think, would see corporations dedicated to what might be called "humanistic capitalism," pursuing limited but well-defined social and economic purposes, developing measures of social and economic purposes, developing measures of social and economic costs and benefits, and making profits distributed to a very wide group of owners, far wider than today, with a much more responsive process for the exercise of management trusteeship. The alternative, one would also think, is the increasing regulation of the corporation and a far larger role even yet for government.

CONCLUSION

Our society, then, is experiencing a change in world view caused by a powerful scientific revolution, providing new knowledge of the universe, of the earth and its functioning, and of man's place in nature. As people's values change, a "Greening of Economics" is occurring as the environmental impacts of economic processes are recognized and weighed more carefully. The result is to redefine capitalism and to question the old culture of a consumptionist society of acquisitive materialism, as people strive to adapt instead to a resource economy of environmental balance that offers long-term prospects of sustaining civilization.

In its larger and deeper aspects, the concern about the environment, about the quality of life, about the culture and its need to change does not mean the end of economic growth but rather the recognition of new knowledge- and service-based wealth of the future. It would be foolish to imagine that such painful developments as the present energy shortage are likely to dispel these powerful forces of new knowledge impinging on our society and the world today. Much more likely, as people grasp more clearly the reasons behind today's energy and material shortages, they probably will question even more the older values of acquisitive materialism and conventional economics for their difficulty in recognizing what wealth is.

Part 2

The Income-Distribution
and Allocative Effects of
Environmental Policies

Assuming we knew how to meet or, where possible, forestall the sundry threats to our environment, how would
such remedial or preventive policies affect the economic
position of the nation, various sectors of the economy, regions,
interest groups, households?

Even such preliminary measures as have been taken or proposed in
the attempt to reduce air pollution from automobile exhaust fumes
or to combat a national energy shortage have provoked vehement
and concerted protests on grounds of allegedly ruinous consequences
in the form of strangulation of certain industries, large-scale unemployment, catastrophic earnings losses.

Clearly, what hits home first, and most forcefully, is—couched in
the plainest possible terms—the question, "How would specific
measures to protect our environment affect us in our pocketbooks?"

Carolyn Bell demonstrates that this seemingly simple question is
difficult even to formulate properly. What is the appropriate frame
of reference? Large as it is, the United States is not a self-contained
unit; there is worldwide interdependence. Are there any isolated
effects, or do all national consequences entail international repercussions, which, even if only "ripples" may bring on feedbacks in their
turn? If so, what would these be like?

By what criteria can we rate different income distribution patterns
as better or worse, and how do we compare them as between nations,
or even domestically between dissimilar settings?

Do we stop at money income, or must we look to what incomes
can buy? When speaking of comparative family income, we must

remember that family units change in response to income changes; over time, therefore, such comparisons may be misleading.

These problems of conceptualization and methodology attach to any attempt to assess income distribution effects of policies of whatever kind—among them environmental policies. But the effects of specific policies depend, of course, on the nature and implementation of the policy. For example, how are we going to "clean up" the environment, by levying special taxes or penalties on polluters? Or by laws and regulations that limit or forbid certain modes of production—with or without compensation to those hurt? From what source—from general revenues? Depending on the approach taken, the ensuing income distribution effects will be very different in their incidence, magnitude, etc.

What if world economic problems should overtake us that dwarf our environmental concerns, both in their effects on income distribution and, much more dramatically, their possible upset of our entire economy or economic order?

William Mobraaten focuses on the problem of how business, especially large, corporate business, raises and allocates capital to render services demanded—through the market mechanism—as a consequence of economic growth. Customers (consumers) and investors (especially stockholders) play the cardinal roles in the process. They, and the "glue that cements [the] entire framework together—profitability" guide and determine management's actions.

Again, as in the foregoing paper, this set of ground rules applies whatever the cause that sets the process in motion. The specific environmental problem complex superimposes a bigger concern that has been in the making for some time, viz., a systemic view as against a single product or service orientation—all the more so, as in the future, the most pronounced and sustained characteristic may not be growth but quality, choice and ingenuity in economizing.

Masson Gaffney takes as his point of departure the present impasse in economic thinking—what with modern fiscal and monetary policy prescriptions (essentially both Keynesian in outlook), and all of the neoclassical conventional wisdom being questioned in the face of protracted "stagflation." He attempts no less than to restructure our basic model, and to prescribe new criteria for radically new full-employment policies. Almost incidentally, pollution problems and other environmental woes undergo a radical scaling-down. Not a mean order!

Harking back nearly a century to observations made and questions raised by Henry George, and about half as long to the theoretical armamentarium of Knut Wicksell, Gaffney constructs a new gauge of the economic efficiency of capital. It is premised upon the absorptive capacity of capital in different forms for human labor. He promises us no less than to cast out some basic fallacies in current economic thinking and to replace these by a "resurrected" theory whereby:

> We can employ ourselves as fully as we wish without any of the unpleasantness we now suffer in the name of jobs: without inflating, without borrowing, without fighting, without polluting, without any compulsion to "grow," "develop" and expand, without wasting, without price and wage controls, without invading more wilderness, without impoverishing posterity, without socializing labor or capital, without *dirigisme*, without giving up freedom, and without overspilling our national boundaries.

Not only can we avoid pollution and other environmental damage in the process of doing so, Gaffney maintains, but growth need not stop; it can take place by simply combining more labor with given magnitudes of capital and land.

This is too challenging a piece of writing to further paraphrase it. We must not whittle away the reader's excitement by revealing more of the clues in advance.

✳ *Chapter 4*

Income Distribution and Environmental Policies

*Carolyn Shaw Bell**

Environmentalists correctly perceive themselves as concerned with distributional problems, that is, how to share the scarce resources of the world. Any specific environmental policy poses a specific distributional question: How will the policy affect the incomes of different people? Such a question requires the technical competence of economic analysis if the answers are to go beyond platitudes or empty generalizations. This analysis will not greatly differ from that given any policy proposal. That is, we may investigate the distributional impact of a ceiling on insured savings or a quota on sugar imports, a local sales tax, or a reduction in local parking spaces using much the same techniques. This chapter will discuss these techniques with special reference to environmental policies.

THE APPROPRIATE INCOME DISTRIBUTION: WHAT AND WHOSE INCOME?

The immediate question for any understanding of distributional effects is, what income distribution? Whose income? Are we talking about the entire world or about one country or, specifically, about the United States? If we consider government policies, we must deal with recognizable political units. But to select only one political entity, which presumably sets policy and which also contains an income distribution, limits the analysis severely.

*Carolyn Shaw Bell is Katharine Coman Professor of Economics at Wellesley College.

Environmental policies involve global, not national, concerns. Those ecologists, prophets, and social activists engaged in consciousness-raising find the notion of spaceship earth, not Project Independence, essential to their cause. It is because resources are contained within a planet and not within a country that resources have, for sure and in fact, finite limitations. Because resources are the source of income, the basic distributional problem also refers to the planet and not any geographical or political subdivision. The world view, however, rarely exists. The severe inequality of income distribution between those in poor countries and those in rich generates conflicting views of environmental problems as well as of proposed solutions. The recent world population conference at Bucharest demonstrated that these divisions reflect not only disparities of income but also of values and expectations among nations.

On the other hand, any attempt to assess the impact of policy on the distribution of income throughout the world will not get far. United Nations data on national product and income for various nations contain vast discrepancies and vary widely in accuracy. Nor do these sources provide much information on the distribution of income *within* these nations. Furthermore, even where we know, for example, that income in Denmark is distributed more equally than in Brazil, this tells us nothing about the world distribution of income. To know that Haiti is a poor country and Mali is a poor country and Austria and Libya are much richer does not let us draw a Lorenz curve describing the incomes of the people in these four countries, taken together. Much less can we derive a Lorenz curve for the entire world (see Figure 4–1). But surely to speak of income distribution globally must mean, as it does at home, income distributed among people, not among nations or governments.

If, however, we consider only domestic policies and the distribution of national income, we must also remember that the United States operates in an international economy. Our controls of automobile pollutants affect U.S. consumers and also automobile workers, in the United States, in Germany, Japan, Sweden, and other countries with industries exporting to the U.S. market. The cost changes, for manufacturers, may remind us of other cost changes and the adjustments that followed. For example, older industries in the United States, such as textiles and leather, migrated to our Southern states as comparative costs between South and North changed, and later succumbed to competition from producers in the Carribean, Hong Kong, and Taiwan. Other industries, light manufacturing and certain electronic components, seem to have rapidly become "older"

Figure 4−1. A Lorenz Curve—Simplest Tool for Income Distribution Analysis

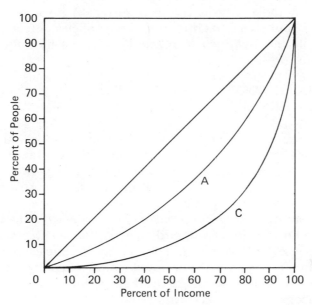

Note: A Lorenz curve, the simplest tool of income distribution analysis, plots the percentage of total income received by equal percentages of people. In Figure 4−1, income is plotted on the horizontal axis, fractions of the population on the vertical axis. The 45-degree line represents the case of perfect equality: 50 percent of the people receive 50 percent of the income, 70 percent of the people receive 70 percent of the income, and so on. The lines *A* and *C* represent more realistic cases. In general, Lorenz curve *C* describes poor populations, where much greater inequality between rich and poor occurs than in rich populations like *A*.

in this respect. These relative labor cost considerations have reflected not only differences in wage rates but differences in working conditions.

But deliberate economic policies also produce differential costs by offering more encouraging economic climates, tax inducements, or the prospect of long-term capital to attract industry. Environmental policies, if they differ in their impact on industry from one municipality or state or island to another, will give rise to differential costs and, as a result, to the location of industry, employment, jobs, and income. Consequently, we may expect to find U.S. producers— both managers and labor-protesting the hardship effects of environmental measures, designed to further the survival of international amenities, as they now protest the hardship effect of tariff-reduction measures designed to further the survival of international amity. We cannot, then, look only at the distribution of income within this country without remembering that our policies affect, in some unmeasurable but not inconsiderable degree, the incomes of those beyond our shores.

INDIVIDUAL INCOME
OR FAMILY INCOME?

We have more queries about "whose income?" Most information about income and wealth within the United States comes from surveys of households or families. Income figures reported by the Internal Revenue Service refer to federal income tax returns, which are quite remote from real live human beings. The major sources consist of the Bureau of Census Current Population Reports, the decennial Census, the Federal Reserve Board, and the Survey Research Center of the University of Michigan. To analyze the impact of a specific environmental policy, therefore, would mean estimating the probable changes in the figures reported by these agencies, calculating new tables of income and wealth distribution.

The exercise is not a simple one. Real income consists not of the dollar sums received but of the goods and services purchased with those sums. Because consumption is a function of income, we may safely conclude that the distribution of real income is fairly accurately represented by the dollar figures, that people with $20,000 incomes enjoy more of the world's real resources, as well as receiving more money, than people with $2,000. But when environmental policies affect consumption, it is not at all clear that the change in real income can be accurately represented by figures on the distribution of money income. This is a profound and disconcerting problem which must be clearly understood.

All surveys of income share a basic anomaly in their approach to questions of real income. Income is earned and received in this economy by people as individuals; only rarely is income paid to two or more persons jointly. But income is not spent or saved by people as individuals; income is not disposed of as independently as it is earned. Most people live with others in what the Census Bureau calls "households" occupying "dwelling units." Most people enjoy—and I use the word enjoy advisedly—*family* income. At any given time a significant portion of the population lacks *any* dollar income, but obviously these children, housewives, and older people receive real income in being fed and clothed and sheltered. However, as individuals, they are totally dependent on the income earned by other individuals and then contributed to the family. Whose income do we calculate, therefore: individuals or households?

Some major difficulties are involved. First, different members of the same household, having different preferences, may extract different amounts of real income from the same dollar total. It follows that the impact on individuals of any measure affecting the distribution of income cannot be predicted from a knowledge of family income. I am reminded of the colleague whose young children wish to deposit the family's output of trash and bottles at the community recycling depot. Their parents don't want to take the time to do this chore, but the children are too young to drive. The amount of family satisfaction provided here by conservation efforts is dubious. Such examples can be multiplied, perhaps especially by conflicts between recreational demands and environmental protection.

Second, if the income distribution chosen is that among *families*, then any change in the structure of families changes income. Consequently, the impact of any policy measure on individual earning or spending will be modified or diverted by shifts in the types of families within the society.

To clarify, let us realize that during the great depression of the thirties, *family* income was more equal than it was during the forties, but *personal* income was not. During the thirties, people lost their homes and doubled up, marriages were postponed, young men and women stayed with their parents. Population grew, but the number of families grew more slowly. The decline in total income was, therefore, spread over fairly large families.

DECEPTIVE SHIFTS IN FAMILY
INCOME DISTRIBUTION

With the onset of prosperity family size decreased sharply. As time grew better and incomes rose, families undoubled and broke up. In the decade from the mid-thirties to the mid-forties, population rose 13 percent, and the number of people aged 25 to 65 increased by 17 percent. But the number of families grew by 23 percent over the same period. This change in structure led to wider disparity of "family" income: the young people just starting out had, of course, much lower incomes than the families they had left.

These different measures of income must be reckoned with in order not to misinterpret the distributional effect of policy. To give only one example, consider the structure of households. If, for one reason or another, more people tend to live singly rather than in families, then larger numbers of certain consumer durables—automobiles, plumbing fixtures, cooking and washing equipment—will be demanded. The sharing that occurs within large households has disparate effects on consumption—economies of scale do not appear with every item on the list of total family expenditure. Ten people living in two households can manage with two kitchen ranges; 10 people living in five households cannot. As only one result, measures affecting the energy used by consumer durables, or the services they yield, will have a wider and more profound impact the greater the number of consuming units, or households, per thousand population.

THE DESIRABLE INCOME DISTRIBUTION

One major area of government policy is explicitly designed to change the distribution of income. First, there is the whole complex of transfers including Social Security, veterans' payments, welfare programs, and other measures enabling or requiring *direct payment* from the Federal Treasury to people. Second, an enormous apparatus exists providing *income in kind* to various designated groups: Medicare and Medicaid, veterans' hospitals, subsidies to homeowners and rural electricity suppliers, guaranteed loans to farmers and college students, and so on.

It is perhaps incorrect to say that this area of federal legislation has been *designed* to alter the distribution of income. Each measure, taken by itself, has involved calculating income effects for Congressional consideration, and usually it has been argued that the law or provision will assist those of a certain income class, or improve the income of others. Nevertheless none of these measures has been rigorously analyzed in terms of its impact on the overall distribution of income, or of its contribution, net, to the division of income among families or among individuals or taxpayers or young people or any other group of people that might be relevant. For the most part, the broad distributional effects of its legislation have not yet been of major concern to any Congress. Nor to its constituents.

This point needs some elaboration. Nothing in our governmental or social structure encourages us to take an overview, to appraise the total impact of our economic system on the welfare of the people in this country. It would be possible for every legislator to have a picture, a scale model, of the income distribution of this country accompanying every legislative proposal. Before voting, the legislator could view the measure against this model, testing for fit, as it were. But such a basic understanding of income, or of any other characteristic of the body politic, does not come as part of any legislator's orientation course or of any citizen's education about the society in which we live.

More importantly, we lack any clear understanding, as a people, how income *should* be distributed. I do not mean merely that we disagree about what ought to be; I mean that we do not understand. Income questions and distributional questions are much more complicated than many people think. Problems requiring technical competence cannot be solved by the simple application of goodwill and common sense. To gain a consensus among Americans of what income distribution *should* be is not merely a matter of values and ethics.

HOW IS INCOME (IN-) EQUALITY TO BE DEFINED?

For example, it is likely that most people would vote for more, rather than less, equality in incomes. But equality is not immediately definable. Take two cases, a situation where one individual is very wealthy and eight others exist at poverty level, and a second situation where nine individuals occupy distinct income classes, three of them being rich, three "comfortably off," and three poor. You may be able to state your *preference* for one over the other, but you cannot readily identify which gives greater *equality* of incomes.

It may be that the distribution of income that suits most people cannot be defined in terms of more or less equality but instead reflects some other value, perhaps rewarding efforts or patriotism or brains or beauty. In times past and in other societies people have chosen systems for distributing the goods of this world according to good behavior or good thinking, both variously defined. Some have distributed the "bads" of this world according to similar criteria, and some, with the help of organized religion, have forecast the distribution of goods and bads in worlds to come. In short, to consider the impact of, say, environmental policies on the distribution of income is to perform a task that is rarely contemplated, let alone carried out, in today's harried world of decision. Perhaps we are better off for *not* considering the complexities of income distribution; but no evidence exists that we have made any considered judgment on this point.

One result is that there is an implicit bias in favor of the status quo. It is much easier to talk about a specific policy—say, a new gasoline tax—in terms of whether it will make poor people more or less poor than they are now. This assumes, insidiously, that there is something good about how they now are. It is much *more* difficult to talk about the impact of said tax on the total distribution of income as envisioned against some standard. But it is also true that any policy involves social change, not social re-creation. We move from where we are, not from a blank slate.

INCOME AND EARNINGS

How, explicitly, will environmental policies affect the incomes received by people in this country? By changing their earnings and the ways in which they spend their earnings. What basic data can we learn that will apply to the analyses of any environmental policy? First, some facts about the current situation—where we are, before we change.

Among 56 million families in 1974, the median family income was slightly over $12,000. One-quarter of these families received incomes of less than $8,000 a year; a quarter were middle income with $7,000 to $12,000 annually, and over one-quarter, or 15 and a half million families, received incomes of $15,000 to $25,000. Twelve percent had larger incomes; most of these fell closer to $25,000 than $50,000 or above. What about the earnings of these low, middle, upper middle and high income classes of families? Where do they get their income?

About half of the families at the bottom of the income scale had no working member, and more than half of those containing a working member were supported by a woman. By contrast, half the families with incomes from $10,000 to $25,000 contained two earners, usually a married couple, and over one-third of the families with incomes over $25,000 similarly contained two working members. The *type* of job which yielded earnings also shows significant differences among income classes. Earned incomes are higher among managerial and professional workers, and such people make up half the working population among the upper income families. They account for only one in eight of the low income workers. Part-time work is also more prevalent among low income families, and so is working less than a full day.

"Other" sources of income—not earnings from a job—occur most frequently at the two extremes of the income scale. At the low end "income other than earnings" refers mainly to welfare or other transfer payments, like social security, while at the upper end of the income scale it is apt to consist of dividends and other property income. The family characteristics associated with receiving small incomes, therefore, consist of relative lack of employment, low paying employment, dependency on one or fewer earners—in short, inability to find gainful *employment* sufficient to provide higher income.

Middle income families show a wide range of family characteristics. Most of the male heads of middle income families have some education beyond high school. Although some 15 percent are either unemployed or not in the labor force, another 50 percent receive all their income from earnings. Dual earner families are significantly fewer than at higher income levels. Finally, the occupational spread is substantial with percentages for unskilled jobs approaching the lower income classes. Reflecting the lesser degree of education, there are very few professional or technical workers in the middle income group.

Environmental policy will affect the distribution of income first as it affects earnings. To the extent that environmental policies change the structure of industry and therefore of employment, they will make relatively little difference to the people at the low end of the income scale. The number of *earners* in the lowest income group is a minority; these families will continue to be dependent on transfer income. It is highly unlikely that environmental policies will produce an increase of job opportunities for poorly educated, unskilled workers, but if they are displaced, semi-skilled and unskilled workers are relatively transferable among jobs.

Environmental policies may have a greater impact on individual workers in both the middle and upper income classes, but for different reasons. If the response to a given environmental requirement is a cut-back in production or a lay-off of workers, sudden and sporadic unemployment may very well result for craftsmen and skilled operatives, numerous among these income groups. But such hardships are not uniquely produced by environmental policies. Other types of policies—and events—produce sudden and sporadic unemployment. For example, the petroleum shortage last year led to lay-offs among hotel workers in Miami and Vermont, but a bout of bad weather can produce equal hardship. Over a longer period of unemployment or when an entire area becomes depressed, the individual worker's mobility seems to be the product of psychological and sociological factors rather than the purely economic attractions of wages and working conditions. The job market is a highly imperfect one, especially with respect to information. People do not necessarily locate where the best job opportunities exist, nor do they necessarily use the best means of finding out about potential job opportunities. In this respect, the adjustment to structural changes brought about by environmental policies will probably be as faulty as the response to any other structural change.

The situation among professional and managerial workers, numerous among the upper income classes, may be somewhat different. Over the past 15 years a new type of unemployment has appeared—that of the "overqualified." It has been seductively easy to say that new environmental requirements will call for engineering skills, managerial skills, systems analysis, computer softwear design, and all of the professional techniques now in use. It does not necessarily follow that Engineer Hutchins can shift his years of design experience to another field or another firm. Nor does it follow that Sales Representative Mahoney can find his expertise in fine chemicals of any use to, say, the drug industry, or the drug policing industry. Although systematic research on the subject is sparse, it seems likely that this new barrier to employment, the unwillingness to hire people trained beyond the level required for the job, may pose significant problems. Clearly it is a cultural and psychological factor, like those that inhibit mobility of the worker, but it pertains to employers.

It is also an ironic byproduct of the credentials trap. The insistence on degrees for every job, and the frequent refusal to accept experience, know-how, or just plain flair as a substitute for the magic letters after one's name, has revealed another side. If the skilled psychiatric social worker cannot be promoted to greater responsibility without the Ph.D or M.S.W., although he or she surpasses the new graduate in ability, undoubtedly society is worse off. But society also loses when the so-called over-qualified Ph.D or the M.S.W. cannot be hired as a psychiatric social worker even though he or she is willing and able to take the job.

Further analysis of the impact on employment will depend on the specific policy under investigation. But the primary focus must be on employment, because earnings from jobs represent the most important form of income for most people in the country.

INCOME AND CONSUMPTION

An equally important impact on our economy comes from consumption spending. If environmental policies change the product mix or the nature of the goods and services available to consumers, then we can expect a variety of effects on people, depending upon how they spend their incomes. Having looked at employment, we need to analyze consumption patterns among different types of families and the impact of environmental policies upon real income, that is, the goods and services families can buy with a given number of dollars. Since consumption patterns by families vary with income, a given environmental policy affecting, say, food will have a quite different impact on families with different incomes. Beyond this gross pattern, however, what else influences how people spend their earnings? For the families in the basic income distribution discussed earlier, some observations can be made about spending characteristics.

Location affects consumption. But by income classes, people live all over the country. It is true that more high income people live in the Northeast and fewer low income; that the Northcentral has more upper middle income families with fewer very rich or very poor, and that the South has more low income families. But these differences are marginal, not glaringly apparent. It follows that whatever impact any economic policy has on the distribution of income, it will be a national concern and not a regional concern. The number of families living on farms is slightly under 5 percent. This ranges from a high of 7 percent of families with incomes of less than $4,000 to a low of 3.4 percent of the families with incomes over $15,000. Again the differences are not crucially significant.

Consumption expenditures also reflect the age and sex of family members, and this does vary by income. Families totally dependent upon women number 12 percent of the total, but almost 40 percent of the low income households. Only 2 percent of the families with incomes over $25,000 are headed by a woman. Besides these, other families with a male head are equally dependent upon a woman. Over two and a half million families which the Census counts as "male-head, married, wife present" report that the wife earns over half the total family income. As regards age, the lower income classes, of course, contain a preponderance of the very young and the very old. Their situation as consumers is tragically different. The very young are earning small amounts because they have just begun in jobs, because frequently their reported earnings refer only to a part-year achievement, because they are still in school, and they will progress onward and upward in the years to come. The very old have nowhere else to go, and for them the low incomes herald no signs of improvement in the immediate future.

As for the size and composition of the family, contrary to the accepted mythology, poor families are smaller than rich families. Partly this represents the presence, among low income families, of the very young and the very old where childless couples are in the majority. But along with the number of *children* present in the family, consumption reflects the number of *earners* in the family. What the family spends reflects the requirements of the workers. People who hold jobs have to spend income on clothing and food in different ways than people who don't hold jobs.

Given all these, and other, influences on consumption expenditures by families within a given income class, the direction of analysis to determine the impact of environmental policies becomes clear. A detailed examination of consumption patterns and their responsiveness to changes in price, availability, or consumer preference must be performed for any realistic evaluation to be made.

ENVIRONMENTAL PROTECTION AS A POLICY

One may expect, reasonably, that any specific economic policy may cause both earnings and consumption expenditures to shift, and there is no particular reason to generalize about the effects of environmental policies. Beyond this, looking at the cost-benefit approach in terms of income and consumption may provide a last word.

The costs of any economic policy consist first of its direct costs, the taxation levied to carry out government programs. Recent evidence from the Pechman study of tax incidence confirms what many have suspected, namely, that the net effect of federal, state, and local taxation is roughly proportional to income. It follows that the tax impact of any program is neutral with respect to the income distribution. There is no reason to suspect that the taxation devised for environmental policies will have any less neutral effect on the income distribution.

It can be argued, however, that the prevention of environmental disruption, or programs designed to protect the environment, should be paid for by what economists call externalities. These are social costs attributed to one particular type of output or one kind of industrial operation, which should be shifted to the users of this output or the product of that industry. In such cases, specific taxes or price adjustments would be designed for particular environmental programs. It would then follow that poor people would pay a greater share of their incomes for such costs than rich people, since the latter spend on consumption a smaller fraction of their total income. Beyond this, however, some useful analyses of consumption and the distribution of income can be made, which ought not to be limited merely to sorting by economic or income class.

For example, if environmental protection means that fuel costs rise, then homeowners and those living outside metropolitan areas will suffer a real income loss relative to renters, and to those living within the inner city areas. If concern for natural resources means that so-called "convenience items"—plastic and paper tableware, elaborate packaging, throwaway containers, and the like—become more expensive, then large families and those with several income earners will suffer more of an income loss than the smaller households with a full-time home manager.

The benefits from environmental policies should similarly be analyzed in terms of consumption patterns and especially consumption preferences. Clearly individuals differ in the value they place on protecting the environment in the first place. Secondly, the amenities of environmental protection mean more to some people than to others. It should be pointed out that many of the adherents of a "no-growth" policy do, in fact, want economic growth, but of those types of output *they* value. To call for an increase in privacy, the preservation of wilderness, or of natural pools for swimming or fishing or simply reflecting does not call for the cessation of economic growth, but merely a shift from one type of output to another. There is, on the face of it, no way to judge between the preferences for enjoying today and the preferences for preserving for tomorrow. But because this is so, then there is no way to allocate the benefits from environmental protection except to society as a whole.

A restatement here may be useful. Economists have been criticized for pretending to a value-free science, but it is not appropriate to criticize economics for attempting to separate values from analysis. To define environmental disruption in terms of external costs allows the analyst to make statements about the size of this cost and its distribution. But no economist and, for that matter, no environmentalist can say, on the basis of pure analysis, that any form of environmental disruption is in itself a wholly bad thing. This remains a value judgment, an ethical judgment, and one therefore that is not susceptible of noncontroversial analysis. To paraphrase Bob Solow, we need to ask ourselves every once in while why we should preserve the water or the land or the hillsides for future generations anyway. In all likelihood they will be far better off than we are, nor is there any reason to attribute our set of preferences to an unknown generation. Though this may run contrary to the fashionable expression of preferences today and perhaps to the values of many readers, it nevertheless bears thinking about.

Summarizing, therefore, the economist's view of the distributional impact of environmental policies, no general or universal rule can be found. Each program, each suggested social change, each potential economic policy must be analyzed individually. Its impact on income distribution will consist of the changes generated in employment and relative earnings and the changes that may be induced in relative consumption patterns. The implications of this for those concerned with designing environmental policy are two-fold. First, the distributional effects will be more complex than a simple characterization of "regressive" or the like indicate. Second, the complexities of consumption patterns argue for much more investigation of the impacts of environmental policies than seems to have been contemplated so far. This is particularly true when the distribution of income is presented not by income classes but by other characteristics affecting consumption patterns, like the number of earners, the sex of the household head, the living arrangements of the family, and so on.

OBITER DICTA

Many statements have recently appeared, ranging from wild insinuations to outright accusations, that the new emphasis on environmental protection causes inflation. The automobile industry has pointed to the so-called "non-productive" requirements for health and safety and the additional costs that are built into automobile prices. The fuel crisis led to many calls for abandoning anti-pollution devices and lowering clean air standards. All such reasoning is fallacious and open to the same criticism, which should be reiterated at every possible opportunity. The causes of our present economic troubles are so complex that to single out environmental policies smacks of irresponsibility. It was not any concern for the environment that led the OPEC countries to form a highly successful cartel. Singling out, for a given price rise, the costs of environmental controls is no more justified than singling out any other component cost: for example, the cost of yearly model changes or of unused engine power in the design of automobiles.

A second closing note follows from this. To be seriously concerned with the impact of environmental policies on the distribution of income, in a day when double-digit inflation is bringing about the most radical shift in the distribution of income that has occurred since the thirties, is taking a very strange view of events indeed. In a sense this entire chapter seems totally irrelevant. Compared to the impact of the current economics of inflation, all the concerns of environmentalists fade into insignificance. We need not worry about *any* income effects of environmental policies at the moment. It is to be devoutly hoped that we can repair the catastrophic disruptions in the structure of the world economy that have led us to this inflationary brink. If we can, then a more fortunate group of people, living in a more stable society, may be able to devote their energies and abilities to discovering the distributional impact of environmental policies. At the moment, our total commitment must be to solve the immediate pressing problems of disastrous price rises. Without some solution, there won't be any economic growth to worry about.

Chapter 5

Corporations as Resource-Allocators

William L. Mobraaten *

CORPORATIONS AND RESOURCE ALLOCATION

It is a popular supposition that corporate managers wield great power over the consumption and distribution of the nation's physical and financial resources. In a narrow sense this is accurate; my own corporation is the largest private enterprise in the world, with assets totaling upwards of $70 billion, yearly revenues in excess of $25 billion; we employ more than 1 million people, and are responsible to nearly 3 million investors. I know that the top management of my business is always concerned that a mistake in utilizing our available dollar and people resources could have severe repercussions for the economy as a whole.

In a broader sense, however, mature corporations like my own are mirrors of past public demand. The bulk of our decisions on priorities and allocation of resources are set in one way or another by the cumulative actions of the consuming public. In a free society, business birth, growth, and death are largely set in the arena of the marketplace. This may strike some as conventional laissez-faire balderdash and gross oversimplification, but in the final analysis I believe it to be accurate. Moreover, I believe the marketplace is the *right* forum for allocative decisions because it best serves the multiplicity of interests involved in such a process.

*William L. Mobraaten is Vice President and Treasurer of the American Telephone and Telegraph company.

THE MARKET AS AN ALLOCATOR

The market approach to resource allocation is both more pervasive and at the same time more subtle than many business managers might seem to reflect in their day-to-day operations. Hardly a week goes by in which the mail does not bring at least one urgent summons to a conclave of right-minded enterprisers aimed at "doing something" about the admittedly disturbing decline in the prestige of American business in the public's mind. The very existence of the National Affiliation of Concerned Business Students is itself evidence of the need for concern. Yet we must constantly remain alert that our concern reflect the real desires of the consumer and not an imposition of an elite definition of what is needed by society. The cry to "reorder our priorities" is too often a code for "do what I think is best." The market concept, broadly defined, offers a much needed guidepost.

How, then, can a business manager look to the marketplace to guide his decision-making? First, we need to define what we mean by "markets." The dictionary definition—"a gathering of people for buying and selling things"—seems clear, but I suspect that in the past there has been too much emphasis on "buying and selling" and not nearly enough on "people." The dramatic instances where the public at large decides it no longer wants or needs a product are, of course, examples of the ultimate decision-making power that is always present. A business fades into oblivion because its managers did not comprehend in time the possibility of sweeping and revolutionary changes in the economic, social, and technological environment. Prudent men considered street railway systems a prime investment for "widows and orphans" just before the advent of the automobile. Between 1915 and 1918, 308 electric street railway companies with nearly $2 billion of capital were forced into receivership. As recently as 1926 the Connecticut Insurance Commission refused to permit institutional investment in electric utilities, but permitted large investments in street-car lines.

These cases are extreme, however, and offer little by way of practical guidance. The public's attitude toward any business is multifaceted, but I believe the main determinant of the public's attitude toward business is its day-in and day-out experience with business' performance. At least some share of the decline in the public's confidence in business reflects the skepticism it has come to feel with respect to the zeal with which we in business pursue our professed aim of giving the public full value for its money. If this is so—and the most authoritative surveys of public opinion that I have seem to indicate that it *is* so—we have some listening to do before we set about to "straighten out" the public's thinking on the economics of enterprise. In other words, we need to interact with the people— the market, if you will—and accommodate our actions to their needs.

SERVICE AND THEODORE VAIL

Perhaps an example from my own company's past will illustrate my point. Theodore N. Vail was its first general manager and later its president. Vail had two careers with us—the first extending from 1878, when he undertook to organize the infant telephone industry on behalf of its proprietors, to 1887 when—uncharacteristically for a Bell System man—he up and quit, and for a very strange reason: the proprietors of the business, it appeared to him, were more interested in profit than in performance.

Vail was gone from our ranks for almost 20 years, but in 1907 he returned to become president of AT&T, the head of a business that had grown enormously since his departure but that was acknowledged to be in trouble—in trouble financially and in trouble with its customers as well.

Vail headed our business until 1919, just a year before his death. In that span of time he restored our business to financial stability and the regard of its customers. He transformed what had been a loose association of companies into a nationwide system, employing common practices throughout its territories and pursuing common aims. He took the lead in articulating the concept of public regulation under which those companies operate today. And he made it unequivocally clear that service was the standard to which the business had committed itself and for which he expected it to be held publicly accountable.

Finally, he left for his posterity a series of remarkable Annual Reports. In an era at least in legend more noted for corporate rapacity than for sensitivity to the public interest, he undertook to set forth in these reports his "philosophy" of the business and his views on the public policy issues affecting its ability to serve well. It is very largely by this philosophy that we still live today.

On December 28, 1883, from the offices of the American Bell Telephone Company in Boston, Vail wrote the managers of the company as follows:

Dear Sir:

Now that the Telephone business has passed its experimental stage, I would like to get your opinion on the points given below . . .

Is the Telephone service, as it is now being furnished, satisfactory to the public?

Are the prices satisfactory to the public, considering the facilities and service that is given . . .?

What has been the tendency of the relationship between the public and the local Co.'s for the past year, i.e., are the relationship between the Co.s improving?

The questions that Vail asked 91 years ago, we have been asking ever since. Not only do we look to our managers to report to us continuously and in detail on the technical performance of our facilities—dial tone speed, the percentage of call completions, the accessibility of our business offices, the trouble report rate, and so forth—but we expect as well to be kept informed with respect to the way the public itself perceives our service.

THE PUBLIC AND RESOURCE ATTRACTION

Public perception of our service is the vital criterion precisely because of its impact on resource attraction and allocation. As an ongoing business enterprise interested in service (and self-perpetuation), we need to assure ourselves of an adequate supply of resources. The problem of allocation is moot absent any resources. Our business is communications. We draw on three basic sources—our customers, our shareowners, and our employees—for the wherewithal to provide that service. Public perception of the need for and desirability of any particular service offering will ultimately decide its fate. If the customer won't buy it, or the investor won't underwrite it, or the business can't attract the needed employees to design and service it, the service cannot become or remain viable. Equally important, the process of attracting needed resources bears importantly on how we allocate those resources.

THE CUSTOMER

The customer's input to the allocation process is twofold: through the usual buy or not-buy decision, and increasingly through the political process. This latter influence is particularly noticeable in a regulated business. In the telephone business, the law requires that we must be allowed adequate total revenues that will provide an overall fair return on our investment. It does not specify how those total revenues are to be derived. The overall revenue requirement is "allocated" to specific services based upon a combination of regulatory and managerial judgments: the cost of providing the service; the relative value to users; political considerations; precedent with similar services; uniformity of price structure; and essentiality of service.

Picturephone offers an example of the customer's influence in the traditional market sense. We felt we had a good product, and actively began field trials. Customers, through their decision not to buy the service at any price approaching the cost of providing it, convinced us that we were ahead of our time in this instance. Research and development will continue in an effort to lower costs, but for the time being we're responding to the evident lack of customers' demand and allocating our efforts elsewhere.

The role of the political process in the allocation decision is receiving more attention today, but in our business the political factor is not new. Basic residential telephone service has historically been priced at an "entry" rate low enough for almost anyone to afford. This goal was promulgated under state and local regulations beginning early in this century, and formalized as national policy in the Federal Communications Act of 1934. Fundamentally, this means pricing more elaborate service features, business services, and long distance calls high enough to make a healthy contribution to the common costs of the business and thus keep basic residential rates relatively low. In a broader sense, the political-regulatory process affects both the kind of services we offer and the prices we can charge. Hence the needs and wants of our customers can and do bear heavily on our ability to marshall resources and our allocation of those resources.

THE INVESTOR

The role of the investor is equally critical to the resource allocation process. The nature of our business is capital intensive; we need nearly $3 in plant investment to generate $1 in revenue. We cannot generate sufficient funds within the business to pay for the plant and equipment that must be in place if we are to serve the growth in demand for communications. Investors must supply the balance of the needed capital.

Under our economic system, we cannot somehow expropriate the required capital. We must convince investors to provide the needed funds. Like any commodity, capital has its price—and in today's highly inflationary economic environment the price is very high. The investor assesses what we plan to do with the money and the return that he might reasonably expect from such use. If the expected return is sufficient, the capital is available; if the expected return is judged to be inadequate, the funds flow elsewhere. The allocation of the funds attracted is keyed to the market through the investor's perception of management's ability to properly gauge profitable opportunities. Any management which ignores or is unable to meet the needs of consumers is unlikely to long remain a favored vehicle for investment capital. This year we needed about $10 billion in construction dollars. We obtained some $6 billion within the business, and outside investors provided the other $4 billion. If we had been forced to "make do" with no external capital, some 40 percent of the investment needed to meet customer demand would have been foregone, with the concurrent impact on the quality of existing service.

THE EMPLOYEE

Going back to our definition of the market—a gathering of people to buy and sell—we note that people are involved on both sides of the transaction. Just as there can be no market without buyers, there can be none without sellers. Our employees are our sellers: they take the capital provided by investors and transform it to the product desired by the customers. They collectively make the managerial decisions that will finally determine how well we meet customer and investor goals.

There is nothing particularly profound in this process, and yet the interaction can be far-reaching. Communications is so much a part of the infrastructure of society that the fundamental decisions on where resources need to be concentrated may be self-evident. For example, after World War I the number of telephones and calls was growing so rapidly that it was obvious management had to concentrate available resources on the switching of calls. The key question, however, was whether that allocation should go into people (telephone operators) or into mechanization (dial switching service). We decided in the 1920s that mechanization was the only long-range solution to the growing demand. We simply wouldn't be able to hire enough operators in the future to handle the switching demand on a manual basis.

Today the big communications machine we call the network runs with far fewer people at the controls than would have been the case had we opted otherwise. The jobs also demand people of higher capabilities, and the job satisfaction is correspondingly greater. Of course, that long-ago decision, as every allocation decision, had prices to be paid as tradeoffs. In this instance perhaps the most damaging was the loss of personal contact with customers on each call handled. On the other hand, we now employ many more operators than we did in the 1920s, and in more truly helpful-to-the-customer jobs, as a result of the enormous service growth over the intervening decades.

Human resources, investor resources, and consumer resources, have all been shaped—and continue to be shaped—by the action management elected over 50 years ago. I feel that the decision then has certainly proved to be the right one, but as a manager today I'm more concerned with the future. Corporate management is much more complex today; how well we meet our commitments in all areas of resource attraction and allocation can have profound social and environmental impact. The market process will do the allocation, but we must accurately interpret what the market is telling us and then act to commit our available resources in the most efficient manner from both economic and human perspectives. These are times that demand innovations in the structuring of our society's undertakings—in business, in government, in education, in the delivery of social services. In the case of my own business, I believe that the allocation process can be enhanced if we all take a fresh look at the role of the consumer, the investor, and the employee.

A LOOK AHEAD: CONSUMERS

Business, my own included, must adapt its practices to better meet the needs of modern-day customers. They're better educated, have higher expectations, and have developed a deep distrust of the motives of business in general. As managers, we must confront their doubts with honest efforts to meet their higher level of expectations. "It has always been done that way" is not a legitimate answer. It's essential that business regain the trust of our customers. We need to find better ways and better communications channels to explain our reasoning on important issues. In short, we need to develop a dialogue with the consumer—a *two-way* conversation—so that our customers are satisfied that their legitimate wants are being met in the most efficient manner. This includes any environmental concerns our customers may bring to bear on the way services are provided.

A LOOK AHEAD: INVESTORS

We likewise have a concurrent obligation to our shareowners. They have advanced their savings to us in good faith. We must manage their capital carefully, and treat it as the depletable resource that it is. The decade ahead will offer no one the luxury of wasting capital resources. Indeed, there is likely to be a shortage of capital to fund the legitimate wants and needs of society. A recent study indicated that over the next 10 years our national store of capital may fall short by some $650 billion—a staggering figure on any basis, but particularly so when it translates to medical facilities not built, energy sources not developed, and environmental concerns that may be neglected. As business leaders we must do our utmost to encourage and enhance the capital formation process. This includes making every effort to earn adequately on the capital invested in the light of current economic conditions. Naturally, as with our customers, so with our investors' environmental expectations that translate themselves into comparative evaluations of competing investment opportunities will leave their imprint on our company.

A LOOK AHEAD: EMPLOYEES

If we are to meet our obligations to our customers and our investors, we must maximize our third resource—the people who will implement those policies. We must attract our fair share of the highly skilled and genuinely concerned younger generation. We must offer opportunities for meaningful input at all levels of the business. We've done some pioneering research in my own company on the work process, and are moving rapidly to implement concepts such as "Work Itself." A major effort is under way to enrich jobs up and down the organizational ladder. We're also conducting a major campaign to inform all of our current employees of the opportunities that are available to them, and at the same time attempting to break the stereotyped conceptions that exist as to what's "men's work" and "women's work." The best effort of *all* available minds will be required if we are to meet the problems that confront us.

ORGANIZATIONAL PRINCIPLES

Even in this brief discussion, the balances and interrelationships are evident. Our investor body can't meet their needs at the expense of consumers or employees; in the final analysis all the interests must be properly balanced. This is a common problem with much broader perspectives than the communications business. There is widespread discontent today, confirmed in poll after poll, with the dominant institutions in our society. Somehow, it would appear, things are not working as they should. To set things right, we first need to know what we want to do: we must set clear and unambiguous goals. This process is a political one, and beyond the scope of this discussion. After charting our course, however, we need a set of operating principles to guide us from where we are to where we want to be. Herein I believe I can again draw on the past history of my own corporation and perhaps illuminate the process for our larger efforts to match the structure of our economy to society's current needs.

Theodore Vail made it unequivocally clear that our goal was "Service." But his greatest contribution was his translation of that goal into a set of operating principles—principles he proclaimed to the world at large in a series of advertisements bearing the slogan "One System, One Policy, Universal Service."

We can realize how radical this philosophy was when we are reminded that it was proclaimed in an era of intense competition in the telephone industry, a period when it was not at all uncommon for a single city to be served—if that is the right word—by two or more competing companies. To Vail, this costly duplication did not make sense, and he said so.

It is because he defined our function in terms of its societal purpose rather than in terms of the hardware it takes to produce it that the Bell System is today, in fact, a system. Service to us is a managed process spanning the entire spectrum of functions it takes to provide it—from scientific research to product development to hardware manufacture to the operation of a nationwide network that, upon the demand of any of its users, will provide any one of the 7 million billion possible connections it takes to link any one of the nation's 120 million telephones with any other. Each of these functions—research, manufacture, operations—enhances the performance of the others and all are subordinate to the single aim that all together serve.

THE SYSTEM CONCEPT

Engineers will recognize what I have described as the "systems concept," the organizing principle underlying the massive production achievements of World War II. Since then it has taken us to the moon and back. But long before the phrase was invented, the systems concept was a way of life in our business.

The relevance it has to the organizational innovations the times demand is indicated by the prominence it was given in the deliberations of the White House Conference on Business in the 1990s four or five years back. There it was urged—most notably and persuasively by Michael Michaelis of Arthur D. Little Associates—that we face up to the inadequacies of an economy for the most part organized—or, more accurately, fragmented—along product lines and therefore lacking command of a sufficient range of resources to mount the basic research and the systematic application of its results that in his view would be required for successful delivery of some of society's basic needs in the years ahead. He cited housing, transportation, health care, and a number of other social services as candidates for the kind of structural innovation he recommended. And, agreeably, as a model for his futuristic vision he cited an organization now almost a century old, the Bell System.

What is ironic about this endorsement is that today the Bell System and the principles on which it is organized are being broadly challenged. History's wheel has turned once again, and today competition—or, in its modern manifestation, regulated competition—is once more a fact of life in our business just as it was in its earliest days. And today our industry is caught up in an intense ferment of discussion over the shape of its future.

The nub of that argument is the question of the degree to which the purported advantages of so-called competition to some people are worth the disadvantages to most people, in terms of higher cost for poorer service, that is the almost certain consequence of the fragmentation of function—and therefore of responsibility—that competition involves. The Bell System is going to fight hard for what it believes is in the long-term best interest of the whole public.

A GREAT DIVIDE

It seems to me that all of us charged with some measure of leadership responsibility have some thinking-through to do in light of the prospect that we may confront—or, as some people say, may already have passed—a turning point in our country's history, a Great Divide in the American condition.

From their first beginnings on the rim of this enormous continent, Americans have continuously and almost heedlessly spent their resources as if there were no limit to their supply and no tomorrow to hold us to account for their spending. One does not have to subscribe to the Doomsday projections of the Club of Rome to recognize the clear signals on every side that we are moving from an age of abundance to an age of increasing scarcity of material after material we had previously considered in almost limitless supply, from an age that set Growth Unlimited as its goal to an age that may not be altogether without its blessings because it will force us to examine—virtually for the first time—the quality of that growth. The first lesson of this new age is one that we've all heard before and never really believed: you can't have everything. It will take some hard thinking and painful choices to decide what it is we really want.

Now I would not presume to prescribe what reshaping of our institutional arrangements this new age will require. Already, however, the energy shortage has served notice on us that it will be an age in which increasingly we shall need to scale our ambitions to the limits of the resources available to meet them. Already we are on notice, too, that to extend those limits—not only in the supply of energy and materials but in the larger future our supply of food as well—will call for organization of the processes of discovery on a much more comprehensive scale than we have found necessary until now. And already we are on notice that our environment is a fragile one, and that its preservation will demand that we scrupulously balance the risks of exploiting it against the purported benefits of doing so.

A THINKING-THROUGH

In the face of prospects like these, it seems to me improbable that we can trust the future entirely to a random interplay of events. Rather, the future seems to call for men and organizations trained in the capacity for thinking in systems.

In light of the changed conditions confronting us, it seems to me we need a thorough thinking-through of which of society's tasks are best performed by private institutions, which by public, and which by possibly previously unimagined combinations of both. Which aspects of our economy need regulation and which do not? Government appears to spawn new agencies quite spontaneously in response to every emerging concern, but are there not some agencies that have long since outlived the urgency that called them forth and some perhaps that have actually completed the job for which they were assembled in the first place? And in the private sector, how long can we permit the presumed badness of bigness to blind us to the fact that there are some big chores ahead of us that can only be done well by large-scale aggregations of capital and skill? And should not each of us, each within his own industry, reexamine its structure and the deployment of its resources in the interest of a renewed commitment to excellence in meeting the public's expectations of us?

SUMMARY

I've tried to briefly outline the resource allocation process and the role of corporations in that process, at least as seen from my particular perspective. I believe the future will demand a much more disciplined management of our affairs than has appeared necessary up to now. We must marshall all our resources in searching for the answers to meeting growing demand. Technology may provide a partial escape hatch, and help to generate the needed improvements in productivity. Systems analysis may be a way of managing the entire process in a meaningful way. I fervently hope that the marketplace will continue to be the primary focal point for the basic allocation decisions. Corporate management certainly will have a large role in the process, with profound social and environmental impact, but that role must be interpretive and one of determining *how* to do the job the public demands and not *what* job should be done.

Finally, a very brief mention of the glue that cements this entire framework together—profitability. Profit has come to be a four-letter word to many of our people, and yet it is the keystone of our entire economy. Adequate earnings are essential if business is to have the resources to take the long view—to plan, to invest in research and development. Already the electric industry has been forced to cut nearly $9 billion from capital expenditures planned for the 1974–78 period. This could foreshadow a lack of sufficient power to meet legitimate economic needs of the future. The impact could ripple throughout the economy. Moreover, the productivity improvement we desperately need in the fight against inflation must stem in large measure from more capital investment. In my own business we've been able to make the very large capital investments that enable us to apply advanced technology to our plant. Today we are handling a volume of business 28 percent higher than we did three years ago with zero increase in employees.

We must keep in mind a fundamental fact: what most encourages investors to invest is the prospect of profit. Business cannot meet its obligation to modernize and grow and create jobs—nor utilities fulfill their obligation to serve—unless that expectation is met. Regulation that thwarts that expectation, or failure of the public to recognize that adequate profits serve consumers as well as investors, will exacerbate the very ills we are gathered here to combat.

✳ *Chapter 6*

Environmental Policies and Full Employment

Mason Gaffney*

A LIVABLE ENVIRONMENT AND PLENTIFUL WORK OPPORTUNITIES ARE BOTH OF THE ESSENCE

In order to protect the environment, we are going to have to face up to the chronic (and now acute) problem of mass unemployment. To save jobs and make jobs we now tolerate polluting mills and vehicles; we chew up more earth each year for energy and materials; we secure and protect mineral rights abroad at great material, environmental and human cost; and we put fat in government budgets, for peace as well as war.

In order to protect and improve our society, too, we must solve the problem of unemployment. Social health and environmental health are compatible, complementary objectives. Some people need work to give meaning to their lives; some to relate constructively to others. Some need work to earn their bread; others to frost their cake. But no society has flourished or long survived when many of its people could not find useful work. When they can't they turn to useless, then obnoxious, then destructive activities. So long as employment is insecure and uncertain, so long will the environment be

*Mason Gaffney is Executive Director at the British Columbia Institute for Economic Policy Analysis. He wishes to express his thanks to Resources for the Future, Inc., for research support. A more technical expansion of the ideas in this chapter is in the writer's "Toward Full Employment with Limited Land and Capital" in Arthur Lynn, Jr. (ed) *Property Taxes, Land Use* and *Public Policy* (Madison: U. of Wis. Press, 1976) pp. 99–166.

sacrificed to it, along with price stability, a measure of freedom, and a measure of world peace.

Along with short work we face a swelling array of derivative evils: crime, alienation and counter-culture, protracted apprenticeship periods, soaring welfare and dependency, frustration of idle house-wives, forced early retirement and geriatric ghettos, imperialism to make jobs and acquire raw materials, weapons constituencies, other pork-barreling, benign approval of waste, slowdowns, featherbedding, fear of change, stunting of creativity through grasping for tenure, seniority and security, suppression of competition, make-work build-ing codes and union rules, loss of flexibility and mobility, and rejec-tion of the free market. All these evils have their independent roots in human weakness, but are inflated by unemployment and the fear of it.

Some unemployment is iatrogenic (caused by the doctor). Critics of welfare point out how welfare payments have boomed into a cause of unemployment. Since work shortage also serves to rational-ize welfare, we have a vicious circle. But there is little doubt which came first, nor is there much doubt that we can solve the problem humanely only by opening more jobs, regardless of the direction of welfare reform.

Each of the derivative evils, like welfare, could be a study in itself. Yet until we face the elemental riddle at the fountainhead of all this trouble, each such study only diverts us from meeting the ultimate challenge for economists that Henry George defined in 1879: "Though custom has dulled us to it, it *is* a strange and unnatural thing that men who wish to labor, in order to satisfy their wants, cannot find the opportunity." "There can be no real scarcity of work . . . until all human wants are satisfied" [1]. That central para-dox for economists remains unresolved. We suffer shortages while men and women are out of work. Why cannot the idle persons find work to meet and fill the shortages?

Is it an excess of productive capacity with inadequate demand? Double-digit inflation bespeaks enough dollars of demand—in point of fact, too many. Environmentalists are aware that the natural re-source bases of production have risen steeply in relative value for many years now, forcing ever-escalating pressures on the land. Busi-nessmen and home buyers are aware of a capital shortage. Raw materials are high, even though their social cost is higher than their revealed market prices owing to massive subsidies and tax favors. It is only labor that appears to be in long supply. There is plenty of de-mand for land and capital, goods and services.

The United States which used to soak up displaced world labor

("Bring me your tired, your poor, . . .") to match its mountains and amber waves of grain, now instead reaches out to exploit the raw materials of others, and wonders if payrolls could grow or even stay the same without them. U.S. wage rates, once the wonder of the world, have declined since 1960 relative to many other countries. The great world financier is beginning again to import capital and fret about rising foreign ownership.

The force behind these changes has to be, and is that the coefficients of land, materials and capital used per worker and consumer have risen sharply for many years. We are bumping into the implacable logic that if we require a vast complement of resources per worker we will chew up lots of resources and push on the limits of Earth and the tolerance of other nations. If we require high coefficients of capital and land per worker, then capital and land set the limits to growth of jobs and consumption.

With labor surplus, and land and capital short, the needed adjustment would be evident to any reasonably bright 12-year old: lower the land and capital used per person. The solution is obvious, intuitive, and altogether correct. In Economese the appropriate phrasing is more labored but not too obscure: We need to substitute labor for land and capital, at the margins of course, making all processes more labor-using. Thus we would increase the use of labor without pushing on the limits of Earth, without invading others' land and without needing more capital.

THE GROWTH ISSUE—A RED HERRING

It is not a question of stopping "growth." There is no need to divide into factions for and against growth. We can grow by combining more labor with the same land and capital. It is simply a matter of modifying processes and products and consumption [2]. Each time the capital recycles it can embody new techniques as well. Growth of capital is not needed for progress; turnover is. And since the way to substitute labor for capital is to turn over capital faster, this also accelerates embodiment of new knowledge in real capital.

We can also create more capital if we wish, as much or as little as we please. We are certainly better off with more, but we can do with what we have. No matter how much we have and create, we will still have people out of work if we continue to match each 5% increment of capital stock with, say, a 10% increment in the capital coefficient per job. Capital formation is not enough. It is not even necessary. We could match the work force to the present or a lesser stock by lowering the capital coefficient. I don't recommend that but it is entirely feasible. Prevailing doctrines greatly overstress the role of net capital formation.

The Keynesian school has taught that the key to making jobs for labor is to make work for capital: investment outlets to absorb excessive savings. It imputes powerful, almost magical leverage to increases in net investment flows, multipliers now built into models used to forecast and control the economy. Newly ascendant conservatives plump for more saving to provide required capital to make jobs. Both schools make net capital formation the focus of concern. This diverts them—and almost everyone—from the much larger matter of how the capital stock is used. To match labor with capital we need to stop increasing the capital coefficient per job. Again, since the way to do that is to replace and turn over capital faster, the result is to increase the gross flow of payroll-generating investment. *Turnover* is the key concept. Most job-making investment flows represent reinvestment of capital recovered by sale of final goods, not net investment of new savings. We can raise *gross* investment without *net* investment simply by turning the stock faster. Of this, more later.

THE MOST WANTED SOCIO-ECONOMIC
GOALS ARE COMPATIBLE

That leads toward a thesis that we can employ ourselves as fully as we wish without any of the unpleasantness we now suffer in the name of jobs: without inflating, without borrowing, without fighting, without polluting, without any compulsion to "grow," "develop" and expand, without wasting, without price and wage controls, without invading more wilderness, without impoverishing posterity, without socializing labor or capital, without *dirigisme*, without giving up freedom, and without overspilling our national boundaries. Economic policy can offer better than the dismal choices among inflation, unemployment, pollution and socialism now being thrust upon us in the name of facing reality.

The problem is too much displacement of labor. It is "too much" because it results from biased institutions, a large set of them, operating over many years, which artificially induce substituting land and capital for labor. The way to solve the problem is to identify and remove the biases. This will increase demand for labor without requiring any more natural resources or capital.

No special rate of growth is required. We simply need to grow (or even not grow) in such a way as to combine each worker with less land and capital than now; to run with a leaner mixture of wealth, richer of labor.

There is no need to go any further and reverse the bias in favor of labor. The operation of a free market with flexible prices to serve as equilibrators should do the job. The idea is to make jobs not by waste, but in the very process of mixing inputs more efficiently. This is the sort of thing that a flexible economy can do—this is why they invented the free market. Just as the United States could retool for war quickly back in 1942, given the will, now we can retool for new jobs quickly given the will, the freedom, and know-how in framing public policy.

The possibilities for reducing resource coefficients of work and consumption are far greater than most people have any idea. We know that change is possible, for change is what got us here from there and what man hath wrought, man can unwork. But we need not go backwards. We only need look to realize that the man/land ratio varies over a wide range all around us today.

Just for example, here are some data on farm land use on the east side of the San Joaquin Valley, California. The data refer to neighboring lands, generally, of comparable quality and in the same markets. The differences therefore display that factor mix is sensitive to shadings of input prices so slight that they are not equalized by the market—differences internal to families and firms such as result from credit ratings, tax positions, political connections and other institutional biases. For example, an immigrant with many children goes heavier on labor, a speculator with friends in the banks and the Capitol favors lands, while a doctor with income to shelter might invest heavily in depreciable capital.

In the San Joaquin Valley, east side, land is versatile among many competing uses. These range from dryland grazing up to citrus, fresh tomatoes, and berries. Dryland grazing might gross $15 from the animal unit; berries might gross $1,500 a year, 100 times as much. The specific prices are subject to secular and cyclical and inflationary change, but the basic principle is not: the same land yields a little or a lot, depending on what you do with it. Table 6—1 is a crop report gathered by the United States Bureau of Reclamation from its Friant-Kern Canal Service Area. Not all the land is versatile among all the options, but a close study of the area has shown that the margins between the uses are ragged [3]. Almost every area has several options, and many of them are choices between the highest and the lowest gross. To get high yields, of course, requires more labor per acre.

Labor's share of gross rises with intensity, defined here simply as nonland inputs ÷ output. For grazing, this is on the order of $6/$15 = 40%. Grazing is land-intensive. For berries it is more like

$1,400/$1,500 = 93%. Berries are labor-intensive. Grazing and other unirrigated uses are not shown in Table 6—1, which shows the high variation of yields on irrigated land only.

Of course the return to land from crops like berries or tomatoes is highly leveraged and volatile, as a short-run gamble, but that is not our concern here. Averaging out the good years and the bad, the return to land from truck crops is very sensitive to wage rates and other costs of hiring like payroll taxes. A slight rise of 7 percent nearly wipes out the rent; a drop of 7 percent nearly doubles it. But the same wage changes would little change the returns to land from grazing. Thus a slight drop of labor costs applies great pressure to shift land to berries and tomatoes and other high-yield, labor-intensive crops, making a very elastic demand for labor.

The scope for this kind of change is manifest in the fact that most of California's prodigious farm output comes from a fraction of her good farm land, that which is used intensively. For example, of the

Table 6—1.   Crop Production, Friant-Kern Canal Service Area

Crop	Acres	Value Per Acre ($)
Barley	15,696	51.09
Corn	10,490	96.68
Rice	907	167.66
Sorghums	17,279	74.77
Wheat	3,176	87.85
Alfalfa Hay	63,460	144.11
Irrigated pasture	17,388	77.66
Beans, dry and edible	4,293	107.14
Cotton, line (upland)	108,928	352.80
Asparagus	1,383	418.70
Beans (processing)	27	900.00
Beans (fresh market)	75	975.33
Corn, sweet (fresh market)	254	205.91
Lettuce	423	336.51
Cantaloupes, etc.	507	547.02
Onions, dry	686	495.70
Potatoes, early	12,711	366.04
Tomatoes (fresh market)	1,343	881.16
Alfalfa	1,279	151.79
Berries (all kinds)	80	1,215.60
Oranges and tangerines	24,952	915.51
Grapes, table	43,795	545.24
Olives	7,172	327.45
Peaches	6,371	644.38
Prunes and plums	3,288	674.00
Walnuts	1,374	338.14

Source: Sacramento Office, U.S. Bureau of Reclamation, 1958. Minor crops omitted. Data refer to irrigated land only.

several million acres of irrigable land in California, there are only about 21,000 acres in plums, 36,000 in freestones, and 65,000 in navels [4]. Most California farm land is used at lower intensities, using little labor to yield barley, alfalfa, forage pasture, hay, sorghum, safflower, rice or cotton.

In irrigated farming water is an indirect land input, since a water right is the right to the water yield of a vast watershed. One might then think the truck crops really use a lot of land in the form of irrigation water. But in fact the high-grossing crops such as tomatoes, citrus, peaches and berries are modest users of water. Pasture, alfalfa, and rice are the heavy drinkers, and they yield only $50–$200 per acre, not one-tenth of the high yielders.

PRESENT LABOR USES ARE REGRESSIVE

The high-grossing crops use more labor per acre not just in the fields, but in the packing houses, the railroads, the stores and the kitchens. A $1500 berry crop will use more labor at every step to the consumer than a $15 weight gain on a calf, do it sooner, and much more often. Thus a higher use of labor in the field increases demand for labor beyond the field. Reciprocally, lower costs between consumer and farmer, raising field prices by say 7 percent, would (in our example) double land returns from berries and increase demand for labor on the farm.

For another and briefer example in Iowa, a more uniform state, Shrader and Landgren have calculated that if all farmers followed the standards already practiced by the most advanced farmers, Iowa alone could supply the nation's output of feed grain [5].

Now that's agriculture, where people often suppose that yields are hard to raise and depend only on genetic miracles, fertilizers and green revolutions. Turning to other human activities, we find even greater dispersion of resource coefficients. Table 6–2 shows value added per kilowatt-hour (or equivalent energy) in various industries. The numbers speak for themselves.

E.F. Schumacher has struck a responsive chord with "Small is Beautiful," relating size of enterprise to high resource coefficients. Although size is only one factor involved, the data bear him out. The use of labor on property tends, over a whole economy, to be regressive. The *U.S. Census of Agriculture* ranks farms by gross sales. "Class I" farms, those grossing $25,000 or more per year, had 22% of the land in farms but only 7 percent of the labor in 1950.

Turning to "industrial" corporations, the regressive use of labor on property may be inferred from data in *Fortune* magazine's yearly re-

Table 6–2.   Energy-Efficiency in Dollars of Value-Added per Kilowatt-hour (VA/KWH,)[1,2,] for Selected Industrial Groups

Industry Group	VA/KWH	Industry Group	VA/KWH
Cookies & crackers	.91	Blast furnaces & steel	
Book printing	.50	mills	.033
Millwork plants	.36	Primary copper	.020
Wood furniture	.28	Paving mixtures	.018
Fluid milk	.13	Paper mills	.016
Frozen fruits, vegetables	.12	Pulp mills	.015
Yarn mills	.12	Petroleum refining	.012
Sawmills	.083	Beet sugar	.010
Wool weaving mills	.048	Brick	.008
Aluminum rolling & drawing	.048	Primary aluminum	.007
		Cement, hydraulic	.006
		Lime	.004

1. KWH equivalents are used where relevant.
2. Source: Dr. John Wilson, citing *U.S. Census of Manufacturers*, 1967, (personal letter from Dr. John Wilson to Dwayne Chapman, Jan. 16, 1974).

Table 6–3.   Profits Per Employee, Large and Small Industrial Firms, Ranked by Net Worth [6]

Group	Net Worth ($000,000)	Profit After Taxes ($000,000)	Employees (000)	Profits/ Employee ($)
Top 10	40,090.	5,470.	1,662.	3,291.
All 500	133,660.	14,839.	9,966.	1,489.
Lowest 10	116.	8.826	29.687	297.

Source: Calculated from data in *Fortune Magazine*, (New York: August, 1964).

port on the largest 500. I tested the thesis by ranking them by "net worth" or invested capital, and calculating profits (after taxes) per employee. Table 6–3 shows the broad results. The choice of profits/ employee to test the case premises that profits in general are the realized earnings of and some index to the real assets of a firm. In fact, if the larger firms use their property less intensively (as this and other evidence suggest) then their realized profits as an index understate the assets of larger firms compared to smaller ones.

GOVERNMENT THE ARCH WASTREL

Can public employment save the unemployed? Not likely: government is the largest firm of all and the least labor-intensive. That's right, the least. It has a reputation for wasting labor, and in some cases conspicuously does. But it is more prone to waste capital and land. It pays the market for labor, while it borrows below the market. As to land, it still holds much more than anyone, tax free and unmortgaged, with little internal pressure or shadow price to reflect the foregone gains.

The military, for example, holds 20 percent of San Francisco and Washington, D.C. virtually idle. The annual value of this kind of lavish land input does not appear in the budget. The National Forests use much more capital (as timber) per man employed than do private ones, especially small private ones, a fact of which Forest Service doctrine makes a virtue. Richard Muth has concluded that the outstanding distinguishing trait of public housing is its higher capital intensity [7]. Civil engineers, generally working for governments, have become notorious for producing white elephants by treating capital—not labor—as a free good, and for overstating future benefits next to present costs by using low interest rates [8]. One can justify any project using a low enough interest rate, and ignoring land costs, and many agencies have, because at zero interest the present value of future rents in perpetuity equals infinity.

Private utilities are capital-using, of course. But governments supply the most capital-using utilities, like water and sewer which are increasingly costly because of urban sprawl. Governments are always called upon to put up social front money, to push back and invade frontiers, territorial and otherwise, where the payoff is too slow for private capital.

Public buildings (other than schools) are often monumental, baroque, cavernous, marbled, and better sited than their function warrants. For productive employment small is beautiful, but government is ugly.

Government freezes up capital in public works, much of it at low productivity. Ironically, much of this is done in the name of making jobs. On balance, it destroys jobs by inactivating capital.

RETHINKING "PRODUCTIVITY" AND "EFFICIENCY"

But how about productivity and efficiency? Is not maximum output per worker the goal of economic organization and the index of success? No, it is not. Many economists have for decades now seriously misled themselves and others by speaking loosely of "productivity" as output per worker, even though their own elementary theory textbooks taught better. Defining efficiency as output per worker is a perverse concept with a built-in bias against employment. Only recently with new studies of energy-efficiency and more sophisticated ones of "total factor productivity" are most people beginning to escape this single-minded preoccupation with economizing on labor at any cost.

Substituting capital and land excessively for labor raises "efficiency" only by wasting capital and land and unemployed labor, and only seems efficient in unrealistic models where land and capital are underpriced and unemployment is ignored. High labor-efficiency then means low land-efficiency and low capital-efficiency, either directly or at one remove in the form of low energy-efficiency, low water-efficiency, low feed-grain efficiency, etc. Capital is not free— saving is a sacrifice, too. Land is not free to a nation—past and present military outlays attest to that. And unemployment is not to be confused with voluntary leisure. The time and talent of the unhappy idle is wasted and worse, used to make trouble for others.

Misled by the goal of labor "productivity" we have exulted in high output per man as a symbol and measure of national and company success, and accepted an extreme substitution of capital and resources for labor. The well-known displacement of farm labor is not an exception, but more like the rule. John Kendrick calculated that the ratio of capital to labor for a large group of industries in the United States rose at an average annual rate of 1.3 percent from 1899−1953 [9]. That means a 100 percent increase over that 54-year period. More recently, the United States Department of Commerce studies nonfinancial corporations, 1948−1971. It found capital inputs growing at 4 percent yearly compounded and labor at 1.2 percent [10]. That means there was 2.5 times as much capital in 1971, with 1.3 times as much labor, or 1.9 times as much capital per worker in 1971. Thus the rate of substitution seems to be increasing.

And that's not really the half of it. These studies omitted the public sector, the infrastructure into which we have poured so much public treasure at low interest rates. They omitted housing, which soaks up so much capital per job created. They omitted the recreation boom which requires so much more land and equipment per consumer hour, and per measure of personal job, than the quiet pleasures of yesteryear. And they omit the swing of consumers toward goods and services like electric power and natural gas, whose production is capital-intensive, and whose prices fall relative to labor-intensive products when the capital input is subsidized. Producers as well as consumers use much more of these as inputs. A primary metal like aluminum will consume 135 kwh per dollar of value-added, compared to 10−20 in a normal manufacturing operation. It is energy inefficient and thrives only on underpriced energy, thanks to which it is cheap relative to competing materials. For years we have been substituting capital and energy for labor and calling it progress and efficiency, only to find that capital and energy are scarce, and labor surplus.

HOW TO INCREASE THE LABOR COEFFICIENT

All right, so efficiency as well as full employment call for increasing the labor coefficient of land and capital. How do we do that? Anyone can see what it means to use more workers per acre—no problem there. Anyone can see, too, what it means to use more men per crew, or use more shifts with given plant, machinery and equipment. Ah, it should be so simple. But who then produces the plant, machinery and equipment—who but labor? There is the problem. Capital is stored-up labor. If we use less stored-up labor per worker, are we not just substituting labor for labor? What is the difference; where the net gain of jobs?

Shop A may equip each of its workers with a smaller or less sophisticated machine, and use more workers. Then Shop B, which produces the machines, needs fewer workers. And Shop A itself may produce cement, the capital for Shops C, D, . . . Z, capital whose obviation would close Shop A. It is tempting to gloss over all that by saying if every shop and farm, mill and mine, office and store, firm and agency, gang and crew, squad and corps, family and kitchen, all up and down the line from the earth to the mouth just used less capital per worker it would all work out. Maybe it would, but maybe is not good enough. If we hadn't enough doubts of our own, modern macro-economics which dominates this field would force us to analyze how capital formation makes jobs.

Modern macro-economics has made much of the fact that labor finds work producing capital, only with the emphasis on the obverse: investment employs labor (to produce capital, of course). Indeed it goes much farther. Investment not only makes some jobs, it is a prime mover, a First Cause that moves independently and exerts enormous leverage over other income-creating flows, which respond dependently. There is a mechanical relation such that aggregate income rises and falls by multiples of changes in investment. Such is the stuff of which macro-economic models are built. Investment is much more important than other flows of equal value because it is autonomous, and determining, they are reactive and determinate. It is fickle and must be wooed, they tag along and may be slighted. The

key to full employment is finding investment opportunities and outlets to absorb the flow of savings. In such a model, reducing capital
coefficients to make jobs is dangerous and self-defeating.

Right or wrong, the orthodox macro-economic model and paradigm, in whose grooves and patterns most thought has become
channeled, is *vertically integrated.* The emphasis is on investment
employing labor, not on the capital coefficient at a given time. It
sees the relations of capital and labor in sequence, rather than in
parallel; labor producing capital, rather than using it or competing
against it. This perception is far too dominant to be ignored or
brushed aside. If we would give and receive signals in macro-economics we must make the same switch, and think vertically.* What is
the relationship between labor and the capital which it produces?
What does it mean to use less capital per worker? How do we accomplish it?

The quantity of labor input, worker-hours, is a product of workers
and time. Similarly the capital input is a product of capital and time,
say "dollar-years." Although capital takes as many forms as Brahma,
the basic idea or transcendental essence is simple enough: capital is
something of value produced but not yet fully consumed by users or
recovered by investors. The more years elapse between production
and recovery the more dollar-years of service are rendered by capital.
Unrecovered capital is said to be "tied-up" or in service.

In addition, often capital income goes unpaid. Then it is plowed
back and becomes additional capital which claims compound interest. In this case the capital input grows more than in proportion to
time. All the needed mathematics has been worked out for centuries
and may be found in any HP-80.**

How to use less dollar-years of capital per worker is now evident:
recover it faster. We can't cut down on the dollars, they have to
cover the payroll. We can cut down the dollar-years of capital combined with payroll by cutting down the years. We accomplish the
goal of reducing capital coefficients by modifying the capital stock
so capital returns home faster to the investor. The capital financing
each payroll is tied up a shorter time with it. The short phrase for it
is, make capital that turns over faster.

At the same time we can use larger crews to operate and maintain
each plant of given value. In pure logic this second idea is implied by

---

*After one gets at home in this milieu he can swing between horizontally
and vertically integrated models, but rarely with the greatest of ease or without
risk of error, and *never* without serious communication problems.

**Hewlett-Packard 80. Hewlett Packard's hand calculator that does what
tables of compound interest do.

the first, but there is no harm in stating it separately (so long as we don't later lead ourselves into double counting). The idea is to shorten the pipeline between work and use, to *move labor downstream closer to the consumer.* That implies, at every step, using more warm labor with the frozen labor in machines, materials, plant and equipment.

SHORTENING THE INVESTMENT CYCLES

The overall idea is to shorten investment cycles, so that value is shorter in transit from maker to user. And then back to earth, dust to dust? Not necessarily. I said "investment" cycles, not physical ones; and "value" in transit, not materials. There is a world of difference between economic flows and materials flows; between economic service life and carcass life. Maintenance, recycling, rehabilitating, remodeling, rebuilding, timber stand improvement, veterinary medicine, salvaging, renewing, reclaiming, scavenging, reassembling, repair, and the like are all investments that extend the useful lives of old carcasses and slow down materials throughput. But they are investments of fairly short payoff and economic life, as a rule, that tie up capital and value a short time and speed up value throughput. It is possible and indeed normal and common to append many short investment cycles in repairs onto the tail end of a longer carcass cycle.

Even outright demolition, scrapping and replacement of a subsystem often extends the usefulness of the whole, like pulling a sick tooth. Replace the battery and save the car; replace old buildings and save a neighborhood and a city.

It is the investment cycle that we must shorten. That lengthens the materials cycle in the instances above. In others it shortens it, as for instance when investment is diverted from new dams and cement-lined canals to water meters; from beef cattle to vegetables; from monuments to tools, and so on. Which is more common would be hard to know. It is clear, though, that as we move labor downstream, nearer the consumer, we need less material overall. Indeed a good deal of labor gets all the way downstream into service industry requiring no materials at all.

Some environmentalists equate short investment cycles with short materials cycles and waste. This is in general a mistaken identity. Producing raw materials from the earth, especially heavy ones, is as far from the consumer as you can get, and the net thrust of policies pushing labor downstream is probably to reduce materials' use. People have difficulty with abstract ideas and seek concrete counterparts. That is understandable enough, but the search must be guided by a correct grasp of the concept. Equating materials flow and economic flow is a misapprehension of the concept, a materialistic fallacy. Value is not just material, it is labor imprinted on material, with labor adding the larger share of value, as a rule. To shorten investment cycles we must lock and unlock the labor with material quicker by moving labor downstream. In the work of Mishan, Kneese, Boulding, et al., materials flow has been elevated to a major issue; correlated, if not identified, with economic flows; and made into a limit on growth and an argument against turnover. It is none of those, and should not divert us.

Lowering the capital coefficient per worker is, to many people, a structural or allocative question, in a box called "micro-economics." But when we understand it from the vertically integrated viewpoint it becomes a macro-economic effect of the most central kind. Turnover means sale and reinvestment. Sale means supply to consumers; reinvestment means payrolls and incomes. Added supply prevents inflation, added payrolls mean more jobs.

"Capital is maintained from age to age, not by preservation but by perpetual reproduction" (J.S. Mill) [11]. Labor consumes capital in return for reproducing capital. The flow of payback from capital sold as goods and services is reinvested continually in payrolls in a steady ongoing process, to create new capital. Investment makes payrolls, but most investment is reinvestment, the recycling of past accumulations. The faster capital recycles, the greater is the flow of labor putting value into the pool of capital, and volume of goods and services flowing out. Faster recycling is capital "quickening." The quicker the capital, the higher rises the flow-to-fund ratio. That means the more employment and production are financed with any given fund of capital, so long as there is idle labor to soak up. There is a lot in this to think about.

It leads to a major proposition: "Turnover limits national income." Otherwise put, "Paybacks deferred are payrolls denied." Hard capital and heavy capital and far-distant capital are slow capital. Soft, light and near capital are quick capital. Quicker capital flows through and delivers value to consumers sooner. Sales mean payback. Payback means money recovered to finance new payrolls. Payrolls mean aggregate demand to match the added sales. It all balances out, but at a higher volume.

A NEW ORIENTATION FOR MACRO-ECONOMICS

Macro-economics is a quest for the bottlenecks of the economy—what keeps us from employing everyone? Turnover is clearly a potential bottleneck. One firm can invest in excess of capital recovery, but only by tapping others. An economy cannot tap others. It is a closed system with a zero sum of capital transfers. The only source of investment funds other than capital recovery is net saving, but net saving is very small next to capital recovery. Essentially labor finds work pouring value into the pool of capital, and sustenance taking it out again. The flow through the pool is virtually the national income (less a few fringes small enough to leave as secondary matters). The flow is capital (K) times its turnover (T) or $K \times T$.

You would expect macro-economics to have inquired into what determines T, but it never has. Its focus has been on another possible bottleneck which is the recycling of money. Capital was pictured (if one thought of it at all) as a pile of finished goods seeking buyers, always ready for delivery, only wanting the trigger of consumer spending to release the flow. Spending controlled turnover, so much so that one need never think it had other controls, much less is a prime mover, as it is, which itself controls spending. The prevailing tendency was to bury the question by implicitly assuming automatic replacement of goods and service flows consumed, so in macro-economic models "consumption" creates income.

The question rarely arose explicitly because if it did the answer was built into the assumptions and would run like this. The cycle of spending has a fatal tendency to run down because of an excessive propensity to save from income, higher than there are investment outlets to absorb. The problem is always to find outlets which are scarce and to be treasured. The goal of policy is always to increase investment opportunities (as by tax loopholes for investors, or public works). Recovering funds from sale of goods adds to gross saving, but saving, net or gross, is not a limit on autonomous investment. There is always a bottomless cornucopia of funds available to invest. Gross saving just adds to the problem—more leakage from the spending stream that has to be offset by using the precious rare investment outlets.

On the positive side, in the Keynesian picture, sale of goods leaves an empty slot to refill, and this is an investment outlet. To the pessimist, however, this is uncertain, since there is an excess of goods anyway. Only the gross saving is certain. It is preferable to sequester capital in very hard, heavy, remote goods from which the payback is slow. Delivery to consumers is also slow, but there is an excess of goods seeking sale anyway so that is no problem. On the contrary, deferring deliveries helps offset the basic depressing imperative of our dying economy to sink into morbid deflation and choke on its own surplus of final goods wanting buyers.

To the environmentalist the "positive" side of the Keynesian picture is unattractive, since the benefit of fast turnover is having things decay and need replacing. But the fault is the picture, not the reality. The true benefit of fast turnover is not the decay of goods but the delivery of value to consumers and the recovery and recycling of capital. The gain is not from wasting, as implied in Keynesian models; the gain is in saving capital, by untying it quicker.

Happily, we can now discard the idea that spending or recycling money is a bottleneck limiting national income. It does not at all square with the facts today, if it ever did. Instead of running down, the turnover of demand deposits has risen rapidly for many years now, even as the money supply does, and banks press on their reserve requirements to meet the demand for loans. Instead of a fatal deflationary imperative, there have been years of violent inflation which failed to solve the fatal unemployment problem. New Economists have mastered all too well the arts of creating and spending money. Delivering the goods is where they fail, and it is real goods ready to consume that turn play money into real money.

Instead of a glut of loanable funds and a shortage of investment outlets there is a capital shortage. Instead of a glut of goods there are shortages, an energy crisis, materials scarcities, limited selections in inventory, delivery delays, islands of famine and fears of world hunger. Labor may be in long supply. Money undoubtedly is. It is land, materials, commodities and investment funds that are short.

Unfortunately, the concerns that prevailed when the twig of the New Economics was bent are built into its axioms, laws, models, circuitry and conditioned reflexes. In addition they drew upon deep springs in the cultural subconscious. "New" Economics was always a misleading name. It was more of a regression.."There is not an opinion more general among mankind than this, that the unproductive expenditure of the rich is necessary to the employment of the poor. Before Adam Smith the doctrine had hardly been questioned; . . . if consumers were to save . . . the extra accumulation would be merely so much waste, since there would be no market for the commodities . . ." [12]. Now everything is different but this mode of thinking which prevails at the top of the economics profession and leads us ever deeper into error and trouble.

The failure of fiscal and monetary policy, in which we once had such faith we talked of "fine-tuning," is by now so notorious we can merely postulate it as a premise. The New Economics foundered as it steered between the shoals of inflation and the rocks of unemployment and ran onto both at once. The New Economics taught that that would not happen. "Fiscal Policy and Full Employment without Inflation" was Samuelson's promise in 1955, and the world believed it. He wrote of the new "mastery of the modern analysis of income determination," and the "momentous Employment Act of 1946 . . . to fight mass unemployment and inflation." Inflation could result only from "overful employment [13]. All that has turned to ashes in the crucible of 15 percent inflation cum mass unemployment.

Faced with failure, leading economists have adopted the posture of scolding others into facing hard reality and making sacrifices. The New Economics once was positive and optimistic, and promised a lot. There were free lunches in those early halcyon days—when you put the idle to work, there *is* such a thing. The Puritan ethic was the goat, obsolete and absurd. But now the New Economics has become a New Dismal Science, a science of choice where all the choices are bad. "One must face up to the bitter truth that only so long as the economy is depressed are we likely to be free of inflation." (Samuelson, 1970) [14] "No one in the world has a recipe for correcting our price performance without some unfortunate increase in unemployment." . . . the public "should be told the facts of life." (Arthur Okun, 1970) [15]. This is not bread, but a stone.

Conservatives are not offering more. ". . . there is no other way to stop inflation. There has to be some unemployment. . . . It is a fact of life." (Milton Friedman, 1970) [16]. "The election will show whether the American people are mature enough to accept a sustainable (low) level of activity." (Henry Wallich, 1970) [17]. ". . . this economy can no longer stand a real boom with low levels of unemployment without kicking off a rampant inflationary spiral." (Alan Greenspan, 1972) [18]. Thus it seems that conservatives unite with liberals in seeing the choice as a trade-off on a Phillips Curve, and differ mainly in preferring to disemploy more and inflate less. There is no effort to rebuild the conceptual framework. "The collective intelligence of the economics profession is unable to fundamentally restructure the intellectual substance of the field. . . . We have a theoretical apparatus that can be used for a wide variety of things. There is no other one, and I do not think we know how to find one." (Otto Eckstein, 1974) [19].

But all that gloom and scolding seem benign next to the words of Lawrence Klein, President-elect of the American Economic Association. "Defense spending . . . has been a large part of the whole expansion of the American economy since World War II." The key question is "whether we should hold down defense spending for either economic or security reasons, and I think not, on both counts. . . . Every cutback of a dollar in defense will cut two dollars from overall GNP and drag down a lot of jobs. . . . If we were to hold spending to $395 billion, the recovery of the economy would fade away" [20]. Reporter Ernest Volkman quotes one Pentagon budget expert, "at least 20 percent of this budget amounts to a federal work-relief program to stimulate the economy. Defence contracts, especially the big ones, have an immense ripple effect" [21].

There you have it, the ultimate insanity to which the New Economics leads, from the unproductive consumption of the rich to warfare for work-relief, waste for waste's sake played with bombs and missiles. Military waste is the last refuge of a bankrupt policy. We have to do better—and we can.

BEYOND THE "NEW ECONOMICS"—SOME POLICY LEADS

New Economists have sharply attacked, rejected and even ridiculed the optimistic J.B. Say for proclaiming that there can be no general overproduction because "Supply creates its own demand." Yet today supply seems to do that and then some. Today one often hears a concern lest increased payrolls just cause inflation. Whether they do depends on where the money comes from. If it is new money why yes, of course. But when the added flow of investible funds has its source in delivery of finished goods to buyers then no, of course not. There is a matching added flow of supply to answer the added demand. Supply and demand still meet but at higher volume. Added flows are synchronized at both ends of the pipeline. The pipeline itself in this metaphor is shortened to speed the throughput and widened to carry more volume.

Keynesian pessimism sees supply overwhelming demand. Inflationary pessimism sees demand overwhelming supply. A confirmed pessimist sees both calamities at once, and there are those who do. Yet each calamity is the counterpart to and solution of the other. Calamity results from neither, but from restrictive and braking policies of other kinds adopted or tolerated by pessimists who believe or proclaim that they must forestall these imagined problems. These are the real macro-economic bottlenecks.

What are they? They include all institutional biases that interfere with the intensive application of labor to land, biases we have accepted and endorsed because we were in doubt about the aggregate benefits of taking the brakes off production and payrolls. There are too many to list here, but a good example is the tendency to base most taxation on the use of land, the activity on land, the payroll on land, the sales, the output, the income generated from land. The alternative is to base more taxation on the value of land, prompting owners to use it harder to serve customers, and make jobs.

They also comprise biases that interfere with the rapid turnover, recovery and reinvestment of capital. Again there are too many to list here, but here are a few. One is the use of low interest rates, or none, in guiding investment in public works, which tie up capital for decades before returning it and may never do so. This bias works in tandem with the bias against intensive use of land which forces the whole network of public capital to be stretched out over much more area than need be. Another set of biases are found in income tax policy which at every turn favors investment in slower capital over quicker [22]. Other biases are subsidies that take the form of cheap money (as U.S. housing programs do); regulatory bias and Averch-Johnson Effect [23]; licensing laws that dispose of resources, franchises, or monopolies subject to heavy capital requirements; ignoring the opportunity cost of public lands devoted to heavy capital works; the "big gadget" approach to pollution control; logrolling, overcommitment, and resulting stretchout of public works; the Highway Trust Fund; and the price-umbrella effect that builds excess capacity into cartels.

A third set of biases are in payroll taxation. In 1975 the U.S. social security payroll tax amounted to about $73 billions, a sixfold increase since 1960, up to about 25 percent of all federal receipts. The personal income tax, largely another payroll tax, raises another 44 percent. The tendency of payroll taxes is to make labor costlier to employers than beneficial to workers, who always have and increasingly exercise the options of welfare and crime.

Once the basic idea is clear a host of policy changes begin to write themselves. Here I offer only a few last guidelines. One is to use the price system and the market place. They are the only means we have for treating the economy consistently throughout as a total system. It would not work say, to harrass extractive industries in order to move labor downstream to the consumer. Some extractive industries like truck farming are labor intensive and close to the consumer. Some "consumer goods," like housing, are capital-intensive and land intensive. We need the price system to sort out all these anomalies and apply steady, consistent pressures of the kind needed throughout every corner and idiosyncrasy of the complex network of the economic system.

Public spending outside the control of the price system calls for some more admonition. Avoid monuments; tools are better. By "monuments" I mean things built with one eye on eternity, like the pyramids, and things that resemble them, like many works of governments and of other large organizations, the family seats of the very wealthy, and overmature timber.

Many monuments are built to make jobs. The intent is lost in the execution, for monuments soak up a maximum of capital per job created, and yield a minimum of subsistence to advance to labor for the next job. Public works to make jobs are one of history's great self-defeating, self-deluding tragic ironies. There is only a one-shot payroll, after which the capital stops recycling for a long time, often forever. One of the great stupidities of all time, surely, was the English effort to relieve the Irish potato famine of 1845–49 by hiring Irishmen to build roads. 570,000 men, a large fraction of the working population, toiled for the Board of Works while food prices took off like a bird and while half the people died of starvation [24]. The people needed subsistence for tomorrow morning, while public policy directed their effort to the next century.

Beware of "frontiers." They beckon like *Die Lorelei.* As a broad generalization, where we use capital to substitute for land, or open frontiers, the capital is very durable. It lies in close with land and resembles it and takes on some of its durability. Wicksell called such objects "rent-goods," because they so resemble land. Examples are surveying and exploring, cuts and fills, drainage, levelling, clearance, foundations, pipes, tiles, wells, pits, shafts, canals, tunnels, bridges, dams, and roadbeds. The permanence of land warrants building long life into capital that develops it.

Subsidies to tap frontiers make land artificially abundant. This is supposed to help make outlets for labor, and in some ways does. But frontiering taps new land at the cost of sequestering capital. Frontiers soak up scarce capital and hold it so it stops cycling and creating payrolls. Abundant land can still be badly used, and centuries of Caucasian expansion in the new world in a futile flight from unemployment have shown frontiers are not enough. Labor doesn't need great reservoirs of underused land so much as pressure to use the land we already have, and working capital to help labor use it.

SOLACE TO ENVIRONMENTALISTS

Environmentalists are distressed at the perpetual invasion of wild land by men seeking employment. They should be glad to learn that that is not where to make jobs after all, anyway.

The traditional last great sink of capital is war, and the policies of mercantilism and imperialism that attend it. War combines the frontier fallacy and the public works syndrome and the waste-makes-jobs doctrine into a claim on the national treasure that can become greatly inflated above the simple cost of police protection. Imperialism has generally been an economic *and environmental* catastrophe for most of the players.

The policy of lowering the land and capital coefficients of labor will help us find full employment on our present land base, permanently, freed from the compulsion to grow and expand and pollute. We can continue to create capital, and we can apply new ideas more quickly than now as faster replacement lets us embody new techniques in capital in a shorter time. Thus we can grow in every good sense by substituting real progress for the random lateral expansion and environmental destruction of the past. We can find full employment in peaceful labor on our share of this small planet, and doing so, drop the burden of imperialism that may otherwise destroy us in the ultimate environmental calamity.

APPENDIX: CONSTRUCTION OF TABLE 6–3

Like any data, these might be massaged a good deal more. In particular I surmise that adding unrealized appreciation to profits would raise the profits per employee more for the top ten than for the others, since six of the top ten are oil companies, and all ten are major mineral owners. But this information is not available.

The lowest ten include one net loser, without which the profits per employee would be $690 instead of $297. However, negative profits are also relevant, and there are twelve firms in the 500 with net losses. Most of these are in the lowest 100, so it is representative to find one loser among any group of ten. Therefore $297 seems more accurate than $690.

Net worth was used for ranking in order to reduce the bias of the regression fallacy. (Had I ranked by profits, the top ten would not have changed much but the lowest ten would have been firms with negative profits.) Although it is only partly successful in that, the trends shown are strong enough to survive further purification.

NOTES TO CHAPTER 6

1. Henry George, *Progress and Povery*, New York Modern Library, 50th Anniversary Edition, 1939, p. 270.

Social Problems, New York, Robert Schalkenbach Foundation, 1939, first published 1882, p. 130.

2. The research group at Resources for the Future has devoted years to belaboring this point in respect to pollution control. The object here is to generalize the point to the whole economy; e.g., Alan V. Kneese and Blair Bower, *Managing Water Quality*, (Baltimore: Johns Hopkins Press, 1968); Alan V. Kneese, R.U. Ayres, Ralph C. D'Arge, *Economics and the Environment*, (Baltimore: Johns Hopkins Press, 1970).

3. Mason Gaffney, "Diseconomies Inherent in Western Water Laws", in *Economic Analysis of Multiple Use*, Proceedings of Western Agricultural Economics Research Council, Range and Water Section, 1961, pp. 55–82, 77ff. See also Irvin H. Althouse, "Water Requirements of Tulare County," Report to Tulare County Board of Supervisors, January, 1942, (mimeo) map in back pocket.

4. *G. W. Dean and Chester O. McCorkle, Trends for Major California Fruit Crops*, California A.E.S., Extension Service Circular 488, 1960. The source has extensive data on other crop averages.

5. William Shrader and N. Landgren, "Land Use Implications of Agricultural Production Potential," in L. Fischer, ed., *Shifts in Land Use.* Nebraska Agricultural Economics Service 1964.

6. See Appendix.

7. Richard Muth, "Capital and Current Expenditures in the Production of Housing" in L. Harriss (ed.) *Benefits of Public Spending* (Madison: U. of Wis. Press, 1973).

8. A collection of such cases is documented in U.S. Congress. *The Analysis and Evaluation of Public Expenditure: The PPB System.* (Joint Economic Committee, Subcommittee on Economy in Government. Washington, D.C.: U.S. Printing Office, 1969).

9. John Kendrick, *Productivity Trends in the U.S.* (Princeton: Princeton University Press, 1961) pp. 148–149, Table 39.

10. Cited in "The Push to get More from Men and Machines" *Business Week*, Sept. 9, 1972, pp. 80–81.

11. John Stuart Mill, *Principles of Political Economy*, I, Ch. V, Sec. 6, (Boston: Lee and Shepard, 1872) p. 47.

12. John Stuart Mill, *Principles* I, Ch. V., Para. 3.

13. Paul S. Samuelson, *Economics*, 3rd ed., (New York: McGraw-Hill Book Co., 1955) pp. 336 and 350.

14. "Nixon Must Alter his Game Plan," *Washington Post*, Aug. 23, 1970 p. G1.

15. *Inflation*, (Washington, D.C.: The Brookings Institution, 1970) p. 9.

16. *New York Times*, Dec. 1970.

17. *Newsweek*, April 20, 1970, p. 91.

18. "The Budget is the Spur," *Newsweek*, January 31, 1972, pp. 63–64.

19. "Resharpening the Tools, *Business Week*, January 5, 1974, p. 56.

20. "The Impacts of cuts in defense spending," *Business Week*, Jan. 19, 1976, pp. 51–52.

21. *Vancouver Sun*, Oct. 15, 1975, p. 37.

22. For a detailed analysis see the writer's "Toward Full Employment with Limited Land and Capital," in Arthur Lynn, Jr. (ed.) *Property Taxes, Land Use and Public Policy* (Madison: U. of Wis. Press, 1976) pp. 99–166, esp. pp. 124–36.

23. Harvey Averch, Leland Johnson, "Behavior of the firm under regulatory constraint," *American Economic Review*, December, 1962, Vol. 52, pp. 1052–69.

24. Cecil Woodham-Smith, *The Great Hunger* (New York: A Signet Book, 1964) pp. 137–160, *et passim*.

✳ Part 3

The Politics of the Environment:
Collective Choice and the Management
of Common Property Resources

The authors of the chapters in this part struggle with the arduous problem of resolving or reconciling conflict situations that arise from our desire to combine in our public decision making about environmental management problems such warranted but disparate concerns as maximum feasible citizen participation, efficiency, soundness in terms of subject-matter dealt with, the sheer procedural feasibility to develop and effectuate solutions that comply with the tenets of representative government; or the planning of resource utilization and tax policy.

Edwin Haefele addresses the management of water resources, Lisle Baker is concerned with land-use management. The former deals with his subject primarily in terms of theoretical models that approach multiple optimization goals through vote-trading between groups, the latter by analyzing and evaluating, also pursuant to a theoretical model, a specific legislative attempt—so far unique in its kind—at regulatory action through taxation.

Haefele raises the paradox of what he considers the virtual incompatibility between maximum citizen involvement and political representation as it emerges from the electoral process. Also he points to the dilemma between subject-matter determined jurisdictional domains, on the one hand, and the need for coherent dove-tailing, systemic solutions spanning several or all of the diverse problem areas, on the other hand.

He raises the interesting possibility of one-man representation at the local level as one conceivable escape from the impasse due to those difficulties, which are compounded by the limitations of bureaucrats in the face of unrealistic expectations.

Baker seeks to shed light on the various ways in which the novel Vermont land gains tax may be felt as regards market demand for and supply of land for various uses, and the induced consequences thereof. While his treatment is prevailingly in terms of deduced market effects, his ultimate inferences look to land as a resource rather than a commodity and the possible general convergence of tax policies and land use planning.

Levy goes behind Haefele's preoccupation with properly channeling citizen participation so as to bring representative judgment to bear. He questions whether, today, even the well informed citizen or corporate officer can possibly know what alternatives he is supposed to be weighing against each other. The issues at stake are too ramified to lend themselves to a ready overview. Unlike Baker, Levy does not look for any constructive contribution from our present tax laws. On the contrary, he foresees such a wide disillusionment due to the growing awareness of manifold tax inequities as to view the public trust in our tax system going downhill. Not until, i. a., new techniques to appraise the issues are devised can the people be expected to wield effective decision-making power.

✳︎ *Chapter 7*

Representative Government and Environmental Management*

*Edwin T. Haefele**

The following drama was played throughout the land in one form or another during the decade of the '60s. An announcement is made in local papers that a dam has been proposed upstream from central city which will (a) control floods, (b) insure an adequate water supply to city residents, (c) provide recreation on the lake created by the dam, and (d) improve water quality in the river downstream. Mr. Average Citizen may read the announcement with only casual interest, comforted, perhaps, that the public officials are doing something worthwhile for a change.

As time goes on, he is puzzled, even bewildered or angered, by a mounting controversy over the dam. The dam is attacked by the people who live on what is to be the bottom of the lake created by the dam. It is attacked by some people who sneer at "flatwater" recreation and speak rapturously of the existing "white" water where the dam is to be placed. It is attacked by fishermen who talk about spawning grounds, by biologists who decry artificial lakes and predict silting, by economists who talk about flood plain restrictions, and by engineers who mention re-aeration of water as a cheaper method of improving water quality.

Mr. Average Citizen, if he does not screen out all this "noise" in his information channels, may well think, "They must have thought

*This paper was delivered at a symposium sponsored by the Westwater Research Centre, the University of British Columbia, and is reprinted from *Managing the Water Environment*, ed. Neil A. Swainson (Vancouver: University of British Columbia Press, 1976).

**Edwin T. Haefele is Professor of Political Science, University of Pennsylvania.

of all that." Mr. Bureaucrat, who did not think of all that, was even more bewildered by the clamor than was Mr. Average Citizen. But Mr. Bureaucrat was resourceful. Nobody was going to finger *him* with the blame; he was, after all, only following the law, and besides, if other people want to get into the act, elementary strategy suggests that one should open the stage door and let them in. Once they are on the stage, they are as committed as anyone else to making the act succeed.

So with one hand, Mr. Bureaucrat handed the hot potato to the politician, and with the other hand, he opened the door to additional interest groups that wanted in on the action.

Mr. Politician, who was born with infra-red vision, can spot a hot potato before it begins to glow. He swiftly fields the hand-off from the bureaucracy, writes some resounding phrases about the "need for public participation," "multiple use," "balanced programs," and lobs the potato (now radioactive) back through the bureaucratic transom. For good measure, he creates an environmental agency co-equal to the agency proposing the dam in the first place, gives no one final authority, and wishes the judges good health.

This chapter attempts to address the resulting problem, which can, perhaps, be categorized by the following three questions: How do we achieve technical efficiency in water quality management? How do we choose the goals for water quality management? Whom do we involve in the process of water quality management?

It will be useful to start in the area of greatest knowledge and move from it gradually out into *terram incognitam.* I have thus arranged the order of the questions and will so address them.

TECHNICAL EFFICIENCY

While there is still substantial argument over the means of accomplishing some of the objectives, it remains true that we recognize the necessary conditions for technical efficiency to be: (a) a geographical area which will allow for control, i.e., a watershed, a tributary, or a reach on which boundary conditions can be specified and met; (b) a criterion for choosing among mutually exclusive projects, e.g., benefit-cost in some form; (c) the absence of any bar *against* certain technical options, and conversely the absence of any external fiscal incentives which bias the technical choice *toward* certain technical options.

These conditions may be thought of as our geographical handle on the problem, our economic handle, and our functional handle. To the degree that any of them are defective, we will fail to achieve technical efficiency in similar measure. Unfortunately, as we all know, all three are defective to some degree.

We have just begun to understand how limited the hydrologic definition of the management area is. Not only is it apt to range so widely that it brings in problems (and people) of minimal interest to the management agency but it also is at odds with the geography of two other interrelated problems—the management of gaseous and solid wastes. These problem sheds will rarely fit the geography of the watershed, yet there may be efficiency gains to be made by considering all three residuals in one management system. The efficiency gains may be significant in an area like Washington, D.C., and the lower Potomac, whereas tying the whole Potomac basin into such a management scheme may make little sense at present, the demands on the river above Washington being minimal.

Our economic criterion, usually some form of benefit-cost analysis, suffers from well-known vicissitudes on efficiency grounds, e.g., choice of discount rates, but is attacked with even heavier artillery when we get into distributional questions. The criterion remains, however, a potent tool by which to make aggregate, economic evaluations of mutually exclusive alternatives. That is a large enough benefit to confer on us and we should not, as the large federal bureaucracies in Washington are trying to do, put more burden on the tool than it can handle. It will not tell anyone which distribution of costs and benefits are "best" nor does it provide a framework to evaluate non-economic costs or benefits.

It is notoriously well known that rarely are management agencies allowed to look at technical options in an unbiased way. Governmental programs typically give grants-in-aid for specific technologies, be they sewage treatment plants, dams, or whatever. Rarely, perhaps never, has an agency been able to review all technical options with a clear eye. The fiscal calculation of matching grants blurs every vision, even the strongest. Leading the solution toward a particular technology would, of course, be forgivable were there any rationality or any larger optimization being served. None comes to mind.

Yet the lack of perfection in our ability to choose efficiently should not be taken too seriously. It remains true, as Kneese, Davis, and others have demonstrated, that we know how to manage river basins so as to make everybody better off. In practice we are still below, probably well below, the kind of efficient management we know how to achieve. Why don't we achieve it? In short, we don't because water quality management is imbedded in a legal and cultural heritage that values technical efficiency less than some other things. Add to that the fact that technical efficiency would displace some people and some areas from a power and influence position they value very highly. Finally, consider the possibility that the legal and cultural context within which these matters rest is, itself, in a pathological state at the moment. The broader institutional structure of governance, particularly in the United States, is inadequate to the tasks that water quality management, or more generally environmental management, has placed upon it. How that came about leads us into an examination of the goal by choosing the mechanisms available to us.

CHOOSING GOALS FOR MANAGEMENT

The common heritage of Canada and the United States consists of what is termed by the present generation of English historians as "the myth of the Anglo-Saxon Constitution." What was a myth in England became a reality on this side of the Atlantic, as both countries established legislative supremacy (limited in the United States case explicitly by a written constitution with a bill of rights patterned closely after the English instrument adopted in 1689) and governments which consciously strove to determine social choices from individual voter preferences. The effort was, in both cases, built from the ground up, i.e., from self-governing colonies and territories. While there are differences, there are greater similarities. One of the similarities is that there is a great deal of power lying dormant in legislative halls. In the United States, the power has, in many cases, been curbed by state constitutional amendment (following the legislative scandals of the early 1800s), but the potential to restore it is still there.

Gradually, however, during the 19th and 20th centuries the remaining power of the state legislatures has seeped away, away to other parts of the state government under a well-motivated attempt to get efficient management, and then dispersed to other levels of government. The fiscal power went to the national government as a result of the passage of the 16th amendment, which authorized the personal income tax. The management power went to special districts, single-purpose authorities, appointed boards and commissions, and to bureaucrats charged with administering laws often vague and unfocused.

The reason for this detour into governmental history is this: to the extent that state legislative power has been absorbed or diffused, the ability of government to choose, to set priorities, has been weakened. The pathology stems from that fact. As one agency gets control of transportation, another control of eduction, as an appointed board issues sewer permits, another reviews zoning plans and a third promotes economic development, the whole question of choosing social priorities becomes irrelevant, and we move ahead by chance. Establishing comprehensive planning arrangements and coordination committees, while of interest to a growing bureaucracy, simply compounds the problem of choosing by burying the process from traditional public pressures. (Indeed, the rise of court suits, civil disobedience, and advocacy planning are all direct results of the traditional streams of advocacy—the party and the parliament—drying up.) If the game is really played in the offices of the bureaucrats or in the hearing rooms of the commission, why bother with parties and legislatures? And, since the bureaucrat and the commissioner are insulated, deliberately, from party pressures, perhaps the court suit was the only way to get into the game at all. Many in the United States have reasoned it like that. If the special interest lobby could sit in the bureaucrat's office and help write the regulations, then perhaps the only recourse for the opposing special interest was to get into the room also. This method of influencing choices is now so common in the United States that sections requiring "citizen" participation in agency decision-making at "every stage" are in several of the new environmental acts at the federal level.

We may have, indeed, gone through a whole revolution of decision-making without the slightest attention being paid to it outside the quarters of the interested parties. It has attractions. The new method allows the politician to get off the hook, by passing the decision-making over to an appointed board or commission. He then can exist on platitudes and good feelings toward all. The political heat is drained off into a kind of infinite sink—a bureaucracy where no one is responsible but all have authority. The interest groups, to the extent that they are organized, (and Olson has shown us which ones will be) can take their chances on the inside, helping to carve the turkey through informal deals and bargains. The bureaucrat cannot lose, as he becomes the indispensible middle-man. And, of course, the outsiders and losers always have the courts.

Again, I must confine my judgment to the United States, but the process that I have just described is going on. It is not working. It will not work. It cannot work. Why not? It does conform to many textbook descriptions of the informal power structure of democracies. Moreover, it is consonant with both "pluralist" and "elitist" descriptions of group politics.

It does not conform nor is it consonant with the structure that some very hard-headed politicians put together in Philadelphia in 1787. One of the prime motivations of those men was to prevent a kind of "courtier" (we would say "bureaucratic") government by men not responsive to, or responsible to, the public will. They built well, exceedingly well, out of fire-hardened materials. Hence, today, when management agencies begin to get into important areas, such as influencing or controlling land use and making life-and-death decisions for communities and areas, they find themselves besieged in the courts. Politicians who practice consensus politics find it impossible to please everyone, and if the legislature did not decide it, the one displeased can often bring the whole administrative process to a standstill in the courts.

Perhaps I belabor the obvious, but the point must be grasped. Decisions made by general-purpose legislatures, whose members are elected, can be overturned in the courts only on the most fundamental grounds of constitutional probity. Decisions made by any other governmental bodies, no matter how carefully designed, can be upset on innumerable procedural and technical grounds by anyone with "standing" in a court of law. An extension of "standing" to a broader and broader spectrum of interests, e.g., class action suits, is going forward rapidly in the United States court system.

We in the United States are being estopped from doing more and more things. Highways are not being built, dams are not being constructed, buildings are not being put up, industries are not being located. Electrical generation capacity is not being expanded. The blockages are not happening everywhere, of course, but they happen in many and a growing number of places.

Two reactions are possible in such a period of impasse. One is to recognize why the original system does not allow decision-making through bureaucracies, and solve the impasse by returning to the original system. The second, and the one we are lamentably following, is to attempt to tear down that part of the original system blocking action by bureaucracy and blast through solutions to the immediate problem. Attempts in the United States to draw these issues up to the federal Presidency, and to use Presidential power (which is still, after 200 years, only vaguely defined) will, if successful, fundamentally alter American government in a way precisely analogous to the efforts of the Stuart kings. The attempt will meet, indeed is now being met by, precisely the same response. Myth or no, in the final analysis, we will either govern ourselves or be ungovernable.

My purpose here is not to dramatize these larger issues as much as to use them to provide the framework for more specific examination of mechanisms for choosing goals. Within the framework one can see the limited role that many sophisticated tools of decision-making, e.g., systems analytical tools with multi-objective functions, can play. If the fight is over the weights to put on each part of the objective function, whether to allow this or that constraint, when there is not one but many decision-makers to contend with and consensus is impossible, these tools do not suffice.

A RESIDUALS MANAGEMENT APPROACH

I add quickly that while they do not suffice, neither are they useless. We are now, at Resources for the Future, developing management models of just such form, i.e., optimizing models with multi-objective function capacity. We are using them, however, in a legislative setting. Let me describe the effort briefly.

Our method has been to construct and experiment with a hypothetical region, modeling its residuals discharge activities and the natural systems which translate those discharges into ambient quality levels. This regional model has been linked to a model that simulates the vote-trading activities of a legislature assumed to be responsible for making the decisions about quality in that region. The regional model has been structured to give a great deal of information in physical as well as economic terms to each legislator. We hope to show that information in this form can be used in a systematic way by real legislatures to assist them in arriving at regional policy. Our legislative model is emphatically *not* an attempt to put real legislatures out of business but is simply a device for allowing us to accomplish two things: first, to design the regional model for use in a legislative setting; and second, to compare the policies adopted by legislatures put together along different lines. The basic function of the simulation program is to identify and accomplish the vote trades which would take place in a real legislature.

In an attempt to capture some of the complexity in the environmental issue we introduce the idea of a preference vector which combines an ordinal ranking and a yes-no vote on a given set of issues. In the legislative model the issues consist of four quality measures of the natural environment* and the four measures of increased cost resulting from improvements in environmental quality.

*These include (a) the level of dissolved oxygen in each reach of the river (calculated in terms of a dissolved oxygen deficit): DOD; (b) increases in the temperature of each reach of the river: ΔT; (c) the level of suspended particulates in the air (measured in micrograms per cubic meter): SP; and (d) the level of sulfur dioxide in the air (measured in micrograms per cubic meter): SO_2. We realize these measures could probably not be used directly in a political process, although the experience in choosing levels of water quality in the Delaware shows a quick assimilation of technical information by laymen, particularly if the technical measures are related to fish population, recreation potential, and health hazards.

Arbitrary preference vectors (reflecting differences of tastes, incomes, etc.) were specified for each area. These are based on arbitrary upper limits on each of the eight measures. Thus, one area's upper limits vector is:

	Area 1	
DOD	3.0	parts per million in reach 4
ΔT	5.0	degrees F in reach 4
SP	50.0	$\mu g/m^3$ in area 1
SO_2	20.0	$\mu g/m^3$ in area 1
Taxes	1%	increase of 1 percent in the area
Unemp.	10%	increase of 10 percent
Elec.	50%	increase of 50 percent to each household in every area
Heat	20	increase in dollars per year to each household in the area

If we allowed area 1 to be our decision-maker, these upper limits would be the constraints area 1 would put on the solution of the regional model. Since area 1 is only one of 25 areas, we wish to construct a social choice process to allow the upper limits vectors of all 25 areas to be expressed. Our preference vectors, one for each area, are designed to do that. For example, we may display area 1's preference vector in response to a current situation as shown in Table 7-1.

The numerical subscripts in the preference vector indicate the ordinal ranking of (in this case) three measures. Thus we are ranking, by assumption, an upper limit of $5°F$ heat rise in reach 4 of the river of first importance in area 1, an upper limit on SO_2 of 20 $\mu g/m^3$ in area 1 as second in importance, and an upper limit of 10% on unemployment as third most importance to area 1.* (For ease of computation we do not rank all measures. Elements without subscripts are assumed to be all of equal importance but less important than any subscripted element.)

Area 1's preferences may be summarized by saying that the citizens of area 1 are dissatisfied with the present situation in three out of four quality measures, while they are satisfied with the present tax and utility burdens on area 1. Since area 1 ranks the environmental measures above the financial ones, however, some additional financial burden would be accepted if necessary to achieve acceptable levels of water and air quality.

---

*The ordinal rankings by real actors would clearly change as one or more upper limits were met and/or other upper limits were greatly exceeded. We have not investigated how such ordinal shifts would affect the algorithm, although it is clear that convergence problems might well occur.

Table 7–1.   Area 1—Preference Vector

	Area 1 Upper Limits	Present Situation	Area 1 Preference Vector
DOD	3.0	5.52	N
ΔT	5.0	9.89	N_1
SP	50.0	17.19	Y
SO_2	20.0	32.69	N_2
Tax	1%	0.0	Y
Unemp.	10%	0.0	Y_3
Elect.	50%	0.0	Y
Heat	$20	0.0	Y

All other areas were assigned upper limits vectors and ordinal ranks to three or more measures. Using those vectors, we can display all 25 preference vectors in response to the present situation (Table 7–2). The Y votes on each row are tallied in the far right column. We see a unanimous approval of all financial measures but much disapproval of the present quality of the air and water. The stage is set, assuming our preference vectors are such that not all can be met simultaneously, for some sort of social choice process to be invoked. Since the number of possible "solutions," that is, technically feasible alternatives, may be said to be almost infinite, the social choice process cannot be simply a blind groping for a solution acceptable to some given percentage of areas, for the process would prove to be inefficient and the "solution" ambiguous at best. Neither can we, without throwing away the concept of social choice, simply stand with arbitrary "solutions" that do not reflect the preference vectors, in the hope that the "objectivity" of any one of these solutions will cow the residents of our region into acceptance.

In a real world situation, whatever official has charge of the model (and a computation budget) might be tempted simply to meet the first and second ranked upper limits of enough areas to insure a majority (assuming there existed some political body through which these votes could be registered). Lacking any such political body, he might "play around" with meeting a few more high ranked upper limits (chosen on the basis of judicious knowledge of which areas could be most difficult if their limits were not met) and balance the additional limits against protests from special interest groups, industrial and environmental.

It may be useful to explore in some detail what procedures could be used to find a solution based on the preferences of the 25 areas. The first method might be to see if all preferences (upper limits) of all the areas might be met simultaneously. If so, clearly it is Pareto-

Table 7–2. Vote Matrix, Present Situation

	1	2	3	4	5	6	7	8	9	10	11
DOD	N	N	Y	Y	Y	N	N	Y	Y	Y	N
ΔT	N_1	N	N	N	Y	N_3	N	N	N	Y	N_3
SP	Y	Y	Y	Y	Y	Y_2	Y_2	Y	Y	Y_2	Y_1
SO_2	N_2	N_1	N	Y	N	N_1	N_1	N	N	N	N_2
Tax	Y	Y	Y_1	Y_2	Y	Y	Y_3	Y_1	Y_2	Y	Y
Unemp.	Y_3	Y_2	Y_2	Y_1	Y_1	Y	Y_4	Y	Y_1	Y_1	Y
Elect.	Y	Y	Y	Y	Y_2	Y	Y	Y_2	Y_3	Y_3	Y
Heat	Y	Y_3	Y_3	Y	Y_3	Y	Y	Y	Y	Y	Y

optimal to meet them. Since such a happy state is unlikely in the real world, we have set the upper limits vector so that it is not attainable in the regional model either. If all preferences cannot be met, then whose should be met, and in what order?

A second method is to meet each area's upper limits by using each set separately as constraints on the regional model. This accomplishes two things: it allows us to make sure that each area's upper limits preferences are internally consistent,* i.e., can be met simultaneously, and it allows us to see the kind of "overlap" or complementarity between one area's upper limits preferences and those of another area.

A third method is to pay more attention at the outset to the ordinal ranking of the different measures by each area. For example, we might try to meet the first and second ranked preferences of all areas, or all first preferences, then all second preferences. Were we thinking about a strong party-oriented legislature or council, "all" might be replaced in the preceding sentence by "majority party." If "all" were possible, the "all" solution might have appeal over the "majority party" solution, but would not necessarily be chosen by the majority party if meeting minority first and second ranked preferences meant giving up on majority party third and fourth ranked preferences. How the majority party acted would depend very much on what powers of retribution the minority party had, when the next election was coming up, and/or other political factors exogenous to our consideration here.

Any of the preceding methods could be employed in connection with the regional model presented in this chapter, but they do not get us very far in terms of the reality of conflicting preferences and

*An area's preferences do not have to be consistent since it could have "if not this, then that" preferences in it. Identifying these beforehand will be useful, however, in a real world situation.

Table 7–2. continued

12	13	14	15	16	17	18	19	20	21	22	23	24	25
N_5	Y	N	Y_3	N	N	N_1	N	N	N	Y_1	Y_1	N_2	Y
N_4	N	N	Y	N_3	N	N	N	N	N_2	N_2	N	N_4	N
Y_2	Y_1	Y	Y_2	Y_2	Y_2	Y	Y	Y_1	Y_3	Y	Y	Y	Y
N_1	N_3	Y	Y_1	N_1	N_1	N	Y	N	N_1	N_4	N	Y	Y_1
Y_3	Y_2	Y	Y	Y	Y_3	Y_2	Y_2	Y_2	Y	Y_3	Y_2	Y_3	Y
Y	Y	Y_1	Y_4	Y	Y	Y	Y_1	Y_3	Y	Y	Y_3	Y_1	Y
Y	Y	Y_2	Y	Y	Y	Y_3	Y_3	Y	Y	Y	Y	Y	Y
Y	Y	Y	Y	Y	Y	Y	Y	Y	Y	Y	Y	Y	Y_2

the loose party structure characteristic of most United States legislative councils. While replicating all of the complexities of United States legislative procedure and structure would be impossible, we can adopt a method which will replicate an important element in them, namely vote-trading. The essence of vote-trading is giving up on one issue to gain another issue you value more.

The basic idea of the vote-trading algorithm is to add constraints to the present situation such that N votes are converted to Y votes in some efficient, non-biased way. Vote-trading is efficient for this purpose because it focuses attention on high-ranked N votes (these are the upper limits violations of most concern to the area). They are the upper limits the areas want most to be put in as constraints on the regional model. However, with vote-trading such a constraint can be put in only if the area that wishes to put it in will accept (also allow to be added as a constraint) another upper limit on another issue that is desired by another area. Constraints are put into the solution, therefore, in pairs.*

Since vote-trading was explained as giving something up for something of higher value, what is it that each area gives up by this trade? To illustrate what is given up, let us pick out a vote-trade from Table 7–2 and see what happens.

	Area 13 Upper Limits →	Area 13 Present Situation →	Area 13 Preference Vector	Area 24 Preference Vector	Area 24 Present Situation ←	Area 24 Upper Limits ←
DOD	3.5	3.4	Y	N_2	3.4	3.0
SO_2	80	103	N_3	Y	38	40

*There is nothing magical about "paired" constraints. Three or more areas could agree on a constraint before it was put in. Paired constraints are simply easier, computationally, to use in the vote-trading algorithm.

The result of the vote trade shown is to put in, as constraints, area 24's upper limit of DOD $\leqslant 3$ on reach 2 of the river and area 13's upper limit of $SO_2 \leqslant 80$ in area 13. What area 13 gives up is a 3.4 DOD outcome, an outcome it was happy with since it was below its own limit of 3.5. Area 24 gives up an SO_2 outcome of 38 in its area, an outcome it was happy with. The outcome of these trades, and further details on the model have been presented elsewhere [1].

There is no reason to believe that any existing legislature or council would use the trading routine we just outlined. There is no necessity for them to do so since the distributional information may be adapted to a variety of decision paths. Let us take some examples. In real councils there is often a desire, sometimes even a necessity, to let everybody win. A chairman might ask each member to write down one constraint that the member really wants, or needs in his district or area. These constraints could be collected and used as the first set of constraints for the model. If the regional model can be solved with those constraints, the effects of the solution could again be examined and one additional constraint added by each member. This process could be continued until the regional model fails to solve. The last solution could be adopted or used as a starting solution to trades or bargains.

Bargaining could occur, either after the process described in the preceding paragraph was completed or *ab initio*. In general terms, bargaining can occur whenever two or more council members perceive that some constraints are in direct conflict. In such instances, real council members may wish to bargain, that is, to agree to slack off their constraints slightly if the other side will slack off its constraints. In doing so, they may wish to use the regional model to help them find the most agreeable bargain—one with minimum change in both constraints, one with minimum variation in percent rise between the two, or whatever other criterion is agreed upon by the pair of bargainers.

It will be quickly seen that such constraint slackening will probably come late in the game, since no one will be willing to change his upper limits until it is clear they either cannot be met as they stand, or that a majority favors a solution in which one's upper limits are greatly exceeded.

The actual use of the regional model, therefore, may vary considerably from one group to another. Some strictures on use are, however, apparent. For example, the distributional information has potentially explosive political content. That fact can be used to advantage for good or ill. Suppressing it may be politically expedient to some but can rarely, if ever, be either ethically or legally justified when taxpayers' monies are being used. It may not be desirable, however, to have all experimental runs made public as long as they are shared by all the council members. (The potential for mischief by a clique within the council or legislature, a committee for instance, would be very large. Such a group could construct a very biased solution.)

Another stricture on use relates to the choice of a method to proceed once unanimity has broken down, as it inevitably will early on in any real situation. One can imagine, in a strong party legislature or council, that the majority party might well wish to give priority to meeting the constraints of its members, with minority preferences being met later if at all. This method is not so bad as it might appear, so long as the distributional impact of their deliberations is known to all council members, *and* the minority party has equal access to the regional model to design counter solutions. These latter solutions will, of course, attempt to meet minority preferences *plus* improving the lot of a sufficient number of the majority members to place the majority solution in jeopardy. That process will, in practice, turn out not too differently from our trading solution.

In more non-partisan situations the idea of coalition building may have appeal as an equalitarian procedure which may be able to reach a dominant solution in the absence of cycling.

In any event there will be some pressure on the operators of the model, who must be like Caesar's wife. Sometimes both majority and minority party staff will be needed to insure ease of access, shared results, and general trust. There will be opportunitites for technicians to facilitate a solution, or to obstruct one by purely technical means which go unnoticed by the members or their staffs. These opportunities and dangers are present in many public service posts and cannot be completely eliminated. Just as both sides in disputes have for centuries employed lawyers, they now must employ programmers, economists, and systems analysts if the technician's temptation to play God (always for the public good, of course) is to be minimized.

In the context of our discussion on choosing goals, a regional residuals management model is but a halfway house on the way to solving our problem. While it does treat residuals in an interrelated fashion and construct a social choice from representative preference, it does not choose boundaries nor does it relate environmental issues and costs to other issues and their costs.

The latter issue is not too significant in the real world, *as long as the same people who sit in this legislature also decide the other issues.* A representative, in other words, can only rank issues if he has access to all the relevant games being played. If a man serves only on the school board, he does not have to judge between schools and environmental improvement. If he sits on both boards, he may have to choose between them, given the inevitable budget constraints faced by all governments.

Thus, since it is unlikely that we will soon put together the dismembered general purpose legislature, (i.e., abolish all special boards and commissions) it may be necessary to change our habits of selecting different people to serve on each of them. Such a course has salutory effects both on citizen participation and the boundary problem and is best discussed under our third and final question.

WHO PARTICIPATES?

I earlier outlined the growth, indeed the necessity of growth, of citizen participation in the beureaucratic governance process. Environmental groups, who feel they had previously been outside the decision process, have come inside with a vengence. I have also suggested that this new emphasis on citizen participation, on widening the numbers of interests and groups, is doomed to failure and why. The bureaucrat's room simply is not big enough to accommodate all, and he has no criterion (nor can he have) to select from competing claims for his attention.

This assertion may be given weight by calling attention to the present plight of the U.S. Corps of Engineers, as they attempt to broaden their evaluation process to economic, social, and environmental effects of their projects [2]. These guidelines respond to Section 122 of Public Law 91-611 (River & Harbor and Flood Control Act of 1970) which asks, among other things, that the Corps evaluate "disruption of desirable community and regional growth." Attempts to comply would have their comic aspects were not the issue so serious. One example will have to suffice. In a small project, within one county, the Corps has several contending, legitimate representatives of portions of the citizenry, saying different things. How is a bureaucrat to judge, assess, evaluate, or weigh these statements? What incentive, other than human compassion and professional pride, does he have for even making the effort? What recourse do those who lose because of his judgment have?

The immediate impact of this kind of dilemma has been to bring project evaluation to a halt while the Corps struggles in the flypaper of such evaluation. The longer run implication, however, is that questions of *quo warranto* and improper legislative delegation of authority will be raised. The courts have always held that legislative authority, being itself delegated from the people, cannot be delegated.* While we have not yet reached that stage, we are verging toward it when we give appointed officials powers to control land use, economic growth, and environmental quality by their actions in water management. Our present tendency, buttressed by whatever level of "citizen participation" the agency can muster, cannot stand against the ancient precepts of representative government. (It is amusing to reflect that we might go full circle, i.e., political activists, in their search for ways for greater participation, may actually rediscover representative government.)

There is, I believe, no need to vex the Corps of Engineers and other agencies with tasks which they are, for good reason, constitutionally barred from doing. Let me suggest an alternative which has the advantage of dealing with the boundary problem as well. The suggestion is that instead of a citizen having many different men represent him—one on the school board, another in the sanitary district, a third in the city or suburban council, a fourth on the planning commission, and so on—the citizen should have one man, a general-purpose representative, represent him in all those governmental bodies. The basic reason for focusing all citizen representation in one man (at the local level) instead of many is to enable the question of priorities, of goals, and resolution of conflicting goals to be managed.

If, for example, a general-purpose representative (GPR) sits both on the school board and the sanitary commission, he can—indeed he must—decide whether to support a new school or a new sewer system if both cannot be funded. Citizens of his area, moreover, have one place to focus their attention on these questions, and they, too, must face the consequence that supporting the school means opposing the sewer.

Before proceding further, there are two general points to be made about the suggestion. The first is to counter the perennial reaction that we ought to have "experts" representing us on the school board, the sanitary board, etc. This reaction is not as common now as it once was, but it still occurs regularly. The point is, of course, that we can hire, to suit, any number of experts of any persuasion. But if government involves the process of reflecting voter preferences, then representatives should be expert in winning elections, since that presumes some knowledge of voter preferences. The second point is more substantive. It is the criticism that I have merely shifted the

---

*Locke's famous dictum *Delegata potestas non potest delegari* is but a restatement of a much older tradition in parliamentary rules. It was an established maxim of Roman law well before the promulgation of the Justinian Code (6th Century).

boundary problem from that of creating the ideal general-purpose local government to that of creating the ideal unit of local representation. The answer is to admit that I have, because the latter problem is solvable; in fact, it has already been solved in many jurisdictions. Congressional districts, state senatorial districts, and state representative districts are constructed of equal population units for the purpose of electing a general purpose representative. The general purpose representative is, in point of history, the oldest form of representation. Political parties are well acquainted with all the problems and possibilities of drawing district lines. The channels of the judiciary are well worn with all the problems of achieving equitable solutions to disputes. In other words, a process is in place which is working, where reform has already occurred.

The use of GPR's could be of value in finessing the environmental boundary problem, by separating the question of the geographical reach of the management agency from the geographical area represented on the policy board(s) to which the management agency is responsible. While the details of this idea are elaborated elsewhere [3], some discussion is necessary here. Let us think of a water control agency, or environmental management agency as a public corporation created at the state level with power to operate anywhere (much as the Maryland State Environmental Services agency is set up) *subject to* policy direction and funding by councils composed of GPR's in all districts affected by the problem. Thus one council involves only the GPR's in the airshed, another council (overlapping, no doubt) composed of those GPR's in the watershed.

The idea may be difficult to think about at first, but the implementation involves nothing more complicated than taking two votes in the hall one of brown-eyed people, the other of brown and blue-eyed people. As the airshed expanded, as it will if the city grows, districts could be added automatically on technical evidence that new areas were being affected.

It will be obvious to many who are familiar with local government that what I am suggesting is in fact already happening in one form or another. Councils of government in the United States are generally composed of elected officials from local jurisdictions. Such men— mayors, councilmen, county commissioners, and the like—already serve as the voting members of transit boards and planning commissions. The GPR is essentially a rationalization and extension of that trend in an attempt to provide maximum chance for the elected official to control what happens in his area, and to receive the reward, or blame for its happening.

The suggestion would have marked benefits for most professional staffs, for it gives them representatives to deal with who are real. Few things are more frustrating than trying to guage community reaction through a board composed of appointees whose knowledge of, and interest in, community reaction is both limited and one-sided. If the GPR system has any merit, it is that it provides incentive for the elected official to know what his constituents want and don't want. It also provides the constituents with an appropriate focus to register their feelings. In an era when the words "participatory" and "democracy" can be joined without any notion of redundancy arising, the incentive and the focus may be worthwhile.

CONCLUSION

We have taken a rather tortuous path through the thorny thicket. Perhaps some of it was unnecessary. If so, I apologize. One of my teachers, the late Louis Wirth, used to say, "The most important part of a man is what he takes for granted." Since we come to this conference from many different paths, it is likely we take difference things for granted. Some of us are interested in solutions of immediate problems, others in asking why do we have such problems. My interest is the latter one, and I have contended at too great length that we have them, in water management, because we are trying to go across the grain of our heritage.

My suggestions for changing direction are but sketchily drawn and will, undoubtedly, not work as presented. That they will not work does not distress me, if they serve the purpose of pointing out a new direction—a direction that appeals to you. Once we have agreed on a common direction, I have no doubt that the means to move there can be found.

NOTES TO CHAPTER 7

1. See Russell, Spofford, and Haefele, *Environmental Quality Management in Metropolitan Areas*, Conference on Urbanization and the Environment, International Economic Association, Copenhagen, June 1972.

2. See "Guidelines for Assessment of Economic, Social and Environmental Effects of Civil Works Projects," Office of the Chief of Engineers, September 28, 1972 (included as Appendix A to this chapter).

3. See Kneese and Haefele, "Environmental Quality and the Optimal Jurisdiction," Conference on Comparative Urban and Grants Economics, University of Windsor, November 1972.

Appendix A

Guidelines for Assessment of Economic, Social, and Environmental Effects of Civil Works Projects

These guidelines are designed to ensure that all significant adverse and beneficial effects of proposed projects are fully considered.*

Effect (impact) assessment is an integral part of the planning process. It serves as one test of the adequacy of that process and of any positive or negative recommendations resulting therefrom. It is fully compatible with multi-objective planning.

Any alternative developed in the planning process may produce unintended effects which are not responsive to the planning objectives and which are not included in benefit-cost analysis. Such effects are the subject of these guidelines.

Effect assessment is an iterative process which consists of the following steps: identification of anticipated project-caused economic, social, and environmental effects; quantitative and qualitative description and display of the effects; evaluation of the effects, whether adverse or beneficial; and consideration of measures to be taken if a proposed project would cause adverse effects.

The sequence of steps in effect assessment is summarized below:

1. Assemble a profile of existing conditions in the planning area.

2. Extend the profile to make projections of "without project" conditions through the expected life of the project.

3. Make "with project" projections, identifying causative factors and tracing their effects for each alternative.

*Pursuant to Section 122 of the River and Harbor and Flood Control Act of 1970, shown in Appendix B.

4. Identify significant effects.

5. Describe and display each significant effect.

6. Evaluate adverse and beneficial effects.

7. Consider project modifications where adverse effects are significant.

8. Seek assessment feedback from other sources.

(Steps 1 through 8 are common to each iteration of the effect assessment process.)

9. Use effect assessment in making recommendations.

10. Prepare a Statement of Findings.

11. Use effect assessment in preparing the Environmental Impact Statement.

This sequence is discussed in more detail in the paragraphs that follow.

Effect Assessment

1. *Assemble a profile.* Portray existing conditions in a profile describing the relevant economic, social, and environmental characteristics of the affected area. Judgment is of critical importance in determining what information will be needed.

A tentative profile should be prepared early in the planning process. Subsequently, as alternatives are considered in greater detail, the profile should be made more precise and focused on identified significant effects.

The boundary areas of the profile will vary depending upon whether the focus of an effect is local or regional; whether the area is defined by political jurisdiction or by hydrologic unit; and by the nature of the project effects.

When completed, the profile should provide a clear understanding of the significant existing conditions, problems, and needs of the affected area and of the rationale for any action, if proposed.

2. *Make projections of "without project" conditions.* Extend the profile of existing conditions to portray future conditions without any project action. Projections should cover the expected life of each alternative considered over a reasonable range of probable future conditions.

Utilize a range of values to compensate in part for the uncertainties of projecting the future.

Projection of existing economic, social, and environmental conditions should yield pertinent information about the conditions, problems, and needs of the affected area in the future and provide a basis or baseline for a comparison of the effects of alternative plans. The projection may suggest issues to be addressed in designing alternative "with project" plans.

3. *Make "with project" projections, identifying causative factors and tracing their effects for each alternative.* Make projections of the "with project" conditions for each alternative being considered, including pre-construction, construction and operation periods through its expected life.

Identify and list project-related causative factors (see Appendix C) and their likely economic, social, and environmental effects (see Appendix D) concurrently with the formulation of alternative plans.

The causative factors and effect elements should be set forth in sufficient detail for each alternative to ensure that all significant interactive relationships are considered. The interrelatedness of economic, social, and environmental aspects cannot be overlooked and must be considered regardless of the category in which any given effect is placed.

Assessments initially should emphasize breadth rather than depth. Refinements should await later stages of plan formulation.

Effect assessment at any stage should be carried to a degree of detail commensurate with the alternative it addresses.

4. *Identify significant effects.* Examine causative factors and the effects they produce for each alternative. Select those effects which appear significant in view of the conditions, problems, and needs of the affected area as projected for the "with" and "without" project conditions.

A "significant" effect is one which would be likely to have a material bearing on the decision-making process.

A determination regarding significance should be made at the earliest stage possible in the assessment process. The determination should be reconsidered at each stage, particularly in the light of public input and reaction.

In the process of formulation, adjustments may be made in the alternative plans that avoid or reduce identified adverse effects. In such cases, only residual adverse effects should be identified for further analysis in the concurrent assessment process.

5. *Describe and display all significant effects.* Describe the effects of the various alternative plans in quantitative terms to the extent possible. Where this cannot be done, effects should at a minimum be set forth in qualitative-descriptive terms.

The effects should be described objectively, and tentatively designated as adverse or beneficial.

Beneficial effects that are identified should be included, to the extent possible, in the benefit evaluation section of the survey report.

Beneficial effects of one kind cannot be considered to cancel out an adverse effect of another kind.

Display the effects of the alternative plans in a form that is easily understood, interpreted, and evaluated, and that clearly shows the differences among them. The display is to be used in consulting with state and federal agencies and public groups with particular expertise. The display also provides one of the bases for assessing alternative plans, selecting a recommended plan, and assisting in public participation.

6. *Evaluate effects.*   Place values on the significant adverse and beneficial effects in monetary terms where applicable, quantitatively where possible, and qualitatively in any event.

The assumptions or criteria on which a judgment is based should be made explicit, since segments of the public may perceive any single effect quite differently.

Significant adverse effects must be sufficiently well displayed to facilitate the weighing of need and type of project modification, if any. No single method for determining relative value is generally accepted. Public policy, community preferences, and the magnitude and degree of severity of effect are factors to be considered.

The aggregate or systems interaction of combined economic, social, and environmental effects along with evaluation of individual effects. In addition, the possibility of individual effects being part of a larger cumulative process should be investigated.

Effects not significant, not relevant, or that can be adequately incorporated in benefit-cost evaluation should not be accommodated in the effect evaluation.

An evaluation cannot be validated without obtaining the review and reaction of other agencies and the public.

7. *Consider project modifications where adverse effects are significant.*   For each significant adverse effect, investigate the possibility of: (a) eliminating the effect; and (b) mitigating the effect by minimizing or reducing it to an acceptable level of intensity; or by compensating for it by including a counter-balancing positive effect.

The costs of such measures, as well as any costs of reduced project performance, provide further bases for comparing alternatives and for deciding how or whether to modify them or to accept the adverse effects.

If effect assessment has not proceeded in step with the formulation of alternatives, the possibility always exists that an identified adverse effect may be of such magnitude or character that it cannot be accepted in the best overall public interest, or be corrected by project modifications. In such a case, one or more new alternatives must be formulated to avoid an unacceptable adverse consequence. "No action" is always one of the alternatives to be considered.

For each beneficial effect investigate the possibility of:

1. Reflecting it in the benefit-cost analysis of the project formulation process; or
2. Describing and displaying the effect for consideration by the public and in plan selection; or
3. Considering it as an offset for a corresponding adverse effect.

8. *Seek assessment feedback from other sources.* Effect assessment procedures require a variety of information sources and continuous feedback.

Informal exchanges with federal, state, and private groups and with individuals should be sought at the beginning of any investigation and maintained throughout planning. More formal discussion occurs in the course of initial formulation and late-stage public meetings.

Consultation with a wide range of interests tests the adequacy of identification of effects, validates their designation as beneficial or adverse, and provides commentary on measures considered for project modification.

Response should be solicited to ensure that effects have not been overlooked or that the significance of effects has not been misjudged.

Fully utilize all the public participation procedures of the planning process. For survey report investigations, known effects and the possibilities for project modifications to overcome adverse effects of alternatives will be introduced at the initial public meeting, discussed in general terms in the formulation-stage public meeting, and detailed at the late-stage public meeting.

For continuing authority reports and Phase I General Design Memoranda, effect assessment will be tailored to the public participation requirements of existing regulations.

Steps 1–7 should be taken before each public meeting to complete a formal iteration of the effect assessment process.

9. *Use effect assessment in making recommendations.* More detailed assessment will be applied to the alternatives, including the tentatively selected proposal, by the time they are presented in the late-stage public meeting. At this meeting, formal presentation of the alternatives and measures to overcome adverse effects will be made and the degree of public acceptance gauged.

The reporting officer should recommend the alternative that is in the best overall public interest considering the planning objectives, the benefits and costs, and the significant economic, social, and environmental effects, including costs of treating those that are adverse.

While assessment and appraisal from all sources influence the alternative recommended by the reporting officer, the burden of judgment and defense ultimately rests with him.

10. *Prepare a Statement of Findings.* Include a summary of the completed effect assessment in the report immediately before the Statement of Findings.

The Statement of Findings presents the rationale of the reporting officer for his conclusions and recommendations in accordance with the "best overall public interest."

11. *Use effect assessment in the Environmental Impact Statement.* The requirements of Section 122 supplement the requirements of P.L. 91–190 (NEPA). Consequently, the completed effect assessment for environmental effects should be used as input for the Environmental Impact Statement.

※ *Appendix B*

Section 122—P. L. 91–611

"Not later than July 1, 1972, the Secretary of the Army, acting through the Chief of Engineers, after consultation with appropriate Federal and State officials, shall submit to Congress, and not later than ninety days after submission, promulgate guidelines designed to assure that possible adverse economic, social, and environmental effects relating to any proposed project have been fully considered in developing such project, and that the final decisions on the project are made in the best overall public interest, taking into consideration the need for flood control, navigation, and associated purposes, and the cost of eliminating or minimizing such adverse effects and the following:

1. Air, noise and water pollution;
2. Destruction or disruption of man-made and natural resources, esthetic values, community cohesion and the availability of public facilities and services;
3. Adverse employment effects and tax and property value losses;
4. Injurious displacement of people, businesses and farms; and,
5. Disruption of desirable community and regional growth.

Such guidelines shall apply to all projects authorized in this Act, and proposed projects after the issuance of such guidelines."

Source: River and Harbor and Flood Control Act of 1970 (P.L. 91–611; 84 Stat. 1818).

Appendix C

Sample Causative Factors

In order to identify and evaluate the effects of a project, describe aspects of the project in terms of factors likely to produce significant effects. Evaluation of effects should not be carried out in greater detail than the project alternative being considered. *The list below is illustrative. It is not to be considered complete or limiting.*

Input Factors

Natural Resources
Water
Land
Resources Products
Gravel
Sand
Coal
Timber
Crushed Rock
Wildlife and Fish
Aesthetics
Flora (Plant life)

Energy Resources
Capital
Labor

Systemic Factors

Physical Alterations
Channelization
Excavation
Dredging
Draining

Structures
Dam/Lake
Levee
Jetty
Channel
Barrier
Road and Utility Relocation

Institutional
Acquisition
Easements
Relocation

Operation and Maintenance Factors

Equipment Service
Resource Management
  Harvesting
  Planting
  Buffer Zone Maintenance
  Grazing
  Fencing

Maintenance
  Recreational areas
  Water Quality Protection
  Dredging Operations
  Navigation Controls
  Reservoir Controls and Procedures

Output Factors

Hydro-power
Flood Control
Navigation
Water Supply
Recreation
Irrigation
Fish and Wildlife
Water Quality
Shoreline Protection

(Example: A project alternative requiring a dam may need a great deal of sand for contrete. Sand, therefore, can be considered an Input Factor. The employment effects of hiring people to excavate and transport sand, the environmental effect of excavation, and the transportation effects of increased heavy traffic on roads leading to the project all need to be considered since they are all effects resulting from the one causative factor—sand. Similarly, the environmental, social, economic effects caused by construction of the dam should be identified and assessed, as should the effects caused by operation and maintenance of the dam and its post-construction outputs.)

Appendix D

Sample Project Effects

All significant effects of project should be identified and assessed. In some cases, a causative factor may result in only one significant effect. In other cases, the significant effects of a causative factor will be numerous and may require consideration in all three effect categories. (Example: a causative factor such as dredging may result in turbidity in the water for a brief period. This should be considered a predominantly environmental effect. Yet, because of the turbid water, a textile factory downstream may have to close down for a few days. This is an economic effect, and should be considered as a result of dredging even though it is a lesser effect than the environmental one. The increased turbidity may also have the effect of reducing water recreation temporarily. This is a social effect of dredging). Judgment must be used as to the limits of tracing out effects. Generally, the degree of detail involved in assessment should be no greater than that of the plan it addresses.

An asterisk denotes items specifically mentioned in Section 122. These must be identified and evaluated. If they are considered to be not significant, that should also be noted. Other effects should be identified and evaluated only if they are considered to be significant. *The list below is an illustrative one. It is not to be considered complete or limiting.*

Social Effects
*Noise
 Population, e.g.,
   Mobility
   Density
   *Displacement of people
 *Esthetic values
 Housing
 Archeologic remains
 Historic Structures
 Transportation
 Education opportunities
 Leisure opportunities (recreation, active and passive)
 Cultural opportunities
 *Community cohesion
 *(Desirable) community growth
 Institutional relationships
 Health

Economic Effects
 National Economic Development
 Local government finance, e.g.,
   *Tax revenues
   *Property values
 Land use
 *Public facilities
 *Public services
 Local/regional activity, e.g.,
   *(Desirable) regional growth
   Relocation
 Real income distribution
 *Employment/labor force
 *Business and industrial activity
 Agricultural activity
   *Displacement of farms
   Food supply
 National defense

Environmental Factors
 *Man-made-resources
 *Natural resources

Pollution aspects
 *Air
    CO
    Sulphur oxides
    Hydrocarbons
    Particulates
    Photochemicals
 *Water
    Pathogenic agents
    Nutrients N and P
    Pesticides, herbicides, rodenticides
    Organic materials
    Solids, dissolved and suspended
 Land
    Soils
 Animal and plant
    Birds
    Mammals
    Amphibians
    Fish, sport and commercial
    Shellfish
    Insects
    Microfauna
    Trees, shrubs and plants
    Microflora
 Ecosystems
    Habitats
    Food chains
    Productivity
    Diversity
    Stability
 Physical and Hydrologic aspects
    Erosion
    Erosion and sedimentation effects
    Compaction and subsidence
    Slope stability
    Groundwater regime alteration
    Surface flow effects
    Micrometeorological effects
    Physiologic changes (e.g., wetlands destruction)

Chapter 8

Controlling Land Uses and Prices by Using Special Gain Taxation to Intervene in the Land Market: The Vermont Experiment *

*R. Lisle Baker***

INTRODUCTION

Concern over escalating land prices and the increasingly rapid conversion of open space to more intensive uses has led to renewed interest in taxation as a technique for land use control [1]. This article will discuss in detail one recent tax innovation: the Vermont tax on up to 60% of gain realized from short-term sales of land, better known as the Vermont land gains tax.

While land value increment taxation has been a subject of some discussion in the past and has become law in several foreign jurisdictions, the Vermont land gains tax is apparently the first of its kind to be enacted in the United States [2].

The land gains tax is so new that hard data about its effects have not been accumulated. The tax, however, raises important issues about the relation of the land market to the land development process, about the participants in that process, and about the rightful ownership of appreciation in land values.

In order to explore these issues more fully, this article will discuss the background of the Vermont land gains tax and its test in the Vermont courts, analyze the tax in relation to a model of the Vermont land market to estimate the likely effects of the gains tax on Vermont land uses and prices, note similar tax innovations now being undertaken or considered elsewhere, and, finally, explore some of

*Appreciation is expressed to the publishers of *Environmental Affairs*, in which a longer version of this paper has been published, for permission to include it in the present volume.

**R. Lisle Baker is Associate Professor of Law, Suffolk University Law School.

the wider implications of the tax in light of issues raised by the Vermont Supreme Court.

THE VERMONT LAND GAINS TAX

Background

Vermont is a rural state with most of its population of only 450,000 scattered in the countryside or in small towns. In such an environment, the green valley becomes a community asset over which even the regular visitor believes he has acquired a prescriptive scenic easement. When such expectations are disrupted by the accelerating conversion of open space to more intensive uses, conflict results.

In 1970, the Vermont legislature responded to this conflict by enacting Act 250, which provided Vermont with a statewide permit system for much of its land development, and required preparation of a three-stage statewide land use plan [3]. In 1972, Governor Thomas Salmon was elected partly because of his support for property tax relief for Vermont landowners and a capital gains tax on land speculation [4].

In April, 1973, the Vermont legislature, with Governor Salmon's support, enacted Act 81, providing increased property tax relief with partial funding from a new land gains tax [5].

What the Tax Provided

The heart of the gains tax was the rate schedule which placed the burden most heavily on the short-term speculator realizing high profits from his land sales.

In addition to progressive exemptions for long-term holdings, the law provided two other primary exemptions; one for gain attributable to a maximum of one acre of land "necessary for the use of a dwelling used by the taxpayer as his principal residence" and one for gain attributable to "buildings or other structures."

Not all short-term and transfers are affected. For instance, transfers without consideration or transfers where no gain was recognized

Table 8–1.   Gain as a Percentage of Basis *(Tax Cost)*

Years Land Held by Transferor	0–99%	100–199%	200% or more
Less than 1 year	30%	45%	60%
1 year, but less than 2	25%	37.5%	50%
2 years, but less than 3	20%	30%	40%
3 years, but less than 4	15%	22.5%	30%
4 years, but less than 5	10%	15%	20%
5 years, but less than 6	5%	7.5%	10%

for purposes of federal income taxation are exempt. Moreover, since the gains tax followed the federal tax rules for definition of basis, land acquiring a stepped-up basis at death for federal tax purposes also acquires a stepped-up basis for purposes of the land gains tax. Unlike the federal model, however, the Vermont tax provides no off-set for land losses.

Since the tax applies only to land, a seller must allocate the gain on a sale of land containing buildings and other structures between the land and the structures on the basis of "fair market value."

The transferor is liable for the tax, but the buyer must withhold ten percent of the consideration paid for the land and remit it to the Vermont Commissioner of Taxes. Within 30 days of the taxable transfer, the seller must file a return with the Commissioner setting forth the amount of the tax due and enclosing the balance owing or making a claim for a refund.

The Challenge to the Gains Tax

Governor Salmon signed Act 81 into law on April 23, 1973. By Bill of Complaint dated April 24, 1973, a Vermont individual, a Vermont limited partnership, and a Vermont Corporation, all allegedly engaged in the sale or development of Vermont land, began an action against Vermont Tax Commissioner Robert Lathrop challenging the constitutionality of the tax and requesting an injunction restraining the Commissioner from collecting or enforcing it [6].

On August 6, 1973, the trial court entered a judgment order dismissing plaintiff's complaint. Plaintiffs appealed, and on February 5, 1974, the Vermont Supreme Court affirmed the judgment of the Washington County Court [7].

The Vermont Supreme Court's treatment of plaintiffs' land development claims is worth noting here. The court determined that deterring speculation through taxation was a constitutionally legitimate state concern so as to justify the variable rate scheme in the tax against plaintiffs' equal protection challenge. The court added:

> . . . we may take judicial notice of an increasing concern within the state over the use and development of land as a natural resource, a concern to which the legislature has responded in other instances with appropriate legislation [Act 250]. . . . Speculation falls within the ambit of such concern as a land use; indeed it has a bearing on many other uses to which the land might be put.

The court apparently came to its conclusion about the land use consequences of speculation without the aid of the trial record or argument by either party, at least to the extent that those arguments are reflected in their written briefs. Whether the court's conclusion was justified is explored next.

LAND MARKET ANALYSIS

The effects of the land gains tax in Vermont have not yet been measured empirically, but the fact that it is designed as a variable exemption transfer tax on land value increments implies effects on the land market. The land market is one of the less studied, yet more important aspects of the land development process because it is through the market that much of the fuel for the land development—capital gains—is realized.

There are other reasons for examining the land market. A sense is emerging that the more traditional land use controls, such as zoning and subdivision regulation, affect the land development process too late to be more than an accommodation to market decisions already made by developers. Hence a desire exists to find a land use tool to intervene earlier. Moreover, part of the concern motivating the Vermont land gains tax (and land value increment taxation elsewhere) is the rising cost of land.

But how does the land gains tax affect the land market? What effect does the process of land transfer have on land uses and prices? To arrive at an understanding of some answers to these questions, it is useful to look at the Vermont land market and then discuss the land gains tax in relation to it.

Some General Observations About
Land Markets

Land prices are determined by market supply and demand [8]. While the supply of land, as distinguished from improvements, is relatively fixed (except where dredging and filling operations can expand it), this supply can be transferred an almost infinite number of times. The transfer process by itself does not use up any land, although activities such as subdivision or construction may effectively pre-empt a particular parcel for a particular use, except where public or private redevelopment occurs.

Thus, when discussing a transfer tax such as the Vermont land gains tax, one should focus on land supply not as the absolute stock of buildable land which stock in fact may be shrinking because of continuing construction, or private or public land use regulation, as discussed below, but on the amount of land offered for sale at a particular time. Such a supply is better termed the "effective" supply of the land.

The other side of the land market is land demand [9]. The desire of potential transferees to purchase land is likely to be affected by a variety of factors. But as a mirror image of effective land supply, the amount of land sought is inversely proportional to price.

Individual land parcel sales will occur as a coincidence of a land-owner's willingness to sell a given acreage at a given price with a prospective purchaser's willingness to purchase such acreage at that price. The aggregate of decisions by individual land market participants is called the land market. Effective supply and demand interact through the market to determine land prices and land transferred.

The Effect of the Land Gains Tax on this Land Market

A quantitative analysis of the effect of the land gains tax requires sophisticated information about the impact of other factors that determine land supply and demand. Until such information is obtained from carefully analyzed field research, the best that can be done as an introductory analysis is to estimate some of the qualitative effects of the tax.

Supply Effects. What is the likely effect of the land gains tax? First, it is important to point out that some land market participants will not be affected by the land gains tax. These include landowners who have held their property longer than six years, some residential sellers and those engaging in tax-free transfers. Those transferors affected by the tax may make one of two responses [10]. An owner may avoid part or all of the tax by withdrawing land from the market, postponing transfers until some or all of the six-year holding period has expired. An alternative response is for the seller to increase the price asked in order to cover the amount of the gains tax.

But not all participants are likely to respond to the tax in the same way. Some participants may elect inflation as a response, other may elect withdrawal.

Which effect—inflation or withdrawal—is likely to dominate is uncertain. Some participants in the land market who have high holding costs, such as interest payments, may find withdrawal an unpalatable alternative. Others with income producing property, such as some farmers, may find withdrawal acceptable. Those to whom withdrawal is not a solution may elect to increase their prices. Whether such land market participants will be successful may depend on how much competition they will face from offerors of similar parcels not subject to the gains tax and how much land demand will absorb price increments. Thus some participants may find both postponement or inflation unfeasible, and may elect in the future to invest outside the Vermont land market.

Demand Effects.   A withdrawal effect is likely to occur when some potential land market participants decide that the risk of land gains taxation on resale of the parcel they acquire (and possible tax-induced effects on prices themselves) makes purchasing Vermont land an undesirable alternative to other investments. Conversely, some participants who desire to remain in the Vermont land market may choose to lower the prices they are willing to offer landowners in order to offset the anticipated tax which they might have to pay upon resale. In this deflationary effect of the tax the amount of land sought by those participants does not decline, but a drop in the offering price occurs. Of course, some participants may elect to absorb any future and gains taxes completely and consequently will not change their market position, but the number of participants who either withdraw from the market or deflate the prices they offer is likely in the aggregate to produce a composite withdrawal and deflationary effect from the tax.

Composite Effects.   What emerges from the foregoing analysis is a sense that the gains tax is likely to induce a reduction in both the amount of land offered for sale and the land sought for purchase, especially among specific participants in the land market, as discussed below. This decline in supply and demand may produce further effects on the land market. A land supply contraction combined with a land demand contraction can produce not only a reduction in the amount of land transferred but also a net decline in prices. A slight adjustment in the relative strength in the supply and demand effects of the tax produces a net price increase. Thus if supply shifts are more severe than demand shifts, prices will rise somewhat, benefiting sellers and taxing "buyers." If demand reductions are more severe than supply shifts, prices will "fall," benefiting purchasers and levying an additional "tax" on sellers. It is important to note, however, that regardless of the price effect of the gains tax, the number of transfers is likely to fall.

The foregoing discussion is potentially misleading in treating even the local land market as monolith. Furthermore, a simple supply and demand analysis has inherent limitations in being focused on only one frame in time. Finally, it does little to illuminate the land use consequences of the tax, whch the Vermont Supreme Court indicated might flow from the tax's likely impact on speculators.

Consequently, it may be useful to look at the likely effect of the land gains tax on some key Vermont land market participants. Such an analysis must deal with several factors. First, while Vermont is a predominantly rural state with much of its land in relatively low intensities of use, it has recently been subject to intense growth pressures, especially from the second-home industry. Second, the gains tax is fundamentally a transfer tax, with many transfers exempt. Third, the tax was apparently targeted (either prospectively or retrospectively) at speculators and subdividers.

A Look at the Land Gains Tax and Key Participants in the Land Market

The reasons land is bought and sold are as diverse as the participants in the market, but it is possible to distinguish as least four categories of participants by the dominant motive for their activity.

1. *Users*: Those who purchase and hold land for use (homeowners, governments) or income (farmers, industries, commercial or residential landlords).
2. *Speculators*: Those who purchase and hold land for transfer after appreciation induced by market forces new public improvements nearby.
3. *Subdividers*: Those who purchase and hold land for transfer after appreciation in part induced by subdivision, rezoning or preconstruction activity they undertake.
4. *Builders*: Those who purchase and hold land for transfer to users or speculators after construction or renovation of buildings or other structures.

How is the gains tax likely to affect these participants?

Users. Those who purchase and hold land for use or income usually enter the land market with the intention of acquiring property for the long term. Consequently, it is likely that the length of the users' holding period would be higher than that for almost any other class of land market participants. Moreover, residential purchasers have the additional advantage of a limited exemption from the land gains tax. Finally, owners of improved income-producing property may find that much of the gain on a sale of such property may be successfully attributed to rising demand for the structure (such as in a rental apartment complex) and not the land itself. Consequently, users probably will not be significantly affected by the land gains tax.

Speculators. Unlike users who can either derive income from their property, or, as in the case of a homeowner, sustain property ownership through outside sources of income, the speculator by definition acquires and holds land for transfer after appreciation induced by market or other forces outside his control. The holding cost for many speculators, including property taxes and interest payments, may make it undesirable for them to hold the land for a long period, leading to an attempt to raise prices. Others may respond by withdrawing land from the market in hopes of waiting out the tax. Consequently, some of the shift in the land market supply schedule will be the result of speculator decisions.

On the demand side, some speculators, especially those with high holding costs, are likely either to find long-term holding undesirable or to find property subject to land gains taxation to be an unacceptable investment. In either case they may withdraw from the land market, as indicated in the original supply and demand analysis. If this decline in demand is significant, it may lead to a secondary contraction in the amount of Vermont land held by speculators. Thus the absolute land supply held by speculators may contract over time, leaving more of the Vermont land bank in the hands of other market participants.

Subdividers. Subdividers differ from speculators because they alter what they purchase. The alteration may be merely surveying a lot or two for resale or it may involve substantial terrain alterations, including installation of streets and utilities. As suppliers, some subdividers may be able to extract from prospective purchasers certifications that a primary residence will be constructed on the lot sold. To that extent, such subdividers would not be affected by the land gains tax. On the other hand, the land gains tax will have a larger impact on those subdividers whose primary market consists of second home sites. As a class, subdividers may be more severely affected than speculators because their holding costs after predevelopment construction loans may be significant. Like speculators, subdividers finding the prospect of waiting out the tax unacceptable, and inflation an undesirable alternative, may elect to withdraw from subdivision activity in Vermont altogether, especially if speculators constitute some of the prospective purchasers of subdivided land.

Subdividers are also likely to be severely affected by the land gains tax if much of any gain realized results from the conversion of a large "economy-sized" parcel into a collection of smaller, proportionately more expensive lots which must then be quickly sold. If many such subdividers decide to leave the Vermont market, the result could mean fewer smaller lots offered for sale. Many subdivided lots, however, are not built upon, especially in the recreational subdivision industry. Thus, if subdivider land demand declines significantly over the long term, the effective supply of subdivided land is likely to undergo a secondary contraction in addition to the primary contractions caused by subdividers electing sale postponement or price inflation.

Builders. The builder's large capital outlay for construction means that he is under more pressure than the subdivider to turn his investment around quickly. However, a large portion of the gain on a sale of improved property, as opposed to subdivided property, may be allocable to the structure, which is exempt from gains taxation. For example, a builder who purchases a lot for $10,000 might erect a structure for $40,000 and sell both lot and structure within a year for a gross return of $60,000. Under the statute, the $10,000 gain realized is allocable between the house and the land on the basis of fair market value. Even assuming that the land and the structure each capture gain in proportion to initial costs, most of the gain will still be allocable to the structure, and therefore exempt from the tax.

Additionally, if the land involved is residential and the seller has used or the purchaser intends to use the property for primary residential purposes, up to ten acres of that land may also be exempt from taxation. Consequently, builders are likely to fare much better than either subdividers or speculators under the land gains tax.

User-Demand. User-demand for land may be affected by prospective gains taxes. Such an effect is likely to be less significant than, for example, the effect on investors, since a user's demand for land is likely to be a reflection of his needs for potential income rather than the incremental costs of the land gains tax on any potential resale. Moreover, as indicated earlier, residential sales involving primary homesites will be completely exempt in many cases and partially exempt in others where large lots are involved.

What is the variation in the impact on various land market participants likely to mean in terms of land use in Vermont?

An answer to that question involves a look at the growth cycle.

THE LAND GAINS TAX AND THE GROWTH CYCLE OR TAXING TRANSFERS FACILITATING INCREASES IN LAND USE INTENSITY

A parcel of buildable open space normally has two intensities of use—one actual and one possible, with the latter limited by natural conditions (such as slope), and private land use regulation (such as conservation easements). Land not so limited is likely to be affected by public control which can set a relatively low potential use intensity through such devices as large lot zoning. When the possible use becomes the actual use what had been merely a latent use intensity becomes realized.

These changes in land use intensity involve transfers either between several land market participants acting in different capacities or between one or two participants acting in a variety of capacities. The transfers involving these shifts in use intensity may be schematically described as indicated in Figure 8–1 with land passing from a latent through a potential and emergent use until the use is realized through construction.

While a single parcel will rarely move from a latent to a realized intensity of use more than once (except where private or public redevelopment occurs), the process can be called a cycle, because the user is both a supplier of buildable open land and purchaser of developed properties. (The use of the term "development" is avoided as much as possible in this discussion because of the risk of confusing preconstruction activity, such as subdivision, with new construction, which often occurs at a different point in time and by the efforts of a different land market participant.)

Users and Speculators are designated land bankers since owners acting in those capacities do not physically convert land from a lower to a higher intensity of use, but provide sources from which subdividers and builders (land converters—effecting a physical or boundary change in the land they hold) might draw.

While each component in the land market is a potential transferor

Figure 8–1. Cycle of Land Market Transfers Affecting Changes in Land Use Intensity

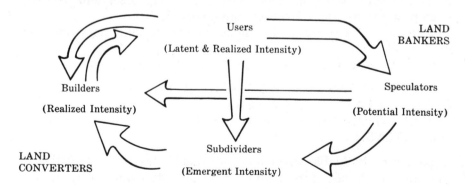

or transferee (the user-user house sale, the speculator-user farmland sale), only transfers resulting in an increment in land use intensity are illustrated. It should be noted that land does not have to pass through the entire cycle. Participants of the system can be bypassed (such as the builder who constructs a planned unit development on land purchased from a timber company), or an owner can elect to act in multiple capacities without even transferring land at all (such as the farmer who builds a house for his daughter). Thus, each participant in the system is a potential transferor or "supplier" of land (*i.e.*, he holds land now which he may transfer) and a potential transferee (he does not hold land now but may do so in the future).

How is the land gains tax likely to affect transfers by these participants? First, aside from the overall market effects discussed earlier, (*i.e.*, modulation of amount of land transferred and modulation of land prices), the gains tax may produce a reduction in the number of transfers "up" the growth cycle, especially where second homes are involved. If the land gains tax affects speculators and second-home subdividers significantly over the long run, the builder may find that he can purchase land directly from users with less competition from wholesalers and retailers (the speculator and the subdivider). Such a reduction could produce a significant opportunity to save transfer costs such as broker's commissions and attorney's fees which are often at least 10 percent of the value of each transfer.

These transfer costs can be an important component of land prices. To the extent that the gains tax causes such transfer costs to be reduced, it may perform a considerable service.

The transfer costs thus saved can mean more profits for either the farmer-user or the builder (or both), assuming that demand for the builder's finished product is not likely to be significantly affected by the gains tax.

But such an analysis, while useful to indicate the importance of transfer costs in the land development process, assumes that the user-farmer can get at least the same amount for his land before the gains tax as after. Is this assumption accurate? If he loses some subdividers or speculators as part of his available market or others offer him lower prices because of the tax's deflationary effect (discussed above) will he be able to sell? If he must sell, will the sale be at a distress price? In other words, how necessary are the growth cycle intermediaries as a means of private price supports for the primary user?

The answer to that question depends on whether the effect of gains tax-induced inflation and withdrawal on other users causes the shift in the effective land supply to match or exceed any shift in land demand. The drop-out effect so postulated will probably not be as severe on the user-seller as one might expect because some user-sellers will elect either to inflate their price or withdraw from the market temporarily. Thus, while the aggregate demand for land may decrease through the loss of certain market participants, the aggregate effective supply will also have dropped, leaving the farmer who must sell in a more favored position than otherwise anticipated. Similarly, builders should not find their market severely curtailed, primarily because of the residential homesite exemption, and also because the land gains tax would constitute a relatively small part of their overall investments. Moreover, the transfer cost savings available to builders through growth cycle bypass may enable them to offer higher prices, leading to a lesser shift in land demand than might otherwise occur. Again, certainty will have to await empirical research, but at this point, it seems that the demand effects of the tax on primary users who wish to sell may not be as harsh as anticipated.

While earlier supply and demand analysis indicated that the land gains tax would produce an overall modulation in land prices, amplifying that analysis by looking at the growth cycle indicates that such a modulation may take place predominately at the expense of the speculator and subdivider and not at the expense of the user or the builder. Thus the gains tax could have the unusual effect of making possible lower land prices for the ultimate users of improved land while increasing the bargaining room of those builders who purchase unsubdivided land, meaning high prices in some cases for user-sellers of unsubdivided land.

Aside from the considerable saving produced by eliminating the transfer costs of moving land "up" the growth cycle (which can distress only brokers or others who live off the land transfer process), the land gains tax may have an important environmental benefit in removing some subdividers from the land market.

To the extent that the gains tax reduces the relative amount of land moving into the hands of subdividers, the gains tax will have accomplished one of Governor Salmon's objectives and helped move Vermont land out of the "lot first" development pattern, which often results not only in an unsound land use plan for a subdivided parcel but also in a significant number of lots that are never used for construction but are no longer virgin open space [11].

It is important to note that even with the expanded homesite exemption enacted in 1974, the land gains tax will apply to precisely the large lot subdivisions that do not now come under the Act 250 process. Hence the gains tax may be a complement to Act 250.

While the gains tax may not significantly affect the amount of construction in Vermont—indeed the structural exemption may stimulate some investors to move into structures if they withdraw from land—the six year holding period and the slow-down in second home subdivision are likely to afford greater opportunities for careful land-use planning, both for particular parcels and for the state itself.

Finally, the structural exemption, as well as the difficulty of making allocations of gain between new construction and land, is likely to permit and perhaps even encourage land owners to improve structures on their land without anxiety that portions of the increments in value will be captured by the state should a sale occur.

To summarize, the structure of the land gains tax implies that the tax will have a beneficial effect on the rate at which open land is converted from latent to realized intensities of use, with the most significant slowdown occurring at the level of emergent use intensities. The gains tax is also likely to permit more opportunities for users and builders to bypass investors and subdividers—the land market middlemen.

Together these projected effects indicate that some open Vermont land which might be purchased by speculators or subdividers will remain in its current use. This can have important effects to the extent that such land is used for agricultural purposes [12].

Do the conclusions of the model bear any relation to what has actually happened in Vermont? Until some broad-ranging research can be undertaken, it is difficult to judge, but it may be useful to look at some indications provided by facts currently available.

Since 1968, Vermont has had a property transfer return which must be filed whenever a deed evidencing a transfer of title to real property is delivered to the town clerk for recording. The town clerk cannot record the deed unless it is accompanied by a completed return and the tax owed, if any. Except for certain exempt transfers, the amount due is .005 of the price paid for the property.

As indicated by property transfer tax returns, the number of transfers declined significantly after passage of the land gains tax. But is this properly attributable to the land gains tax or to other causes? 1973–74 marked a severe credit crunch involving both high interest rates and tight money. Consequently, while the figures could be taken to confirm this article's economic analysis, judgment should be withheld until more sophisticated field information can be collected and analyzed.

In addition, the land gains tax has not resulted in the amount of revenue originally anticipated, producing $1,288,520 in tax liability for fiscal year 1973–74. But again, without more data it may be a mistake to ascribe the shortfall to the transfer-reducing and price-modulating effects of the gains tax predicted by the analysis.

THE IMPLICATION OF STATE LAND VALUE INCREMENT TAXATION

Some of the important issues raised by devices such as the Vermont Land Gains Tax were discussed in the challenge to the tax in the Vermont Supreme Court, which upheld the tax against its challenge by Vermont land developers. Much of the court's opinion has already been discussed elsewhere [13]. However, several key issues remain to be analyzed, including the "taking" issue.

The Taking Issue
The plaintiffs in their original bill of complaint alleged that the land gains tax violated the Fifth Amendment's prohibition against taking private property for public use without just compensation [14]. However, they did not elaborate in their bill on the nature of the interference with this constitutional provision. In their later briefs, appellants abandoned the taking issue altogether (except in the guise of a double taxation argument) and the court did not take it up itself. Nonetheless, because it raises questions about the ownership of appreciation in land values, the issue is worth exploring further. (If that appreciation is not "property" no "taking" has occurred when it is taxed.)

Land Gains Taxation, Transferable Development Rights and the Landowner's Entitlement to Land Value Appreciation
A number of commentators have noted a trend toward a view of land as a resource rather than a commodity [15]. The recent proliferation of environmentally-based controls imposed has prompted warnings of a backlash from aggrieved landowners who find the rewards going to a favored and diminishing few who can jump the increasing number of barrels on the land development ice [16].

In order to deal with this problem commentators have been focusing on the idea of transferable development rights as a means of preserving urban landmarks, open space and farmland, environmentally fragile areas, or as a means of dealing with the "equal protection" aspects of the taking issue generally [17].

Transferable development rights proposals generally involve either government acquisition in districts where development is undesired followed by resale to developers in transfer districts or government restriction in preservation districts, followed by free market transfer of the restricted right to owners in transfer districts. An extended discussion of the merits and demerits of transferable development rights is beyond the scope of this article. In short, however, the scheme is predicated on the assumption that the owner of land is entitled to profit from it, or as Professor Carmichael has put it

> Development and redevelopment will doubtless continue to be a strongly protected incident of land ownership. This incident is certainly a principal basis of expectations within our system of private ownership rights, and its destruction would not be tolerated [18].

It seems likely that the widespread adoption of some form of TDR scheme would fulfill his prophecy since even landowners barred from developing their land by sound environmental or other regulation would still profit by its nondevelopment.

If land is going to be viewed as something precious in which future generations have a legitimate interest which should be protected, it may be premature to enshrine the current owner's development expectancy into alienable and publicly protected "rights." A counter-current is at work, fueled by the widening understanding of ecological principles, promoted by social theorists, given respectability by commentators, and supported by court decisions such as the famous case of *Just v. Marinette County* [19]. In the *Just* case, the court redefined the owner's property entitlement, in the context of a county ordinance barring lakeshore land filling without a permit, to land in its "natural state" [20].

In the view of the counter-current, changes in land use intensity are presumptively "ameliorative waste" [21] of the interests of later generations rather than "development" or "improvements" [22].

Pending a resolution of this fundamental question of the owner's entitlement to profit from changes in the intensity of the use of his land, it is useful to ponder the Vermont land gains tax. Rather than choosing one school of thought over the other, the land gains tax implies a concern for the legitimate land use interests of future generations and also a recognition that land in Vermont still is very much a commodity. It consequently taxes only some appreciation in land value, then only as realized, and even then only that appreciation that seems "unearned." Until the "new property" emerges, the tax may be a useful intermediate step.

Finally, the land gains tax helps to focus on how taxation relates to the other two principal tools of land use control—condemnation and regulation.

When eminent domain is involved, the government compensates the affected landowner. When regulation occurs, neither pays (directly). But when taxation occurs, the affected landowner pays the government. As noted above, however, the courts defer to governmental exercise of the taxing power as long as equal protection issues are met and "confiscation," as yet relatively undefined, has not occurred. Thus until more guidance is forthcoming from courts or commentators, governments who want land use controls that help pay their way are likely to look at taxation in general and the Vermont land Gains Tax in particular.

CONCLUSION

The Vermont land gains tax is an unproven but promising innovation in the arsenal of land use controls. It intervenes in the land market— a market that may have had more influence on land uses than many realize. Unlike most conventional land use controls and property tax exemptions, the land gains tax strongly affects both land demand and land supply—not mainly supply. The exemption structure of the tax targets it effects most heavily on the speculator and the subdivider, the middlemen in the growth cycle, improving chances for profit and planning for land users and builders. The tax raises questions as to who owns the appreciation in land value and as to the nature of entitlements to make changes in land use intensities. Furthermore, it leads to renewed examination of taxation as a device for land use control. Finally, it may lead land use planners and tax collectors for a jurisdiction to begin to think of ways that they can work toward similar, rather than separate and often conflicting, goals.

NOTES TO CHAPTER 8

1. *See* Urban Land Use Policy, 207–276 (Andrews ed. 1972) Delogu, *The Taxing Power as a Land Use Control Device*, 45 Den. L.J. 279 (1968); Gurko, *Federal Income Taxes and Urban Sprawl*, 48 Den. L.J. 329 (1972); Zimmerman, *Tax Planning for Land Use Control*, 5 Urban Lawyer 639 (1973).

2. For other commentary on the Vermont land gains tax, *see* Rose, *From the Legislatures: Vermont Using the Taxing Power to Control Land Use*, 2 Real Estate Law JOURNAL 602 (1973); Note *State Taxation—Use of Taxing Power to Achieve Environmental Goals: Vermont Taxes Gains Realized from the Sale or Exchange of Land Held Less than Six Years*, _____ Vt. Stat. Ann., tit. 32, §§10001–10 (1973), 49 Wash. L. Rev. 1159 (Aug., 1974);

3. *See* 10 V.S.A. §6001 et seq. (1974). The permit process and land use plan have been discussed in detail elsewhere. *See* F. Bosselman and D. Callies, The Quiet Revolution in Land Use Control, 54–108 (1971); Myers, So Goes Ver-

mont (Conservation Foundation, 1974); Levy *Vermont's New Approach to Land Development*; 59 A.B.A.J. 1158 (1973); Walter, *The Law of the Land: Development Regulation in Maine and Vermont* 23 Me. L. Rev. 315 (1971).

4. Myers, *supra* note 3 at 34.

5. Act 81 of the 1973 Vermont laws, amending 32 V.S.A. §§5951, 5960(e), 5967–68, 5973; *adding* 32 V.S.A. §§5976–77 and 32 V.S.A. §§10001–10010; repealing 32 V.S.A., §5966. The gains tax is 32 V.S.A. §§ 10001–10010 (1973).

6. Record at 2–9, Andrews v. Lathrop, 315 A.2d 860 (Vt. 1974). Plaintiffs' bill made two principal allegations: (1) as a revenue bill, the gains tax was improperly enacted because it failed to originate in the Vermont House of Representatives as required by Chapter 2, section 6 of the Vermont Constitution; and (2) the gains tax rate schedule and exemptions made the tax unconstitutionally discriminatory under the equal protection provisions of the Vermont and U.S. Constitutions.

7. Andrews v. Lathrop, 315 A.2d 860 (Vt. 1974). For discussion of Act 250, *see supra* note 3.

While the developers lost in court, they won a small victory in the 1974 session in the Vermont legislature. By legislation effective July 1, 1974, section 10002 of chapter 236 was amended by providing that the residential exemption was raised to a maximum of five acres. Moreover, that exemption was extended not only to individuals already owning a primary residence in Vermont at the time of sale, but also to purchasers who intended the subject dwelling to become their principal residence.

The burden on subdividers was also alleviated somewhat. The amendment provided that where there is no existing dwelling completed and fit for occupancy as the purchaser's principal residence at the time of transfer of title, the purchaser can certify that construction on the dwelling will commence within a year of the date of transfer of title and will complete it and occupy it within two years of transfer.

8. *See* Corty, *The Land Market and Transfer Process*, in Rural Land Tenure in the United States 195 (A. Bertrand and F.L. Corty, eds. 1962).

9. Land demand may be a function of population growth and migration, economic growth, costs of borrowing, transportation problems such as no gasoline, market expectations and the availability of attractive alternative investment. *See generally*, Corty, *supra* note 9 at 195, op cit.

10. The land gains tax paid is apparently treated by the Internal Revenue Service as a selling expense resulting in a decrease in the net gain taxable for federal income tax purposes. Thus changes in the supply schedule may be less severe because the land gains tax has partially replaced what might otherwise be taxable gain or income for federal income tax purposes.

11. This problem is acute in the second-home lot development where only a few subdivided lots are ever built upon. According to one recent source, six recreational lots were sold nationwide in 1971 for every home constructed. *See* Task Force on Land Use and Urban Growth, Citizens' Advisory Committee on Environmental Quality, The Use of Land: A Citizens Guide to Urban Growth 264 (1973).

Thus to the extent that more Vermont open space stays in unbroken parcels until it is ripe for development, the opportunity is increased for the land plan for a Vermont parcel to be successfully integrated with subsequent construction. This is particularly important since a poorly designed subdivision can do more environmental harm than ugly buildings on it. The Use of Land described the process this way:

> If past experience is any guide, many of the lots now being created will never be used at all: in this case, it is, "lots first, buildings never." The lot lines will remain on the record books, though, and land titles will become ever more clouded as decades pass. Tough for the land buyers? Yes. Tough also for the environment as is shown by any number of "dead subdivisions" created forty years ago. If a few scattered lots are built upon, the subdivision may become a sparsely settled rural slum. . . . Once the countryside has been given over to quarter acre or 1-acre lots (and most recreational lots sold in 1971 were one-quarter to 1-acre in size), you can forget thoughts of clustering, variable densities, common open spaces, and the like . . . the lot lines will survive to block sensitive use of the land.

Ibid., pp. 275–76.

For additional discussion of the environmental problems of poor land planning, *see* I. McHarg, Design With Nature (1969); Toner and Thurow, *Let Nature Decide the Land Use*, 40 Planning 17 (January 1974).

12. The traditional method of dealing with the preservation of agricultural land has been to lower tax rates to reflect the agricultural use. See generally *Note, Property Taxation of Agricultural and Open Space Land*, 8 Harv. J. Legis 158 (1970). Such measures have, however, been criticized as relieving the sale induced by high taxation, but not protecting against the unrefusable offer. To the extent the gains tax intervenes in demand for such land, it may begin to attach the "forgotten" side of the preservation issue.

13. See articles noted at note 2, *supra.*

14. For a general discussion of the Taking Issue, see F. Bosselman, D. Callies, J. Banta, The Taking Issue (1973); reviewed by Hagman, 87 Harv. L. Rev. 482 (1973).

15. G. Lefcoe, Land Development Law (2nd ed. 1974); C.L. Harriss, ed., The Good Earth of America (1974); F. Bosselman & D. Callies, The Quiet Revolution in Land Use Control (1971).

16. In a sense, this constitutes the "equal protection" component of the "taking" issue. For an elaboration, *see* D. Hagman, Windfalls for Wipeouts in C.L. Harriss, ed., The Good Earth of America, 109–133 (1974); Hagman, *A New Deal: Trading Windfalls for Wipeouts*, 40 Planning (Sept., 1974).

17. Costonis, J., Space Adrift-Landmark Preservation and the Marketplace (1974); Costonis, *The Chicago Plan: Incentive Zoning and the Preservation of Urban Landmarks*, 85 Harv. L. Rev. 574 (1972); Carmichael, *Transferable Development Rights as a Basis for Land Use Control*, 2 Fla. St. U.L. Rev. 35 (1974); Costonis, *Development Rights Transfer: An Exploratory Essay*, 83 Yale L.J. 75 (1973). *See also* Urban Land (January, 1975) which contains an extensive bibliography and is entirely devoted to the subject.

18. Carmichael, *supra* note 18 at 47.

19. *See* McHarg, *supra* note 12; International Independence Institute, The Community Land Trust, a Guide to a New Model of Land Tenure in America (1972). Large, *This Land is Whose Land? Changing Concepts of Land as Property,* 1973 Wis. L. Rev. 1038 (1973); *See also* Bosselman and Callies, *supra* note 16 at 314–318; *also* Bosselman, Callies and Banta, *supra* note 32, p. 240;

> The idea that a regulation of the use of land which prevents the owner from making money can amount to a taking assumes that a landowner has a constitutional right to use and develop his land from some purpose which will result in personal profit, regardless of the effect that such development will have on the public. Such a holding gives land as a commodity a constitutional status higher than other commodities—a status land no longer deserves.

20. 56 Wis. 2d. 7, 201 N.W.2d 761 (1972), recently followed in New Hampshire in *Sibson v. State of New Hampshire* (N.H. Sup. Ct. March 31, 1975).

> The Justs argue their property has been severely depreciated in value. But this depreciation of value is not based on the use of the land in its natural state but on what the land would be worth if it could be filled and used for the location of a dwelling. While loss of value is to be considered in determining whether a restriction is a constructive taking, value based on changing the character of the land at the expense of harm to public rights is not an essential factor or controlling.

56. Wis.2d at 23, 201 N.W.2d. 771 (1972).

21. The concept of "ameliorative waste" is a useful way of focusing on the fact that changed in land use intensity have been fostered in part by the favorable bias inherent in terms like "development" and "improvements." What is more important is to decide whether the change is worthwhile in the particular case. For a discussion of "ameliorative waste" *see generally* American Law of Property, §20.11 (1952). In effect the doctrine states that acts may be waste even though they increase the value of the land because they injure the successor's interest. §20.11. *See also* Melms v. Pabst Brewing Co., 104 Wis. 7, 79 N.W. 738 (1899); Crewe Corp. v. Feiler, 28 N.J. 316, 146 A.2d. 458 (1958).

22. If this counter-current prevails, in the future years, we may see special taxes for the conferral of development rights. Certainly if land in its "natural state" is all the owner can claim as his entitlement, then any increment in use intensity beyond that entitlement constitutes a benefit conferred by the government which might be recaptured through taxation to the extent of the benefit received.

Chapter 9

Problems of Social Accounting: An Accountant Looks at Cost-Benefit Analysis and Popular Decision Making

Morton Levy*

In the public domain, that receptacle for the "externalities" of our private actions, even the concepts, let alone measurements, of "benefits" and "costs" are hard to come by.

ASSESSING THE BENEFITS

It is fairly well recognized that certain benefits may be exceedingly difficult to quantify. What are the benefits of the San Francisco Bay Area Rapid Transit (BART) system? And to whom do they accrue? Will business in San Francisco (and therefore tax revenues) increase? Would there not be corresponding decreases in business activity in outlying areas? What is it worth to an individual to get to work 10 minutes faster? What is the net saving in commuting costs? Who achieves that net saving considering the subsidies necessary to maintain virtually all rapid transit systems? Who got and who should get the benefits of increased property values along the BART right-of-way? What will happen to the hopefully no-longer-needed parking lots in San Francisco? Just how much will the benefits be from a reduction in air pollution because of the hoped-for decrease in auto usage? The list could go on and on.

DETERMINING THE COSTS

The difficulty of determining reasonably accurate cost data is less well-recognized. Let's start with two well-known axioms from Cost

*Morton Levy is Executive Director of the National Association of Accountants for the Public Interest.

Accounting 1A: first, that no two cost accounting systems are the same; and second, that no two cost accountants working within the same system would likely come up with the same answer.

What kind of costs are we talking about? In the case of BART, the obvious starting point is clearly capital costs. Right? Wrong! We would have been discussing *estimated* capital costs, which turned out to be an unfortunately small percentage of actual capital costs. And I feel confident that the proclivity to substantially mis-estimate costs is not peculiar to BART or the San Francisco Bay Area. I recall reading that the Department of Defense occasionally has the same problem!

And what is the cost of noise pollution caused by the BART trains? What is the cost of the time spent in the years of debate prior to the approval of the system and the seemingly endless inquiries and investigations of its inadequacies?

Any attempt to quantify the costs and benefits of a program such as this must of necessity involve countless and often interdependent assumptions. I suggest that the mere attempt to do so may be a disservice to that group or community which has decision-making responsibility.

EXAMPLES: EMERGENCY CHILD CARE
AND NONVIOLENT CRIME

Let's simplify the subject by limiting our consideration to direct dollar cost determinations. Two cases with which we have been involved in San Francisco illustrate the difficulty in accurately determining such costs, even on an historical basis.

We were asked to determine the dollar costs incurred in San Francisco for the emergency care of dependent, abused and neglected children in connection with a plan to change that method of providing such care to one which would be more compassionate and humane.

To accomplish this it was necessary to examine, accumulate, and allocate costs from about a dozen city and private agencies involved in the program. These included the Youth Guidance Center, Juvenile Hall, Probation Department, Board of Education, Utilities, Department of Social Services, Department of Public Health, Foster Care, and the Police Department. We also had to determine and allocate a rental factor for the structures used to house the children. Each of the factors contained in our computation involved many factual assumptions and subjective decisions. A team of three highly trained certified public accountants (CPA's) worked on this case for many weeks. I am confident that any other similarly trained team of CPA's could have arrived at an answer perhaps 50 percent higher or lower than ours. The attempt to quantify prospective programs would have been even more difficult and considerably less reliable. The additional consideration of *social* costs and *social* benefits would have been far beyond the training, skills, and capability of the accounting profession.

We are currently wrestling with the problem of attempting to determine the costs of arrests and processing of those accused of victimless crimes in San Francisco. The first phase of this project, relating to prostitution, has been completed in an admittedly limited fashion by considering only direct costs. Even so, we were faced with the task of attempting to cost the following components: the 17-man prostitution detail of the Police Department; transportation costs to the Hall of Justice; booking of defendants at the city prison; preparstion of bail receipts; indexing defendants; quarantine time; venereal disease examinations; preparation of court calendars; court time; court trials; jury costs; public defender costs; police overtime for court appearances; and county jail costs.

Our attempt to deal with the costs for all victimless crimes will be infinitely more complex and substantially more arbitrary. Can we allocate total Police Department costs on the basis of the percentage of arrests for victimless crimes to the total arrests for all crimes? Would the ratio of charged defendants be more meaningful? How about the ratio of convictions? Or some weighted average? If we must revert to the methodology of phase one, then how can overhead be fairly allocated to classes of crimes? Would the elimination of victimless crime laws result in any reduction of Police Department personnel or would such persons merely be utilized for other purposes? I might add that we expect to merely list certain types of costs to society, such as loss of wages of defendants, the difficulty of convicts in securing employment, etc., without attempting to quantify them.

APPLICATIONS TO CORPORATE
SOCIAL POLICY

If Cost Benefit Analysis is useful at all, it might be particularly suited to the subject of corporate social policy (as a program). The costs probably represent little more than the salaries, fringe benefits, and related overhead of the numerous corporation urban affairs officers. And the benefits have yet to attain measurable size! Might a symposium on corporate social policy be, in fact, a waste of effort in that it is likely to be playing the corporate game with their (the corporations') cards and their dice—at a time when innovative thinking and planning are desperately needed?

BUSINESS INTERESTS AND SOCIETY'S: THE DANGERS OF CORRODING PUBLIC TRUST

Does the very debate on corporate social policy or corporate social responsibility obfuscate what are, or should be, the legal responsibilities of corporations? A corporation exists to make profits for its owners and, more importantly, its managers. That is a major part of our capitalist system. To expect this nonmoral thing to exhibit a powerful social conscience reminds me a bit of the young boy accused of the murder of both of his parents, who threw himself on the mercy of the court because he was an orphan!

A corporation should not be humbly asked to stop polluting the air and water as evidence of its social responsibility. It must be stopped from polluting because it is not its air and water—it is yours and mine. And the way to encourage responsible conduct is through laws providing for imprisonment of responsible officials and stiff non-tax-deductible fines.

And when more of the leaders in the business community accept the fact that their long-range success is intimately related to the continued existence of our economic system, then even problems like equal employment opportunities for minorities and women will be quickly solved.

There is one more important element to my program. We should rely much more heavily on taxes than we do now. The "list price" rate system (under which few sophisticated or well-advised taxpayers) pay "retail" rates is a massive deception in practice. And it's not because of loopholes in the tax law. The special deductions, credits, exceptions, and exclusions are carefully thought out and intentionally enacted. With rare exceptions, they are not unforeseen weaknesses or unplanned accidents. And they may not even be conspiracies! They are the inevitable result of using the tax system to ecourage or discourage certain investments, and to solve social and economic problems. The personal tax structure has been largely responsible for the maintenance or even acceleration of maldistribution of wealth despite our progressive tax rates. I predict the coming years will witness a substantial erosion in a priceless national asset: a system of taxation that is based on voluntary compliance. The cumulative effect of increasing awareness of the unfair nature of many of our tax laws could well lead to massive voluntary noncompliance. What would happen if corporate and personal taxes were based solely on income? I don't mean to imply that the development and conversion problems related to such a system would be a simple matter. It would be terribly complex and difficult to achieve, both politically and administratively. But it would totally disclose and expose—to the people—the costs of previously hidden tax incentives. The additional tens of billions of dollars of additional tax revenues could be openly used to encourage desirable social and economic and investment policies. Then rational decisions could be made after full and open debate on such matters as oil exploration, low-cost housing, or municipal finances.

I think it is time to stop deluding ourselves that wise decisions can be made by the use of ethereal tools such as cost/benefit analyses—at least until such time as we can develop the techniques and systems and skills to uncover dollar costs alone. Then we can, with reasonable precision, say that this program costs so much, and here are the costs of alternative programs. Given the social objectives we are trying to reach, which is the best program to get us there? We might then be truly able to return the decision-making process to the people.

Part 4

Some Current Technological Issues
in Environmental Protection

Though focusing on the technological component in environmental policies, the authors in this section recognize as well a necessary spillover into, or feedback from, the sociopolitical framework in which decision-making is embedded. None of the contributors ignores these facts of life, though they differ in the weight they attach to them.

Steven Ebbin devotes the bulk of his chapter to discussing various dimensions and problem areas of nuclear power generation, and the need for their full and open assessment. His strongest pitch, however, is in support of a truly comprehensive, systematic, and multifaceted exploration of *all* possible sources and processes to generate power.

Thomas Williams' chapter has similar overtones. Though given over in its entirely to discussing the main components of the solid-waste peril, and the widely divergent positions taken by different sectors relative to desirable public policies, several almost marginal observations appear no less worthy of attention than the main course of the argument. They have in common an implied warning of two attendant dangers. On the one hand, too narrow a focus on the technological side of the issues may cause us to lose sight of their far-reaching dimensions. On the other hand, any temptation to let one's position on a technological issue be governed by a narrow ideological stance is apt to be a hindrance rather than a help in arriving at sound solutions.

The need for a holistic and balanced view, and a caution against "tunnel vision," emerges equally from a reading of either chapter. Likewise, both chapters convey the impression that the more public attitudes as well as the attitudes of different sectors can come to see the commonality of the problems, the less will be the need to rely on regulatory action by government.

Sheldon Samuels' chapter presents ideas some of which are in sharp contrast to those of the other writers.

Samuels takes a positive view of the corporate role but warns against "negative collectivism." He advocates a multiplicity of actors, as against supposedly but not truly representative positions which mindless monoliths are likely to take. He strongly reaffirms the regulatory role of government—largely on grounds of countervailing power. Even within government, he sees certain guaranties in the multiplicity of agencies and authorities. He pleads for a considerably wider purview than economic cost-benefit reckoning. He identifies a whole spectrum of evaluative guages, and he stresses the importance of the right timing, to wit: in the early phases of production planning, as essential in sound environmental decision-making.

✳ *Chapter 10*

Democracy and Technological Determinism

*Steven Ebbin**

In referring to the science communities in the mid-1960s, Ralph Lapp dubbed them the "new priesthood." That priesthood has grown even more powerful since then by the reluctant acceptance to co-equality of the engineering fraternity. Together, they form a formidable bloc, controlling, as it were, several important federal agencies and their supportive technologies as well as private industries and billions of R&D dollars. Long-time fears of technocracy may indeed have been realized. Though scientists and engineers have not been elected to public office in any notable numbers, their influence on political decisions is tremendous indeed. No doubt our society has been and will continue to be increasingly dependent on their products to meet what have become widely accepted needs, which in my view, requires the acceptance by them of a reordered sense of social responsibility. Claims of value-free science are, I believe, obsolete and will not serve the interests of a society that much oriented toward reliance on technology. Yet, despite the great contributions by science and technology, we need to maintain our perspective and not to confuse scientific and technological knowledge with wisdom. Technology based on supporting scientific knowledge can tell us how to do some things. It cannot tell us whether or not to do them nor can it tell us why; these decisions must be made by the public. Business, for its part, must decide whether or not to assume certain economic risks, but it cannot be left to business to make decisions about society's course; those, too,

*Steven Ebbin is Director of the Environmental Studies Group, Policy Studies in Science and Technology, at George Washington University.

are decisions for the people. The role of government must be to weigh the tradeoffs on behalf of the public and in light of public opinion. It is, after all, on the shoulders of people, all kinds of people, that fall not only the beneficial anointments of science and technology but the burdens, the risks, the costs, and the negative impacts as well. The people, not technologists, must decide. Scientists and technologists can only tell us what they think will happen if we take one course or another.

A NEW RESPONSIBILITY FOR THE 'NEW PRIESTHOOD'

This suggests a new role, a new responsibility, for scientists and technologists, and that is a role in carrying out independent assessments of the potential impacts of a technology on the human and physical environments.

The energy crisis seems to point this up particularly well. Our dependence on natural fuels is threatened by the growth of populations and the growing demands of the so-called developing nations for their fair share of scarce resources. Resentment grows at the disproportionate expenditure of energy stores by the more affluent, developed countries, and competition for these limited non-renewable resources grows stronger placing resource supplying nations, to the extent that they can work in concert, at a considerable economic and political manipulative advantage. To counteract this effect, we turn to science and technology to develop an array of alternatives, or in the peculiar parlance of the Nixonian view of the world, to develop self-sufficiency. Project Independence is a concept with appeal to many Americans, but it is probably not feasible in an interdependent world. "Project Interdependence" may be more in point. To retreat behind a wall of independence would be to isolate ourselves and would hold negative implications for our own viability as an exporting nation and for the ability of our customers to trade with us.

Our reliance on technological development will continue to grow in a competitive economic system which depends on better products and better means of making them. One important basis for making public—that is, political—decisions based on the technological efficacy and on a knowledge of the impacts of those technologies to meet our energy needs is the development of independent technology assessment mechanisms.

Such vehicles are essential if we are to avoid duplicating the negative aspects of our past experiences in energy policy formulation, particularly those involving nuclear energy. (Because much of my recent research has involved the processes of decision-making within the Atomic Energy Commission (AEC), many of the specific examples referred to in this chapter will deal with nuclear power. But most, if not alll, of them can be generalized to relate to decision-making about most large-scale technologies.) The Atomic Energy Commission is the only technology-specific agency of the federal government; it controls and promotes and sets standards and criteria; it polices its own technology. It grants permits for construction and licenses for operation of all nuclear power plants and it controls the fuels on which they depend. It has its own committee of the Congress, its own dependent industry, its own R&D facilities and reliant R&D community, its own dependent academic community—including teachers, researchers, graduate students, equipment, and courses—and its own fully reliant consulting industry. It is, in short, in full control of the information upon which decisions are based, and because of this it sets the limits and defines how the public will participate in its processes. It also resists independent assessments of the technology it controls, substituting smooth public relations for meaningful review and real citizen participation in its decision-making. Through the use of its extraordinary control over the course of development of a single technology, it has been the primary contributor to a national commitment to reliance on nuclear energy as a major energy source.

It would be unfair to criticize the agency or its managers for their evident successes. No question can be sensibly raised as to the fine job which the AEC has done in developing nuclear power as a source of energy. The AEC maintains an active and dynamic research and development program and is clearly the world leader in nuclear power matters.

Where the agency is subject to criticism—and I believe this holds valuable lessons for us as it relates to technology in general—is that its monolithic control over the technology has had an unhealthy relationship to the technology and its implementation. Problems with the technology have arisen, yet the AEC has taken steps in the past to obscure them from public view and has sought to stifle or punish those who dared heresy by bringing those problems to light. Goffman, Tamplin, Rosen, Ritterbush are names which come to mind in this context. Emergency core cooling systems, radiation criteria, thermal effluents, the fuel cycle, fuel densification, and waste disposal are issues that come to mind. An absence of candor and a promotional posture has cost the agency heavily in public trust and credibility, possibly to the expense of us all. If atomic energy for peaceful purposes is a good thing, it is sensible to recognize that even good things are subject to problems and concerns and that obscuring those problems does little to solve them.

I cannot say that I oppose nuclear power plants. After studying the issue for the last two years or so I do not find myself frightened by nuclear power as an energy source. But I do, as do many other informed citizens, see that there are real concerns with the present state of the technology and I will not, as others will not, be lulled by reassurances from the agency that all is well with nuclear power and that we can rely on the agency to care for our health, safety, and welfare despite a history replete with secretiveness and obfuscatory actions. As a citizen, I, like others, want to be informed and to make my input to decisions whether or not there will be a nuclear power plant in my neighborhood or whether or not tax dollars are spent to promote nuclear power. As it stands now, that is not the case. Moreover, in the absence of an *independent* assessment of nuclear power it is difficult to make an informed, intelligent judgment about the merits of public policy decisions with regard to its use. My representatives, those who serve and have served on the Congressional Joint Committee on Atomic Energy, do not bolster my confidence by their enlightened and skeptical consideration of the impacts of the technology, nor by their vigorous pursuit of their oversight responsibilities. They may be right, and nuclear power's problems may be easy to resolve, but their uncritical acceptance of nuclear power and their evident propensity to ignore and squelch the opposition does not win my confidence. Even given a proclivity to believe, it is not possible to ignore incident after incident calling claims of safety and efficacy to question.

INDEPENDENT TECHNOLOGY ASSESSMENT: ITS CRUCIAL ROLE AND ITS PREDICAMENT

It is clear that the mechanisms to carry out independent technology assessments do not yet exist. It is not, in my view, tenable for us to rely on government agencies nor on the standard kind of consulting firms for independent assessments of technology's impacts on the human and physical environments. All too often, evidence shows that federal agencies tend to represent specail interests. The Atomic Energy Commission is a good example, but there are, of course, many other examples. Consulting companies lack the independence as seekers of continued business and also find it difficult to maintain access to first rate scientific talent. They depend on the next job and all too often seek to satisfy the client at the expense of independent analysis.

The National Academies of Sciences and Engineering could provide the basis for such independent analysis. But they are unwilling to become what they see as "job shops." That is not to suggest that they do not already provide significant analytical capability in assessing technology. Nor does it suggest that the Academies have not already provided a significant input to the development of technology assessment as a valuable tool. Some elements of the design of technology assessment indeed emanated from the Academies, not only from their 1969 reports but from the accomplishment of the Jamaica Bay/Kennedy Airport study (1971) which many view as the prototype for technology assessment.

In our recent study of the nuclear power controversy and the uses of scientific and technological information by citizen groups in interventions before the Atomic Safety and Licensing Boards (ASLB) of the Atomic Energy Commission, we (Raphael Kasper and I) were impressed with some of the contentions of intervenor groups and with the fact that no impartial studies of their concerns, fears, and points of contention exist nor does the funding or institutional capability to accomplish them. As it is now, citizens are fully reliant on the Atomic Energy Commission and the nuclear industry for evaluation of their own technology. The AEC's role as the major and, in some particular areas, the exclusive funding source for research in the nuclear sciences has created a situation in which almost every nuclear scientist or engineer is under grant or contract to the AEC, or in the employ of the AEC, the nuclear industry, or a national laboratory. "It is difficult to find experts on nuclear power," we wrote, "who do not have close ties with the nuclear industry or the AEC since government funding for nuclear power research comes, for the most part, from a single source." The existence of only a single funding source is, in our view, a major and perhaps insurmountable obstacle to a free, open, and informed debate within the scientific community and therefore in the public arena, on matters involving safety and other aspects of nuclear technology. The tentacles of the "nuclear establishment," in fact, reach into the very heart of the academic community, dependent on sources for funding of equipment purchases, nuclear materials, course design, research, graduate students, assistantships, scholarships, and fellowships, almost all of which ultimately are dependent on the AEC. This creates a situation not conducive to scientific independence, free exchange of views and certainly not deviation from the prevailing "truths." Similar situations among scientists in the Soviet Union have been decried by scientists the world over as "Lysenkoism." It is notable, in my view, that according to one of the attorneys for an intervenor group in the nuclear power controversy, 75 percent of the scientific and technological information upon which their case was based was received in unmarked plain brown envelopes, evidently from employees of AEC and the national laboratories. What a commentary!

REMEDIES HARD TO COME BY

While I think that the ERDA (Energy Research and Development Administration) legislation recently passed by the Congress is a step in the right direction, I am not sufficiently hopeful that in its present form it is the final answer. One danger not faced by the legislation is that ERDA will integrate the Reactor Development Program of the AEC in its entirety. No guarantees are provided in the legislation—though several members of the Senate are concerned and have expressed that concern—that ERDA will devise a balanced energy research and development program. Since the best organized and operating arm of ERDA will almost certainly be the nuclear part, it is clearly to be expected that it will dominate the new agency for some time to come. Changing the name of the zebra does not change its stripes or its genus. Other areas of energy R&D will most certainly be overshadowed and outgunned in any struggle for ascendency, attention, and funds.

Moreover, the legislation calls for the creation of a separate commission to be called the Nuclear Energy Commission. Under their aegis will remain the regulatory, licensing, and adjudicatory functions now part of the AEC.

In my testimony on March 12, 1974, before the Senate Committee on Government Operations, I recommended a separation between regulatory and adjudicatory functions—an independent adjudicatory mechanism to provide a fair and judicious body of administrative technological judges before which could be argued, in democratic fashion, the pros and cons of the nuclear power licensing controversy and other aspects of energy matters in contention. I argued then, as I do now, that the police (regulatory) should not be part of the "courts" (adjudicatory—ASLB) mechanism and that where it is, contentions placed before such bodies for resolution will not be given equal consideration. If the regulators say an application meets agency criteria and should be approved, can the adjudicators in the employ of the regulatory agency treat that information impartially, as just one of several inputs into their deliberative process, giving it weight only equal to other inputs? Of course not!

BALANCED VERSUS NUCLEAR ENERGY DEVELOPMENT—THE PEOPLE'S INFORMAL CHOICE IS OF THE ESSENCE

Moreover, I asked the Committee to consider calling the NEC the National Energy Commission rather than the Nuclear Energy Commission, thereby giving substance to the concept of balanced energy considerations, discontinuing the special status afforded nuclear technology and effectuating the legislative intent reflected in the ERDA-creating portion of the Bill. My own feeling is that the same comprehensive energy development mission assigned to ERDA should apply equally to the regulatory commission. The regulatory functions of the Commission should be applied not only to nuclear power but to all energy sources extant and prospective. I believe the NEC should embody the regulatory functions of the Bureau of Mines, the Federal Power Commission, and other appropriate agencies as well as those of the Atomic Energy Commission. There is little justification for the consideration of policy and regulation of single, specific energy sources when it is increasingly clear that national energy policies must be comprehensive and consistent if they are to be effective.

In a democratic society where technology plays a major role and has a major impact on people's lives, government operations and decision-making require that an informed citizenry be afforded access to independent, unbiased assessments of the technology. To achieve this, it will be necessary for us to develop reliable institutions, sharply departing from those that exist now. What is needed is not a decision-making mechanism but a means to provide better informational inputs for decisions.

We recommended in our book on the nuclear power controversy the formation of independent assessment centers to perform and arrange for analyses of the impact of technology on the physical, social, and human environment.

Such centers would operate independent of any mission-oriented agency and would form a nucleus for carrying out *ad hoc* interdisciplinary studies of the consequences of actions involving the use of technology. Supported by Congressional appropriations and by State contributions, the centers would thus provide an input to the decision making process which is presently non-existent. Rather than being structured along traditional geographical lines (by state or region), the centers could be organized about areas of similar environmental characteristics or problems. Thus, areas of the country with similar problems (water resources, air quality, land use, urbanization, etc., for example) could be joined in a single center independent of their geographic location. The staffs of the centers would assemble assessment groups to perform analyses of particular environmental problems. Groups performing assessments would be comprised of experts from a broad variety of disciplines relevant to the problem being assessed and would be on reimbursable loan from the teaching and research faculties of universities and from research institutions for the duration of a particular study. In order to avoid the development of entrenched and bureaucratic staffs with prevailing attitudes or positions within the centers, the staffs of the centers should serve with limited tenure for a specific term, perhaps three years, and should then be assisted by the centers in locating new positions. It is probable that the value of experience gained in such a position would be of considerable import to government agencies, universities and private industry. The studies carried out by the *ad hoc* interdisciplinary teams, in addition to providing necessary information to decision makers and the public, would, if the centers and their teams were maintained scrupulously independent of any vested interests, avoid the now prevalent problem of continuous and acrimonious conflict over the motives of scientists and engineers providing information to policy makers (for example, about the effects of nuclear power plants or other technologies). The centers could each interact closely with each other and with the Congressional Office of Technology Assessment, when that Office begins operating. Interdisciplinary analyses performed by the centers would integrate the best available expertise and knowledge about the human and physical environment and other effects of a technology, and, perhaps, initiate new investigations in areas where definitive information is lacking. The analyses would clarify areas of agreement among experts; they would, as well, spell out areas of disagreement or uncertainty so that decision makers, in weighing the remifications of various alternative actions, could base their decisions upon an understanding of the state of knowledge concerning the effects of those actions. It must be emphasized that the assessment centers would make no decisions but would provide information to the decision makers about the known and potential impacts of technology. Analyses would be made available to the public and would thus provide a definitive basis for citizen group involvement to supplement what is, at present, a largely visceral basis for such involvement.

The need for environmental assessment centers has been recognized in a bill which would amend the National Environmental Policy Act to encourage the establishment of state and regional environmental centers which is presently pending before the Senate Committee on Interior and Insular Affairs (S. 1865, 93rd Congress, 1st Session, p. 7, lines 7–10.) The purpose of the legislation is to provide for and supplement existing programs for the conduct of basic and applied research, investigations and experiments relating to the environment. The Administrator of the EPA would be authorized to distribute $10 million annually through FY 1976 on the basis of population, total land area, the nature and severity of the environmental problems in the areas served by the centers, and the ability and willingness of each center to address these problems. Some of this money would be only available to those centers for which the concerned States themselves provide the requisite matching funds.

The legislation holds that the centers would have "a nucleus of administrative, professional, scientific, technical, and other personnel capable of planning, coordinating and directing interdisciplinary programs. . . ." The proposed legislation is similar to what has been proposed here although it places greater emphasis on traditional state and regional boundaries than we feel is necessary or advisable in the examination of environmental matters.

In that same report we noted:

> . . . that the current hearing process is marked by a lack of a fair and unbiased adjudicatory body. Accordingly, we recommend the formation of governmental bodies of adjudicators independent of any mission-oriented agency to hear and rule on the arguments of competing interests in nuclear power licensing cases. Bodies of this sort, independent of any mission-oriented agency, would serve as a mechanism for the consideration of licensing of nuclear power plants, though there is clearly implication for the adjudication of other types of environmental or technology based disputes. The adjudicators would make recommendations to the licensing authorith; the licensing authority would not be legally bound to follow the recommendations of the adjudicators, although, if it ignored the recommendations, it would be required to explain, in detail, the reasons for its action and to demonstrate that it was not acting in an arbitrary or capricious manner. The body of adjudicators could be empowered by legislation to serve more than one Executive branch agency. As with the assessment centers, except for a skeletal staff of managers, there would be no long-term appointments to this body of adjudicators, in order to avoid the formation of any set and definitive opinions about the issues to be considered. In any given case, three judges, including two with relevant scientific or technical competence and as is presently the case with ASLB's, one with legal competence, would be appointed to preside over a proceeding designed to fairly and judiciously consider issues raised by all of the parties involved and to raise any questions or issues which it felt were not adequately posed by the parties. Adjudicators would be chosen from a panel in much the same way that ASLB members are chosen; the significant difference from current practice would be that selection would be within a mechanism with no relationship to the AEC or any of the parties involved in the case.
>
> There are, of course, precedents for such independent adjudicative bodies within the Federal structure. Both the Federal Mediation and Conciliation Service and the National Mediation Board, which mediate labor disputes, contain organizational elements applicable to this concept. Decisions of the adjudicators, of course, would be subject to court review.

Of course, if this mechanism is to be successful, it will have to develop a reputation for integrity, impartiality, reliability, fairness, relevance, understandability, and openness.

PRECEDENTS AND ANALOGIES

But technology assessment is not a new concept. To one degree or another, usually to a lesser degree, industry and government have carried out informal seat-of-the-pants kinds of assessments. Sometimes they have been called market surveys; sometimes they have been called economic analyses or market projections. But they have usually been directed at how a technology can be expected to work, or at what the economic potential is likely to be, who will buy it, how long they will keep it, and when will they replace it. They have not really considered the full range of impacts which a technology can have on the human and physical environment cycle and what alternatives to it exist.

Technology assessment is an input to the decision-making process. It is not the decision itself and it does not compel the decision-maker. It informs him about what he can expect to ensue from one decision or another. But, he still makes the decision, hopefully a better, more informed, more intelligent one.

Technology assessment emphasizes substantive input to decision-making as distinguished from the emphasis of PPB and operations research on the process of decision-making. Technology assessment emphasizes the analysis of impacts on human and physical environments within which humans live. It also emphasizes the consideration of an array of alternatives, thereby directing itself outward rather than inward, that is, to the environmental impacts rather than to an assessment of the workability or efficacy of technology.

It is important that technology assessments be written in such a way as to make the results fully comprehensible to those citizens willing to make and effort to understand them. Technical jargon and complex scientific and technological concepts can and must be presented in terms familiar to lay people with a modicum of interest and educational background.

The results of technology assessment should certainly be made fully available to the public so that the public may use them in formulating their own positions about the acceptability of a technology or in intervening in administrative or judicial proceedings. Contrary to the views of others, however, I do not believe that the actual performance of the assessment study is something that lay citizens can do. What they can be, and should be, is the primary users.

The energy crunch provides us with the challenge. Many are the potential alternatives for energy resource development: solar energy, winds, tides, etc. All have their advocates. Insofar as we encourage government and industry to explore and seek to develop new energy sources, this is all to the good. But new technologies should not be adopted without careful assessments of their impacts.

Chapter 11

Solid Waste Management-Resource Conservation and Land Protection

*Thomas F. Williams**

The status of solid waste management today is illustrative of the environmental transition which our country is attempting to make—a transition from an era of the random and careless use of resources, accompanied by equally aimless and damaging disposal practices, to an era of resource conservation, accompanied by environmental awareness and the foresightful use of technology.

Federal attention was first placed on the problem in 1965 with passage of the Solid Waste Disposal Act, which authorized the creation of a modest program of technical assistance to states, local governments, and interstate agencies for the planning and development of solid waste management programs, and to promote national research programs to find better methods for controlling, processing, recovering, and recycling wastes and for disposing of residues.

In 1970, this Act was amended by the Resource Recovery Act, which stressed the need to develop resource recovery in solid waste management and directed that studies be made, with requirements for reporting back to Congress, to determine the best means for recovering materials and energy from solid waste and to recommend public policies, including economic incentives that would encourage the reclamation and recycling of solid wastes. It required, also, a comprehensive investigation of hazardous waste management practices in the United States.

This is not the occasion to go into the rocky history of the federal

*Thomas F. Williams is Director of the Technical Information Staff, Office of Solid Waste Management Programs, U. S. Environmental Protection Agency.

solid waste management program, except to make, perhaps, one important point. The very uncertain, uneven, and reluctant support that solid waste management as a national issue has received until very recently, from both the executive and legislative branches of government and from the environmental community is a mirror reflection of our society's uncertainties as we grope our way toward environmentally more responsible methods of conducting the nation's business. It has been only in recent months that the federal program has succeeded in delivering to the Congress and the public the results of the studies required by the Resource Recovery Act of 1970 and, hence, to delineate the full spectrum of environmental and resource use concerns that surround the issue.

THE SOLID-WASTE MANAGEMENT RESOLVE—PRODUCT OF VARIED INSIGHTS

Toward the end of last year several important forces converged which catalyzed public and Congressional interest in the issue—the Environmental Protection Agency's reports to Congress on the significant energy and materials savings which could be realized through source reduction and resource recovery practices; the report of the National Commission on Materials Policy, which was required by the 1970 Resource Recovery Act; the rather belated realization on the part of environmental public interest groups that solid waste management is, indeed, a core ecological issue with public health, economic, and political ramifications of very significant proportions; and, of course, the gasoline shortage, which forcibly reminded the public that the natural resources available to us are finite.

From this point I should like to discuss briefly, first, just how the solid waste management picture looks to us in EPA at this time, and then to discuss the three major conceptual issues with which the public and the Congress are concerned as we begin to try to cope more adequately with the full dimensions of the solid waste management problem.

According to a study conducted last year by the National League of Cities/United States Conference of Mayors, almost half of our cities will be running out of current disposal capacity in from one to five years. The report refers to this state of affairs—and it is difficult to disagree—as a crisis. In cities, solid waste volumes are estimated to have doubled in the past 20 years. Between 1958 and 1976, packaging consumption, 90 percent of which is disposed, will have increased an estimated 63 percent. An estimated 16 to 24 percent of the nation's solid waste is potentially recoverable and reusable; yet cities are forced to expend $6 billion annually for collection and disposal.

It is no wonder that a recent survey of mayors and city managers reveals that a majority of those surveyed in medium and large cities consider solid waste management to be their most pressing problem. They are at the final link of the great American production-distribution-consumption-throwaway chain, with no one to whom to pass the buck.

Ours is a nation which each year produces, consumes, and throws away more and more. Multiple packaging, built-in obsolescence, and the convenience of disposable consumer items contribute to enormous amounts of waste. With only 7 percent of the world's population, we consume almost half of the earth's industrial raw material. Most of these—in the form of worn-out equipment, discarded bottles, cans, packaging, and yesterday's newspaper—end up sooner or later on the nation's ubiquitous dumps.

We are recycling a lower percentage of our resources than ever before in history.

The United States annually consumes about 190 million tons of major metals, paper, glass, rubber, and textiles. Of this amount, 143 million tons come from virgin resources; the remaining 48 million tons—about a quarter of the total—are obtained from resource recovery operations. Virtually all of the recovered materials are derived from discards of industrial processing, fabrication, and manufacturing activities, rather than from obsolete products discarded into the waste stream.

Studies indicate that the failure to control the amounts of wastes produced in the first place and to recover resources that have become wastes have far-reaching environmental consequences. When two production systems are compared—one using virgin materials, and the other, secondary materials—the system using wastes causes less air and water pollution, generates less solid waste, and consumes less energy.

A report released last year by the National Commission on Materials Policy, called for under the Resource Recovery Act of 1970, clearly outlines where we are headed: toward greater dependence on other countries for vital materials and predictable worldwide shortages for some materials, especially as competition for them increases with increasing industrialization in other parts of the world.

The United States has run out of its own chromium and manganese, vital to steel-making, and we import most of our bauxite.

Of the 13 basic raw materials required by our modern economy, we depended in 1970 on imports for more than half of our supplies of six of these. By 1985, it has been projected that we will be primarily dependent on imports for supplies of 9 of 13 basic raw materials—including bauxite, iron ore, and tin.

The mixed wastes from our larger urban areas, which are now an environmental problem, could generate 230 Btu's of energy—the equivalent of 400,000 barrels of oil per day, which is nearly a third of the Alaskan pipeline's projected flow. Seven percent of our iron, 8 percent of the aluminum, 5 percent of the copper, 3 percent of the lead, 19 percent of the tin, and 14 percent of the paper consumed each year could be supplied from what is now waste. And these are simply the obvious potentials, based on the recovery of mixed residential and commercial wastes, and using technology already demonstrated. Recovery of materials or energy values from industrial sludges that now go to disposal, from crops and animal wastes, and from forestry residues could easily triple the potential.

So, the resource wastage and the environmental degradation sides of the solid waste coin are related by an undeniable logic that, historically, we have failed to perceive. The more we open our eyes to the real and diverse costs of improper disposal practices, the more compelling energy and materials recovery initiatives become. Until we are able to fully disabuse ourselves of the illusion that available resources are endless, and that open dumping of wastes of all varieties is all right, we will be slow to make the institutional changes that will be required to convert wastes into resources.

Our municipal waste management problem alone makes it very clear that we have to reexamine and alter many of our traditional habits and attitudes, if we are to adequately cope with the related problems of resource conservation and environmental protection.

SOME COMMON (ENVIRONMENTAL) SENSE RULES AND CONCERNS

The problem and the opportunities extend, of course, far beyond the municipal solid waste problem, for we have been profligate, historically, at both ends of the environmental spectrum and at all points in between as well, The strip mine symbolizes the careless and cavalier way in which we have generally obtained resources—probing Mother Earth, not like a surgeon, but like a butcher, for her riches. The coal mine waste piles of Appalachia, the uranium waste piles in Colorado, the dumps of all varieties in every region of the country—too often polluting the air and surface waters and continuously leaching a witch's brew of acids, organics, heavy metals, and other assorted contaminants into the ground waters—suggest that we have moved too far from a sensible reverence for the earth and the life it sustains.

We have also demonstrated an arrogant disregard of a fundamental truth—that most of what we convert into pollution, in whatever form, whether dumped into the air, water, or land, represents the waste of valuable resources.

In between the strip mine and the dump, we have carried out the nation's business as if the supply of energy and materials were limitless. In our design of almost everything you can name—from the buildings in which we live and work and the vehicles in which we transport ourselves, to the hospitals in which we are born and the vaults in which we are put to final rest—we have always given far too little consideration to the conservation of materials and energy. We have, in short, conducted our personal, our governmental, and our industrial affairs as if energy and materials were meant to be squandered, as if the land, air, and water—the earth itself—were merely another disposable commodity.

What could be more symptomatic of our environmental dilemma than the fact that we have to range ever farther over the surface of the globe for our raw materials, and dig ever deeper for those which still remain within our borders, at the same time that our communities are finding it ever more difficult to find land in which to bury these same resources?

Moreover, we have just awakened to the fact that the more successful we become in dealing with air and water pollution and in curbing ocean dumping, the greater will be the pressures for concentrated disposal on land of a whole new dimension of toxic, hazardous, and "ordinary" wastes which, traditionally, have been more or less scattered and diluted into the air and water. Even now we have between 15,000 and 20,000 known disposal sites, of which only a handful qualify as sanitary landfills in a true sense, where site selection, operation, and monitoring are all carried out properly. We've just begun to explore the conditions under which leachate from municipal waste, as well as from hazardous waste, may threaten the ground water and, hence, the drinking water.

OLD FALLACIES AND NEEDED NEW ANSWERS CONCERNING THE MOST PRESSING ISSUES

Now, there is little resembling common sense in the way we have dealt with the solid waste problem in our country. The whole complex process, viewed holistically, resembles a vast comedy of almost incredible absurdities, and, to cap it all off, as recently as about a year ago, the issue was being described by statements such as: "Solid waste managment is strictly a local problem," "There are no health effects associated with inadequate disposal," "Recycling is at least a generation away," "There is no need to improve resource recovery technology," "There is no real shortage of any of the materials or energy that could be recovered from post-consumer waste," and on and on. And I must say that when 1973 began, even among most practicing environmentalists, there seemed to be precious little interest in the problem.

The three most difficult conceptual issues with which the framers of new legislation are grappling are: first, the adverse effects on environment and public health of hazardous industrial wastes and, for that matter, of municipal waste which, under certain circumstances, can be said to be situationally hazardous, particularly in relation to the leaching of toxic substances into ground water; second, how to bring about as quickly as possible the recovery of energy and materials from post-consumer wastes, which requires that we overcome institutional and other barriers which, despite strong public interest, inhibit the widespread use of resource and energy recovery systems in our metropolitan areas; third, the issue of source reduction—that is to say, the questions of how to reduce unnecessary materials consumption in the first place, and how to eliminate materials and products which may cuase irreparable harm to the environment.

HAZARDOUS WASTE: A MATTER FOR REGULATION

There is little question that the issue of hazardous waste will call for a regulatory approach, such as has been employed in air and water pollution, to bring state, local, and federal enforcement efforts to bear on industrial and other sources of harmful effluents. Corporate policy considerations and the issue of what has been termed "corporate responsibility" here will depend largely upon the extent to which corporate and public attitudes have been modified since serious enforcement efforts began against the sources of air and water pollution. Disagreements among the public, environmentalists, industry spokesmen, and governmental regulators are, of course, inevitable; but the need for controlling the random disposition of hazardous and industrial materials on the land is just as sound as the need to keep them out of the water and out of the air in the first place, so it is quite likely that enforcement programs will be mounted, and that those responsible for disposing of residuals will comply over time with varying degrees of alacrity.

The second major area, resource recovery of post-consumer waste, is quite different in that everybody seems to want to do it. While there is still a gigantic gap between the promise and the reality in this area of solid waste management, the promise has become much brighter in the last year or so. The most developed aspect of recovery, and the area with the greatest near-term potential, is mixed waste recycling. This breaks down into energy and materials recovery, and materials recovery subdivides further into mechanical and separate collection approaches. Separate collection systems have much wider application than mechanical systems. Today, for instance, more than 130 municipalities are collecting newsprint separately for recycling— up from just a few less than two years ago.

To what extent separation by the householder and separate collection by the municipality might apply to other items in the waste stream, such as aluminum cans, steel cans, glass bottles, and so forth, is really not fully understood. The industry-sponsored organizations who are promoting resource recovery of municipal waste tend to strongly favor technological approaches applied after the wastes have been homogenized by the compactor truck and deposited at a recovery/disposal site. I feel that separate collection of newsprint is not the limit of the citizen's willingness to cooperate in preparing materials for recycling. Those officially responsible for municipal collection and disposal, however, do not seem, in general, inclined to "experiment" with further separate collection options, which are generally considered approaches that are regressive in nature, having been carried out in the past and abandoned. Newsprint, which is easily separately collected as an uncontaminated waste, is currently the sole exception to this general attitude about separate collection versus technological recovery of wastes already homogenized and collected.

Just a short while ago, even separate collection of newsprint was being challenged by those who felt that it would cut down too much on the energy recovery systems being proposed widely by both government and industry with the advent of last winter's gasoline shortage. In actual fact, if newsprint were separately collected, the Btu loss would be around 10 percent, which would leave still great amounts of energy to be recovered from contaminated wood and paper products, plastics in the waste stream, yard wastes, and other organic materials, which, under current conditions, could not possibly be recycled in economically feasible ways. From an environmental viewpoint, it is important to note that returning newsprint to buyers for use again as newsprint or in other applications is, from an environmental viewpoint, more desirable than recovering the Btu's through combustion.

EPA has identified about 50 major metropolitan areas where mechanical energy/materials recovery seems feasible. These areas account for about 180,000 tons of waste a day, 66 million annual tons, or more than half of the municipal waste stream.

Less than 1 percent of the energy and materials available from the municipal waste stream are being recovered today. Dry fuel production and steam recovery incinerators have been demonstrated and are actually being employed in a few cities. Energy recovery by dry or wet shredded fuel production as steam and as pyrolytic gas and oil should become viable, demonstrated technical alternatives by 1976 or 1977. Mechanical materials recovery systems are somewhere between the demonstration and the operational phases. Technological methods of reclaiming steel objects from the municipal waste stream are well developed. Aluminim and glass separation techniques look promising, but are still in the development or demonstration phases. Fiber recovery by a wet pulping method has been shown to work; it produces a low-grade but high-consistency secondary fiber.

Shortages have increased secondary materials prices to record highs, and although it is not likely that they will remain at current levels, it is also unlikely that they will decline to the lows of the last decade. There is growing evidence that utilities and private fuel users are beginning to view solid waste as an attractive fuel. High materials and energy prices, along with demands for environmentally sound disposal practices, will no doubt force municipalities to place more attention on recycling as it becomes more economically competitive with disposal.

Public support is very high and, in some locations, the public has shown a willingness to support resource recovery approaches, even when the immediate cost is slightly higher, than that of conventional disposal systems.

A number of states are directing their interest to statewide resource recovery activities. Connecticut and Wisconsin have developed comprehensive planned recovery systems, with state-level facilitating mechanisms.

Over a half-dozen companies claim that they can now design, finance, construct, own, and operate recovery systems. Some have developed proprietary systems; others will put together a package using off-the-shelf technology.

RESOURCE—RECOVERY PROBLEMS: MANAGERIAL AND FINANCIAL RATHER THAN TECHNOLOGICAL

The problems of ensuring the widespread application of resource recovery systems are not primarily technological. The non-technological issues which must be overcome lie in the areas of planning, marketing, financing, and management, all of which are made more difficult by the fact that they will require a degree of interaction between municipal governments and private industry which has not traditionally been required of either.

There is little doubt that new legislation will address itself to ways of increasing the incentives for municipalities and industries to engage in widespread post-consumer resource recovery operations. The options range from giving the Environmental Protection Agency the authority and resources to improve and amplify its current technical assistance efforts and resource recovery demonstration programs, through loan guarantees to private industries, to providing outright construction grant financing to cities, as has been done in the water pollution area. For a number of reasons, this latter option, however, is not likely to be chosen.

The third area of emphasis—source reduction—is the one that touches most directly at the heart of the environmental issue. To reduce waste generation at the source is an attempt to achieve the ultimate in waste management. The furor it has caused has been placed mostly on packaging, but this may be deceptive, for the issue touches on a central question which has very disturbing implications for those who hold the traditional view that high energy and high materials use and high consumption are necessarily the hallmark of a technologically advanced society. Behind the excess packaging and the returnable versus the non-returnable beverage container arguments lie more serious issues concerning, for example, long-lived tires, more durable appliances, smaller cars, more renovation in general and less demolition, and could involve the redesign of many thousands of products to make them require less energy and to last longer.

CAN THE MARKET BRING ABOUT REDUCTION IN WASTE GENERATION IN THE FIRST PLACE?

Those who contend that the marketplace will automatically take care of such questions say that the rising cost of materials, energy, and waste management will inevitably lead to increased resource conservation, to more efficient materials use throughout the economy. Ranged on the other side are those who contend that market signals may not necessarily result in socially optimal uses of material and energy resources.

It should not be surprising that the first line of battle on the source reduction issue is drawn on the question of packaging, because packaging activity in the United States has been growing at a very rapid rate over the past decade. Shipments of containers and packaging were valued at $19.7 billion in 1971, an increase of 5 percent since 1970 and an increase of 82 percent since 1960.

The growth of packaging consumption has led to increased consumption of raw materials and energy, and an increased rate of generation of solid waste and other adverse environmental effects. In 1971, packaging accounted for approximately 47 percent of all paper production, 14 percent of aluminum production, 75 percent of glass production, more than 8 percent of steel production, and approximately 29 percent of plastic production. At that time, total packaging material energy consumption represented an estimated 5 percent of U.S. industrial energy consumption.

Post-consumer solid waste resulting from the discard of packaging material was estimated at between 40 and 50 million tons in 1971. Packaging was thus estimated to be between 30 and 40 percent of municipal solid waste, based on the EPA estimate of 125 million tons of municipal solid waste in 1971.

In rough summary, it can be concluded that packaging consumption has grown considerably since 1958—that in many cases it has far outstripped the consumption of the product being packaged, that its growth has resulted in increased uses of materials and energy, that its growth has been concurrent with greater concentrations of industry, and that its cost has increased relative to the cost of the product being packaged.

The environmental community, in general, has pointed to resource recovery as the only environmentally sound option for conserving resources and decreasing the pollution caused by solid waste.

RETURNABLE CONTAINERS—SOMEHOW AN IDEOLOGICAL ISSUE?

The leading edge of the packaging controversy has to do with the returnable versus the nonreturnable beverage container. For many years those who advocated use of the returnable beverage container based their case primarily on the litter problem, and those who felt differently countered by offering litter-control programs of one kind or another and by pointing out that littering in general was a personal problem that could be overcome only through public education. But in recent times the battleground has shifted. When energy and materials consumption and attendant environmental damage are taken into account, it is clear to EPA that the returnable container is superior to the nonreturnable container.

A likely outcome of nationwide mandatory deposit legislation would be a situation in which 90 percent of all containers used were refillable bottles, and each bottle made 10 trips. This would result in an energy use reduction of approximately 194 trillion Btu's of energy, the equivalent of 92,000 barrels of oil per day. If everyone used refillable bottles, and each bottle was used 10 times, the savings would rise to 110,000 barrels of oil per day.

Some segments of industry challenge the relevance of these data. Their criticisms run from rather rhetorical pronouncements on the returnable being the ultimate threat to the free enterprise system to more defensible assertions about potential impacts upon employment, capital investment, and tax revenue losses.

THE SOLID-WASTE PROBLEM SEEN AS A HARBINGER OF GREATER CHALLENGES TO COME

This past summer, when the Public Works Committee of the Senate held hearings on new solid-waste legislation, spokesmen from industry, with support from unions, concentrated virtually all of their attention on the returnable bottle issue and strongly opposed any provision in federal legislation which would inhibit in any way the use of nonreturnable containers. Even more, they favored legislation which would strongly discourage such legislation at the state and local levels of government.

Earlier this year the Environmental Protection Agency testified before Congress on beverage container legislation in favor of the concept of a national deposit requirement, provided there were a gradual time-phased implementation of the law to ensure that the obvious environmental and resource benefits would not be purchased at too high a cost in economic and labor dislocation.

Precisely what kind of new legislation on solid waste management the Congress will enact is certainly not known at this time, but it seems unlikely that any regulatory power in the source reduction area will be given to the executive branch of government, but at the same time, quite likely that new measures to encourage resource recovery of municipal waste will be enacted, with the strong support of industries, which feel municipal waste recovery will take the pressure off the source reduction issue. From the viewpoint of many environmentalists, this does represent progress. It wasn't long ago that industry support for municipal resource recovery was lukewarm at best, in part, presumably, because the recovery of waste resources could have adverse effects on those who extract and process virgin materials.

Corporate spokesmen who, a short time ago, were not pushing hard to promote the recycling of post-consumer solid wastes have changed their position dramatically and now publicly favor municipal energy and materials recycling and allege that successes here would do away with the need for the "market interference" that they feel legislation in favor of the returnable container would entail.

It is not at all surprising that those engaged in manufacturing the containers would oppose any attempts to place restrictions on non-returnable beverage containers, since such measures would disrupt their operations and create losses and shifts in employment. But the broad-scale corporate public information and lobbying efforts on their behalf suggest that, symbolically, the returnable bottle touches on nerves still sensitive to the currents of yesterday, when waste and wealth were evidently viewed as inseparable.

Upgrading our collection and disposal systems to environmentally acceptable levels and maximizing the amounts of waste we recover are essential to achieve proper land use, to achieve more fully the fruits of air and water pollution control efforts, and to reclaim needed resources.

However, these are only partial steps toward diffusing the world's environmental crisis; the ultimate aim must be the reduction of both the waste we generate and the amount of resources we consume. Cleaning up pollution and making a world fit for human beings has to involve something more—and something harder—than just solving a technological problem. Turning back the tide of our environmental ills, learning to use technology wisely, requires new codes of law, alterations in the market mechanism, institutional restructuring, and transformed decision-making processes. What happens in solid waste management in the years immediately ahead may determine to what extent we are willing to admit it.

✳ *Chapter 12*

Environmental Risk in the Workplace

*Sheldon W. Samuels**

Fifteen years ago another conference met on the campus of the University of Chicago. It was convened for those who felt a close intellectual or personal kinship with one who could not attend: Albert Schweitzer. The topic of that meeting was to look at the problem of peace—not just for one species: man, but peace in nature. Schweitzer's concept of the individual "will to live" accounts for the hostility in the world. Reverence for life—his companion concept—must balance that will without overwhelming it [1]. Hence the problem.

Some of us came away from that meeting with positive feelings about a broad vision, a set of concepts which a younger generation calls the Earth Ethic, an ethic that generation hasn't really defined—except by reference to selected ecological facts and principles which by themselves cannot be applied universally to the human situation without doing violence to an understanding of the uniqueness of man in nature. Perhaps, before all of us have become the victims of environmental filth in the workplace, smog and the chemical feast at home, we can bridge the difficulties of that definition. The bridge is very important for our society is engaged in a far from fully understood struggle for its existence: a war with our environment. It takes the form of material shortages, the energy issue, the dispersion of hazardous risks here and abroad, to unprotected workers, global pollution, and other crises.

Prior forms of warfare revolved around the question of who could

*Sheldon W. Samuels is Director of Health, Safety and Environment in the Industrial Union Department of the AFL–CIO.

win. In this type of war, the question is how to survive. The survivor—out of biological necessity—will be the most humane, while at the same time most efficient, society.

THE CORPORATE CONTRIBUTION

It may sound strange coming from me but part of the answer lies in the potential of the mature or socially responsible corporation, that thus-far mythical corporation free of mindless collectivism with the resulting mayhem and murder. To-date, that threat of negative collectivism, as Professor Hayek calls it [2], is to be formed less in the obvious, traditional forms of American communal action, described by deTocqueville [3], than in the virtually uncontrolled institutions of the corporate world: the trade and commerce associations. Ironically, the ideology professed by these organizations supposedly is based on the supremacy of "the individual." Yet they best typify the forms of collectivism described by Hayek: institutions whose consensually low common denominator allows little greater unit discretion than that of the slime mold.

The modern corporation is the newest institution in our society. We don't really understand it. Nor can we agree on what it is or even how to look at it. One thing we do know is that while the courts may treat it as a person, it is a mistake to believe that it is in any way anthropomorphic. It's a legal cloak which all too often permits a few to jeopardize the wages of the worker, to deprive stock holders of dividends, and society of a productive enterprise.

Positivist economists, such as Milton Friedman, see the corporation as an element in the science of managing capital, which means that social responsibility is equated with simply obeying the law and the rules of the game. There is much to be said for this approach. Certainly it is honest, and as descriptive economics contrasts favorably with the public-service concept that "PR" people use to paper over reality. In any case, the social responsibility of a corporation as a purely theoretical consideration makes little difference. But, like it or not, the corporation is caught in the communal maelstrom.

The difficulty is that the corporation not only helps make the law, like other elements in the social process, but it interprets the law and—by force of its size and importance—may even determine the law. Given a situation in which the reward-and-punishment system is purely economic, indeed, in most industrial situations, short-term, microeconomic, that may mean that immoral if not criminal acts may take place (in the name of a corporation) that our current mores do not recognize as such. Moreover, certain activities take place that are recognized as wrong, but are beyond the power of regulatory agencies to correct.

Every organization has the problem of the "yes" men. Their retention at times may be profitable or simply the easiest accommodation. But in respect of the problem complex of health and environment— given the new realities—we can no longer afford them. "Yes" is often the criminal response. Those who utter it, even if few in number, may have a sphere of influence so out of proportion to their number that entire companies may have to be characterized as criminal. When an industry is unusually concentrated, that may mean—as in the case of heavy metal mining and smelting—that an entire industry becomes tainted.

Decent men in management are often heard to say: "I didn't know" when faced with environmental reality. They "didn't know" because the yes men they hired to investigate and monitor problems are incapable of objectivity and candor. Bad decisions thus become unquestioned operating procedures. As a consequence, for example, the decision *not* to hire a full-time medical director has been made by nearly every major corporation in this country. Many of the corporations with medical directors hire yes men, who in turn hire indentured scientists from other disciplines. Whether through such staff or consultants, the corporation achieves at best a very short-term benefit.

Not all corporate mistakes occur internally. Corporations often seek the assistance of external structures. Unhappily, they are selected because they replicate the same attitudes that prevail within. In the case of trade and business associations, what is replicated is the collectivist attitude of the lowest common denominator. These organizations speak for the corporate community despite behavior that is not countenanced by many if not most member companies, despite the consequent and often inevitable confrontation with society, a confrontation that increasingly precludes the corporation from positive participation in environmental risk determination.

The consequence is that the viability of the member corporations frequently is threatened with expensive, after-the-fact redesign of processes, forced withdrawal of expensively developed products, plummeting product acceptance and rising disruption in the workforce. "Mindless collectivism" is a mild description.

RISK ACCEPTANCE

The awesome question before us is really that of who shall live and who shall die. The answer is approached from four perspectives: the scientific (biological), the social, the moral, and the feasible (technological).

While most environmental discussion appears to be focused on the scientific aspect, it is in the realm of feasibility that most of the battle must be waged. Contrary to the conventional wisdom, such decisions are made in actuality at the social and moral levels. Thus, essential issues revolve around what risks we have decided we will accept rather than around what we can do. The control regulation or standard is an expression of that willingness as the determinant of the technical feasibility to be achieved. The methods for resolving the moral and social outcome, then, become a critical decision-making process: the determination of socially acceptable risks.

For reasons, which are only partially rational, we have looked to the science of economics for guidance is this process. Historically this is because we have never quite given up Jeremy Bentham's dream of reducing each pain and pleasure to a quantifiable expression [5]. Bentham's calculus reminds us of the modern discussion of risk benefit analysis, another version of cost benefit analysis. Thus, most attempts at determining the socially acceptable risk really amount to exercises in determining what is economically acceptable, with results fraught with largely unexamined difficulties. As the studies by the Occupational Safety and Health Administration (OSHA) demonstrate, the predominant data base is micro-economic in character. Macro-economic considerations and social costs are given lip service.

Part of the difficulty lies in the outlook and limited competence of government. Part of the difficulty is much more fundamental.

K.W. Kapp observes that "the main stream of economical analysis still avoids placing man, with his actual needs and requirements, in the center of its theoretical considerations." It does this through the process of externalizing "social costs" [6]. Economists have generally failed to develop what may be called Relative Economics, a system which would emphasize the individual in the analysis. A worker with totally disabling asbestosis contracted as an employee of Pittsburgh Corning in Port Allegheny, Pa., was recently forced to accept $36 per week as compensation, supplemented by community welfare funds. The total award cannot exceed $12,000. (He and his fellow workers were told by the company doctor that their exposures were not dangerous).

Now what does $36 per week mean? on the basis of personal inquiry, I can testify that it means the impoverishment of an entire family. It means that the priority of medical care is not the prolongation of life, but easing a painful death. That man hasn't the lung capacity to say "Corporate Responsibility" without discomfort. Nor is he likely to try.

In 1965 the B.F. Goodrich company in Louisville began paying compensation to workers afflicted with vinyl chloride disease. The first case died of anginsarcoma of the liver. They did nothing significant to clean up. In fact, the men lost a strike in which one issue was a place to eat that was free of polyvinyl chloride dust and vinyl chloride fumes. It was simply cheaper to let them sicken and die.

Paul Brodeur has written a text in relative economics entitled: "Expendable Americans" [7].

Now how do we rationally approach problems such as these? A common-sense step is to avoid building industries around unnecessary uses of a toxic substance: pre-market screening. Yet when a group of Dow scientists blew the whistle on vinyl chloride *in 1961*, this did not stop the incredible proliferation of PVC as a substitute for hundreds of *nontoxic* materials.

What if it becomes socially necessary and therefore socially acceptable to use PVC? Do we have a technique for determining the "necessary" extent of toxic substance use, a technique to determine an *acceptable* risk?

What is *acceptable* in the current crystalization of morals, essentially unchanged since the beginning of our society, is an expression of thinly veneered bestiality. The level of risk expected of American workers is not voluntarily acceptable to them.

If the history of the labor movement has any meaning, to use a favorite expression of Selikoff, it is that workers must struggle against being forced to eat bad bread [8].

Determining what is socially necessary and therefore a socially acceptable risk is difficult. The concept connotes the possibility of mutual agreement. But it denotes no means for arriving at a rational and humane conclusion on when and how to intervene in the control of a hazard.

The nature of the intervention is an essential, but controversial, part of that conclusion, since intervention is dependent primarily upon government action.

INTERVENTION DEPENDS ON GOVERNMENT

It is often and persuasively argued that the public interest can be served ideally through the natural regulatory mechanism of the marketplace rather than by government. But because the free market is a myth, regulation through the marketplace, in essence, replaces the government with the very centers of concentrated collectivism that experience tells us must be controlled by government because nothing else is big enough to do the job.

More, bitter history teaches us that it is wrong to assume, as does the notion of the market as a regulator, that the self-interest of the corporation is to provide the largest number of consumers with goods of high quality, utility, and safety at attractive prices, and that this self-interest—stimulated by the awareness of the consumer—is an automatic mechanism of consumer protection.

Such self-interest fails as a regulator because the consumer can seldom "beware" of the hazards he must guard against or have a choice in any case. Even when aware, the worker and the community are seldom in a position to work for, or provide services only to, the humane employer.

Indeed, the heart of government regulation must be to force access to information, to force competition, and to force honest business practices.

The complication, the redundance, and the creeping pace of government regulation comes less from the inability of government to achieve a regulatory mission than from the success of the corporation in making the regulator dependent upon the largesse of the regulated. Even among research agencies, those that protect the regulated—such as the National Center For Toxicological Research (NCTR)*—have no difficulty finding support. Agencies that protect the consumer—such as the National Institute For Environmental Health Sciences (NIEHS)*—struggle for their very existence.

What we must deal with if government is to become an effective intervenor, is not the work of one agency but of many agencies at more than one level of government.

There can never be a government agency so organized as to totally encapsulize any single mission. Environmental, economic, and every other concern raised in the public interest—and the programs designed to implement them—must be the inseparable concerns of each structure. The purpose of governmental organization and re-organization then, should not be to segregate but to focus and re-focus a cluster of concerns within one agency or another.

Secondly, within the universe defined by the focus, basic governmental functions (research, rule-making, policing, education, and adjudication) need balancing mechanisms to control the negative

*NCTR is a joint venture of two enforcement agencies: the Environmental Protection Agency and the Food and Drug Administration. NIEHS is part of the health research apparatus in the Department of Health, Education and Welfare.

collectivism that would otherwise result. These, traditionally, take the form of legislative oversight and executive accountability. More is needed: public involvement, peer review, interagency and private sector competition, and administrative separation.

Information gathered and brought to the attention of the focal agency by other agencies and by non-governmental institutions with environmental concerns is essential, but it takes provisions for a formal and somewhat detached mechanism to insure active collaboration.

Fostered competition is in the public interest. This is particularly true in the public sector since a monolithic government entity could easily smother the detection of problems, let alone their solution.

A carcinogen or any environmental hazard is best regulated by limiting the jurisdiction of any one agency and the encouragement of competitors. The policeman must have a limited role in determining the rule he enforces, the procedures under which the enforcement takes place, or even the definition of the problem for which regulation is intended to alleviate. Not even all police powers should reside in one regulative agency. Competition between EPA, OSHA, FDA, and other regulators has proven to be in the public interest, albeit often confusing.

Neat organizational charts seldom reflect good government. Amalgamation and consolidation has often meant a decrease in the extent to which a regulatory mission has been achieved, even though there may have been increased efficiency—along with a poor final product.

Competition should exist not only between agencies with the same or overlapping functions, but also when functions are ostensibly separate. Research agencies such as NIOSH (National Institute for Occupational Safety and Health), NIEHS, and NCI (National Cancer Institute) *do* compete with regulatory agencies. This competition is a necessary check and balance. The regulator must gather facts on the basis of which he must choose to act or not to act. He must not become the exclusive source of those facts nor be allowed to define conclusively the constellations from which they result.

The private sector becomes an additional factor in the competitive context in which data and decisions should be developed. Competition between the private and public sectors is a critical brake on the collectivism that might otherwise result.

Competition, of course, is only one restraint upon government. Public institutions independent of the political spoils system—though politically accountable—also are essential.

The broader the scope of the decision, the broader the political accountability required of the decision-maker. But, ideally, the "higher" echelons have as their primary tasks the insulation of the civil servant from political pressures and the efficient administration of the decision-making process. Decisions in grey areas, because of their essentially social-political nature, should be made by a politically accountable personage or structure.

There isn't any substitute for a competent civil servant. Even political decisions require objective data, defined options, a narrowing of the number of decisions to be made within the capacity of the executive at each level of consideration.

THE PLACE OF ECONOMICS

Intervention requires various inputs that differ depending upon the stage of action. Economic considerations should be minimal in most early situations. Relatively easy, non-political decisions based essentially on biological parameters can be made early. The grey areas are concentrated at the end of the process, where the concept of socially acceptable risk must guide the politically sensitive administrator, with the inviolable limitation that what is done must be done publicly without covert considerations of any kind. If the decision is to prevent only Y deaths because of a decision to spend only X dollars, this must be an explicated fact.

Only the very naive may think this decision can simply be one of subjectively discussing and accepting—as is often suggested—a given percentage of death and disease at a given so-called feasible limit of exposure, where feasibility is a micro-economic exercise. Obviously, the social value of the uses of a toxic substance must be considered in calculating a socially acceptable risk. Some or even all uses might be eliminated. This could reduce the size of the population at risk. But it could also destroy the livelihood of workers. Both are important considerations. Hence, the decision had better be taken early (e.g., pre-market) than late (e.g., post-production).

Further considerations of import are: other environmental effects; substitutability of the product, raw material, or process; externalized social costs; desires and needs of the population at risk; genetic and other long-term effects on the human stock; feasibility of potential technology; future raw material needs; and economic and social development.

SOME BASIC CONCEPTS

Critical examination of the basic concept of development is imperative when applied to the economic and social scene. Economics as a science has much to learn from biology. There is a historic and relevant dialectic on biological change: preformation vs. epigenesis. The question was whether growth proceeds essentially by increase in volume or increase in volume + differentiation (internalized development). The epigeneticists seem to have won. There has been a rejection of Galen's notion, namely, that growth (to use Galen's example) equals the blowing up of a pig's bladder [9].

I think that there is an analogy here with the current, simplistic views of "economic" growth as reflected in the preoccupation with Gross National Product, production units, retail sales, and similar indices of volume in plant-level economics.

Economic development is not the blowing up of a pig's bladder. Without internalized development there cannot be that kind of change in the quality of human life identified with satisfactory social development. The concept of social acceptability must encompass an epigenetic view of human material development. It cannot be restricted, for example, to the micro-economics of polymerization of vinyl chloride (PVC).

As we stated in our economic analysis at the VC hearings before the Department of Labor, at worst the OSHA 1 part per million regulation may increase the cost of a product (this has not occurred), and may thereby reduce the rate at which its market expands (the actual market has increased). We pointed out that in addition, it may also reduce the rate at which a number of other macro-economic effects would occur, such as: (a) problem of disposal; (b) depletion of raw materials; (c) diversion of capital for control equipment; (d) diversion of human resources for planning, construction, and operation of controls; (e) loss of dollar exchange in importation of the basic petro-chemical stock (or its domestic replacement); (f) costs to the health delivery system at a given level of risk; (g) concentration of production among current producers who may be least efficient, removing the stimulus for the entry of new firms and more efficient technology.

The last is particularly important because, as we predicted, the industry (trade association) proposal which would have permitted concentrations 10 times the current limit encouraged the concentration of production in the existing plants of a few firms that dominate the trade association. This would have occurred by subsidizing inefficient plants with externalized social costs and ignoring the cost of controlling adverse health effects. The trade association made its case about the level of control which is necessary and feasible through the use of fallacious medical data and a "study" which predicted mass unemployment based on consciously skewed assumptions. Subsequent to the promulgation of the standard, four technologically new and efficient PVC plants owned by firms that played a minor role in the hearings came on line that can meet the standard. They were planned prior to the hearings, and their technology was known to their competitors. One old plant is threatened. Thus the trade association was even wrong at a plant, i.e., a micro-economic level. Without considering any other set of factors, they did not propose a socially acceptable risk.

In the determination of socially acceptable risks, there are at least four other considerations that must be brought to bear.

First, it is not possible to quantify and compute everything that goes into the decision-making process; moreover, not everything that is quantified has not the same value, level of precision, or commensurability. Methods must be appropriate to subject matter and the precision with which analysis can take place. Different subjects entail different methods. Their outputs are not comparable. Although they may be considered or "displayed" concurrently, they cannot be used in the same equation.

Second, it is dangerous to assume that the assessment of the quantifiable and commensurable factors of risk need take the form of cost/benefit analysis, a limited technique borrowed from economics. Other computative techniques need exploration: ranking (e.g., biological over economic) and the determination of the morally critical datum (e.g., species—lethal levels of mutagenicity).

Third, non-economic factors cannot be handled as if they did not exist or as if they can be converted into economic units. Life has *no* monetary value. Hence, the impossibility of a demonstrable Benthamite calculus by conversion.

Fourth, some of the economic consequences are relatively greater than others. But the weighing of these factors cannot be premised simply on computing the greatest good for the greatest number. This view must be balanced by consideration for the "relative" economics measured by the impact on the rights of a smaller group of individuals or even a person.

A FURTHER CONSIDERATION: POSITIVE PUBLIC ADVOCACY

Human rights arise out of need. They are not inherited like a predisposition for warts. The right of individuals, peer groups, and peer group leaders to participate in a decision-making process which would control their hazards and their benefits *must* be exercised if social decisions are to be made equitably and political accountability is to have meaning.

Administrative procedures, implementation of "freedom of information" legislation, and the judicial process provide opportunities. They are not adequate in themselves to insure fruitful participation. Nor is it sufficient to merely increase the volume of educational materials and the number of informational opportunities for the press and public. These techniques fail to identify and assist the expression of the shifting interests and concerns found in our heterogeneously structured culture.

Although the right of government to manipulate political pressures by manipulating the anxieties of the various publics is correctly questioned, there should be no question of the duty of government to go beyond the public notice and the press release to identify and assist social structures in coping with technological impacts.

It is necessary to specially train field workers for this task. They must not themselves "skew" the information, arbitrarily favor one group or another, or themselves become organizers of citizen action. Rather they must find peer leaders of every kind who can have an interest in specific issues, provide opportunities in training for the citizen role, and then maintain a flow of information on the facts, issues, and opportunities for participation.

The object of such programs, where they have been successful, has not been to train scientists but knowledgeable citizens who are able to grapple with social issues and have not by lack of action chosen to endorse a technocracy. Without this kind of program, decision-making is willy-nilly left to the experts alone.

Labor groups, environmental organizations, social clubs, small businessmen, farmers, and ad hoc associations are examples of structures needing assistance in the exercise of their rights.

CONCLUSION

To reiterate, the most difficult decisions to be made by government will not be scientific in nature. Social and moral decisions will be made that can channel and shape the development of our control technology, which itself will become a major determinant of our future welfare. In this process, labor's contribution is unique.

Among the several publics, the worker is most exposed to environmental insult in the community and in the shop while being most vulnerable to the economic consequences of control. He and his institutions are of necessity, therefore, in a position of forced objectivity. Thus his is a critical voice to be heeded.

The participation of organized labor is not automatic. A positive effort must be made, an effott which I call "positive public advocacy." This is an essential government responsibility: involving the public in decision-making processes such as the assessment of environmental risk.

The passage of the Occupational Safety and Health Act of 1970 has resulted in a steady progression of "discovery" in the world press: the carcinogen-of-the-month, old horrors revisted (lead and mercury poisoning) and millions of workers and their families at risk from asbestos exposure.

Movement is slow in a democracy. Forms of collectivism, such as the trade association, appear without inherent mechanism or control. Unrestrained collectivism—which can be controlled—is characterized essentially by the lowest common denominator. These denominators in a collectivist structure have incredible leverage. They can become—as the years of secret studies by trade associations of vinyl chloride demonstrated—an almost insurmountable obstacle at the heart of the inquiry: the transmission of information and its examination.

As a consequence, the ideology prevailing when Percival Pott discovered occupational cancer 200 years ago, and the ideology of Bentham persist. But their influence is waning, in part because the worker is an increasingly effective agent of change. More and more he is becoming intellectually and economically able to act. He will not tolerate hundreds of thousands of cases of occupational cancer to be condoned by collectivist decisions on socially acceptable risks.

NOTES TO CHAPTER 12

1. Cf. Albert Schweitzer, *The Philosophy of Civilization*, trans. C.T. Campton (New York: Macmillan, 1957).

2. Cf. Friedrich A. Hayek, *The Road to Serfdom* (Chicago: University of Chicago Press, 1944).

3. Cf. Alexis de Tocqueville, *Democracy in America* trans. Reeve/Bowen (New York: Knopf, 1945).

4. Cf. Milton Friedman, "The Social Responsibility of Business Is to Increase Its Profits," *New York Times Magazine* (September 13, 1970), p. 32.

5. Jeremy Bentham, In: *The English Philosophers from Bacon to Mill*, ed. E.A. Burt (New York: Random House, 1939), p. 802. Cf. W.C. Mitchell, "Bentham's Felicific Calculus," *Political Science Quarterly* 33 (June 1918).

6. K. William Kapp, *The Social Costs of Private Enterprise* (New York: Schocken, 1971), p. xxiv.

7. Paul Brodeur, *Expendable Americans* (New York: Viking, 1974);

8. Personal communications, Prof. Irving J. Selikoff, Mt. Sinai School of Medicine.

9. Galen, *On the Natural Faculties* trans. Brock (Cambridge, Harvard University Press, 1947), p. 27.

10. Submission for the Record of the Vinyl Chloride Hearings, OSHA, Dept. of Labor, by the Industrial Union Department, August 23, 1974, p. 4.

Part 5

The Social Management
of Technology

Across generations, and across any and all "gaps" between
them, there is likely to run a common childhood memory
that is powerfully alive in the minds of most if not all of us,
regardless of age: it is that of the genie that got out of the bottle. Just
a fairy tale from *Arabian Nights*, to be sure, yet ominously revived
and somehow identified with and brought back to many minds by
the image of the mushroom-shaped cloud whose first appearance
over Hiroshima, just three decades ago. So new and awesome at the
time, it has become a permanent fixture of everyone's private chamber of horrors.

To this day, the full impact of this first public unveiling and un-
leashing of the destructive potential of nuclear power—in all its
physical, biological, psychological, and ethical dimensions, and in
many more respects—remains unclear.

Admittedly, this is an extreme and one-sided example. Yet, in
some ways the seemingly most beneficent and all-around-desirable
technological breakthroughs, e.g., some of the life-preserving and
prolonging advances in medicine, may prove to be "genies." In fact,
human interventions of any kind that entail changes in a given state
of affairs partake of this nature: what with our all too limited fore-
knowledge of *all* their consequences, both proximate and induced.

Far-fetched as this detour may seem at first blush, it is very much
in point as an approach to the essence of Technology Assessment
(TA). For, having stolen the fire from the Gods, Prometheus—man—
cannot evade responsibility for its use. And just as ignorance of man-
made law does not stay its enforcement, so our all-too-limited

awareness of all the consequences of our actions, especially in the realm of innovation, does not protect us from their occurrence. The only thing we *can* do is to *try and know* what we are doing ere we rush into action—which is a very different thing, again, from accepting nonaction in the face of problem situations as the blissful or virtuous state. Metternich's precept: "Govern and change nothing!". represents merely the other horn of the human dilemma.

Walter Hahn, in broaching the whole subject of TA in its historical evolution, sums up its essence in a homely way by citing the old adage: "Look before you leap!"

Obviously, this is a simplistic generalization, and Hahn takes pains to explain what TA really is, as well as what it is not. The breadth and comprehensiveness of the new operational concept may surprise many readers, as will the differentiation from older and therefore better known concepts, such as technological forecasting or other futuristic research.

Perhaps the greatest surprise to the noninitiate may turn out to be the facets of intellectual and social impact analysis that TA aims to provide.

In addition to the importance of TA to corporate planners, Hahn tells the story of its institutionalization in government and across national boundaries. He stresses its systemic character and comments on its role in planning, its objectives, methods, and the involvement of the public. Last, not least, he provides us with a wealth of references.

Joseph Coates develops the public policy aspects of TA, notably the crucial TA role that is exercised by the fairly new Congressional Office of Technology Assessment, as well as in agencies of the federal government and at other levels of government. He illustrates the process and the component parts of TA, and acquaints us with some concrete projects, with special reference to the TA agenda of the National Science Foundation and selected publications of topical TAs undertaken elsewhere.

Byron Kennard views TA primarily within the political context. With all the special interests involved, he considers grassroot participation of the essence. Wide open processes, with due opportunities for the voluntary groups who speak *pro bono publico* to be heard, suggest to Kennard institutionalized channels for two-way communication as the ideal arrangement. He views it as a precaution to be taken in the public interest prior to the adoption of public policies in virtually any and all fields.

✳ *Chapter 13*

Technology Assessment and Corporate Planning

Walter A. Hahn *

The central idea behind technology assessment (TA) is far from new: look before you leap! But this idea has a modern twist as TA looks at any physical or mental construct of man to evaluate its social, economic, environmental, and even its political consequences. In particular, TA looks beyond the immediate or intended effects for unintended, long-range consequences and for events in conjunction with other activities—the so-called second order effects [1]. To some planners TA will appear old hat with a new name. To others it is an extension of present practice. A few will view it as unwelcome competition or will fear that it will hinder planning and its implementation.

This chapter suggests that technology assessment is here to stay and that corporate planners, as well as others, ought to know all about it. For TA will become a key element in corporate and other planning. Planners have much to contribute to the development of good TA—through their concepts, methodology, and institutions. This chapter will briefly cover the origins and development of the TA movement, describe its present institutional and conceptual status, and offer some observations relevant to corporate and other institutional executives and planners. Documentation is deliberately detailed to supply readers with a core bibliography of original materials.

*Walter A. Hahn is Senior Specialist in Science and Technology, Congressional Research Service, Library of Congress. The views expressed in this paper are the author's alone; they do not represent the position of any government agency or the U.S. Congress.

AN IDEA DEVELOPS

To say that "TA is here" is not an overstatement. On October 13, 1972, President Nixon signed Public Law 92–484, the Technology Assessment Act of 1972, creating the first new organization in the legislative branch since 1971. Almost 100 technology assessments have been conducted by offices in the executive branch. Several states and a number of industrial corporations, here and abroad, have established groups to do work classified as (but often not named) TA. Academic courses on the subject, symposiums, and meetings abound, and a rising flood of papers and articles is appearing in the popular, trade, and professional media. A TA international society exists, complete with a quarterly journal and plans for an international conference.

Origins of a Concept

Technology assessment in concept and in name originated in the Congress. The term first appeared in a report of October 17, 1966, of the House Committee on Science and Astronautics [2]. On March 7, 1967, Representative Emilio Q. Daddario introduced a bill (H.R. 6689) proposing the creation of a "Technology Assessment Board" reporting to the Congress. In a subsequent formal statement, Daddario defined technology assessment in these words:

> Technology assessment is a form of policy research which provides a balanced appraisal to the policymaker. Ideally, it is a system to ask the right questions, and obtain correct and timely answers. It identifies policy issues, assesses the impact of alternative courses of action and presents findings. It is a method of analysis that systematically appraises the nature, significance, status, and merit of a technological program. . . . [It] is designed to uncover three types of consequences—desirable, undesirable, and uncertain. . . . To assess technology one has to establish cause and effect relationships from the action or project source to the locale of consequences. . . . The function of technology assessment is to identify [all impacts and trends]—both short-term and long range. . . . The focus of Technology Assessment will be on those consequences that can be predicted with a useful degree of probability [3].

Numerous discussions and studies were initiated by Daddario to develop the idea and to assess its merits for meeting the acknowledged need of Congress for improved analytical research and information. These activities plus a chapter in the report of the White House National Goals Research Staff [4] convey the basic technology assessment ideas, issues, and opportunities as seen by 1970.

Several bills and hearings and more conferences and reports followed as the idea advanced and consensus developed over the next two years. A complete legislative history of technology assessment proposals is contained in the Senate Rules and administration Committee's Staff Study of November 1, 1972 [5], and an abbreviated listing appears in Senate Report No. 92—1123 [6]. These activities included a 1967 seminar held to evoke professional views [7], a study by the Legislative Reference Service [8] (now Congressional Research Service), another by the National Academy of Sciences [9], and a third by the National Academy of Engineering [10].

A Consensus Emerges

In August 1971 Representative John Davis, replacing Daddario as Chairman of the Subcommittee on Science, Research, and Development initiated a series of activities [11] which eventually resulted in House passage of H.R. 10243 on February 8, 1972, on a roll call vote of 256 to 118 [12]. The bill as reported called for an 11-member Technology Assessment Board composed of two senators and two representatives, one from each political party in each House, the Comptroller General, the Director of the Congressional Research Service, four members from the public (to be appointed by the President), and the Director of the Office of Technology Assessment (OTA). Several sections of the bill were amended on the floor, and the final version eliminated the Presidential appointments [13].

The absence of public scientists and engineers from the structure was one point of major discussion in the March 1972 Senate hearings on the House-passed bill [14]. In the Senate bill that emerged in September, public and professional participation was restored by adding a Technology Assessment Advisory Council of 12 members, "ten members from the public, to be appointed by the Board, who shall be persons eminent in one or more fields of the physical, biological, or social sciences or engineering or experienced in the administration of technical activities, or who may be judged qualified on the basis of contributions made to educational or public activities" [15] plus the Comptroller General and the Director of the Congressional Research Service. In addition, party parity was restored to the TA board by provision for the appointment of six senators and six representatives, three from each party in each House. Also, the Director of the OTA was named a non-voting member of the TA Board.

Office of Technology Assessment

The Office of Technology Assessment thus includes the Board, the Advisory Council, and a Director and staff. OTA explicitly has available the services of the General Accounting Office and the Congressional Research Service and "shall maintain a continuing liaison with the National Science Foundation" [16] concerning research on technology assessment. A quotation from the Act most accurately conveys the OTA mission:

Sec. 3(c) The basic function of the Office shall be to provide early indications of the probable beneficial and adverse impacts of the applications of technology and to develop other coordinate information which may assist the Congress. In carrying out such function, the Office shall:
(1) identify existing or probable impacts of technology or technological programs;
(2) where possible, ascertain cause-and-effect relationships;
(3) identify alternative technological methods of implementing specific programs;
(4) identify alternative programs for achieving requisite goals:
(5) make estimates and comparisons of the impacts of alternative methods and programs;
(6) present findings of completed analyses to the appropriate legislative authorities;
(7) identify areas where additional research or data collection is required to provide adequate support for the assessments and estimates described in paragraph (1) through (5) of this subsection [17].

All indications are that OTA will consist of a small (20—50) professional staff and that most of the assessments will be conducted by ad hoc teams of contractors and consultants. The Office will not operate laboratories, pilot plants, or test facilities.

The previous section on the legislative history of OTA mentioned that a "consensus" was building. The Senate Staff Study summarizes this movement as follows:

This consensus is revealed in the long hearings record, numerous studies, meetings, discussions and articles, both within and outside of Government, that have led to the subcommittee's considerations of these bills. Nine propositions are stated below which omit many qualifications, comments and alternatives. But this succinct form reveals the basic notions of the consensus:
1. The pace and scale of technological innovations are increasing ever more rapidly.
2. The social, environmental, and economic impacts of these innovations are growing in complexity (most are beyond man's immediate senses); these impacts have very far-reaching and sometimes irreversible effects, which may be highly concentrated in urbanized areas as well as throughout the natural environment.

3. Today's changing values and life styles enhance dissatisfaction with the negative effects of technology and foster both an anti-technology mood and a demand for relief.

4. There is concern that this attitude will create a climate for technological "arrestment" at a time when new technologies (and/or new applications) are vitally needed to remedy the ills of past technological excesses and to provide satisfaction of new requirements.

5. Private sector, executive department, or State and local government approaches to the control of the effects of advancing technology are no longer adequate. Congressional leadership and policy guidance are essential for management of affairs so national in scope and with growing international implications.

6. Advances in the behavioral and systems sciences, in economic and environmental analysis, in technological forecasting, and in many other fields are creating a new capability and sophistication to deal with these large, complex and dynamic problems and opportunities.

7. As the executive branch expands its present assessment, research, and analysis activities, many of the basic policy issues involving the public interest and welfare can be resolved only by the Congress.

8. To identify these issues, to marshal specialized resources, and to be responsive and serve its unique interests full time, the Congress should have a specific organization to respond to these requirements.

9. The need is clear and present. Technology assessment appears to be a concept that can help and should be tried. The Congress now has the opportunity—perhaps the responsibility—to act and to apply the concept and capability for the benefit of all the people [18].

THE ANATOMY OF TECHNOLOGY ASSESSMENT

Thus far the term "technology assessment" has been used to describe a broad, multifaceted, policy-oriented concept. The National Academy of Engineering suggested two useful and self-explanatory classifications for assessments: problem-oriented and technology-oriented analyses. In addition there are many writers who use the term TA synonymously with the set of methodological approaches to assessment. At the Engineering Research Foundation Conference on TA in Andover, N.H. (September 1971) this author proposed that the general term "TA" as loosely used by sponsors, doers, and users of TA be recognized to include four "types" of TA: policy-oriented, issue (or problem) oriented, technology-oriented, and methodology-oriented [19]. Regardless of the particular emphasis, all types share the central idea of identification of the second order and other indirect and long-range consequences of technological innovations and the use of this information for public policy-making.

Categories and Constituencies

Acknowledging oversimplification, these categories correlate meaningfully with the focus of attention of the several interest groups involved in TA. Policy-oriented TA is of major interest to the legislative and, to some extent, executive branches of the several levels of government. Assessments to determine the impact of the use of old, new, or proposed technological structures, products, or processes are more usually associated with industrial or government regulatory agencies. Problem- or issue-oriented TA's arise from the feeling that "something is going wrong," often articulated by industrial citizens, groups, or public-interest organizations. This has been referred to as "people's technology assessment" [20]. This last category of assessments will most likely, but not exclusively, be the focus of court involvement. Persons in academic and not-for-profit organizations emphasize the conceptual and methodological aspects of TA and push for the development of the techniques, quality assurance, and objectivity so necessary for the viability of TA.

The foregoing overlapping and interacting categories may have some utility for understanding TA as it develops. But they should not be viewed as early elements of a "TA theory." Technology assessment today is a very necessary, pragmatic activity to aid decision (policy) -making in complex and pervasive situations. It utilizes many "theories" and practices. It demands participation by persons of many different professional disciplines. It also requires participation by generalists, by interested parties, and by persons skilled in balancing resources and in integrating the contributions of many disciplines and non-disciplines simultaneously. In particular, it requires persons who can synthesize all of the above and communicate the result to decision makers and affected parties. Although technology assessment is not planning, some of the similarities between the two activities are becoming clear.

TA is not. . . .

Technology assessment also is *not* several other activities. It is not technological forecasting—". . . the estimating of probable availability or use of a technological innovation at some specified future point in time" [21]. TA is not technology transfer nor is it futures research or futuristics. Many writers do consider technology assessment to be a unique form of policy analysis.

The reader is further warned that technology assessment is not limited to technological things—man-made materials, tools, machinery, structures—as many of us most commonly use the word technology. It includes evaluating the impacts of man's intellectual and social (so-called soft) inventions and innovations as well, viz., credit, information systems, suburbs, organ transplants, environmental and other standards and regulations ... [22]. Although depending heavily on their use improvement, TA is also not synonymous with social indicators.

CURRENT STATUS

Congress

The focal point of technology assessment in the United States is the new Office of Technology Assessment in the legislative branch. The policy-making and controlling element for OTA is the Technology Assessment Board. Its 13 members include:

(1) six Members of the Senate, appointed by the President pro tempore of the Senate, three from the majority party and three from the minority party;

(2) six Members of the House of Representatives appointed by the Speaker of the House of Representatives, three from the majority party and three from the minority party; and

(3) the Director, who shall not be a voting member [23].

Before the close of the 92nd Congress the 12 congressional members were appointed, but the Board did not meet. One representative and one senator were not reelected, and two new appointments were made early in the 93rd Congress. The Technology Assessment Act specifies that the Chairman shall be from the Senate during the odd-numbered Congresses, and the Vice Chairman from the House. The Senate members of the Board met on January 6, 1973, and elected Senator Kennedy as Chairman. Congressman Mosher was later unanimously elected Vice Chairman by the House members of the Board.

Early in November 1973, the Legislative Branch Appropriations Bill was signed by the President. This bill contained $2 million for the Office of Technology Assessment for FY'74. Once these funds were made available, the Board met and appointed Emilio Daddario as the first Director of OTA. The appointments of the 10 public members of the Advisory Council (each for a term of four years) and office staff followed in early 1974 [24].

Executive Branch

As mentioned earlier, there are a number of scattered technology assessment activities throughout the executive branch. Dr. Vary Coates of George Washington University recently completed an excellent survey of these activities [25]. Dr. Coates classified 9 of the 97 projects surveyed as "wide scope assessments"—ones that gave "open-ended consideration of possible impacts in several categories, employed a multi-disciplinary team, and whose intention was to support and influence public decision-making." On the average, these assessments involved 4.5 different disciplines, cost $381,000 each, and took 16 months to complete. Forty of the studies were "partial assessments," giving consideration to preselected secondary consequences in one or more categories. They averaged two disciplines, ran from $85,000 (by universities) to $139,000 (by industry), and lasted around 18.5 months each. A third class of 14 studies was called "problem-oriented," which focused on societal problems where technology is a cause or a possible solution. These averaged 6.3 disciplines, cost $678,000, and took 18 months to complete. Technology assessment is neither quick nor cheap!

The States

In December 1971 a working conference met to discuss "Technology Assessment in State Government" [26]. The conference concluded (in part) that the state governments had a parallel function with the federal government as part of the "federal system" of performing technology assessments. Several states—for example, Georgia and Hawaii—have already established components to conduct TA, and several others have similar plans.

Industry

In industry the picture is less clear. Several large companies are heavily engaged in TA-like activities but title these strategic planning, social responsibility of business, corporate citizenship, environmental or consumer affairs, and many others. Some industries claim they have been doing "TA" for years and point to their market research or product-testing activities, while others focus upon their public information group. Only two tentative generalizations seem possible at this time. First, those corporations that are aware of TA seem to favor it at the corporate executive level ("it's good business," "it's here, let's make it work 'right'"). At the "P and L" and research laboratory level there is more concern for possible increased costs or regulation ("technology arrestment"). Secondly, industry has only recently really become aware of technology assessment, and through direct means and through trade and professional associations, corporations are scrambling to know about it and plan their actions accordingly.

An International Movement

TA is clearly an international movement. The Organization for Economic Cooperation and Development countries held a meeting on TA in Paris in January 1972. The Engineering Research Foundation sponsored a third annual meeting in August in Henniker, N.H. In September the "Salzburg Assembly: Impact of the New Technology" (SAINT) met in Austria. That same month the North Atlantic Treaty Organization, with the U.S. National Science Foundation and the newly formed International Institute for the Management of Technology (Milan), sponsored a TA advanced study institute involving representatives from over 20 nations. The newly formed International Society for Technology Assessment (ISTA) attracted over 500 members in its first year, almost half from outside the United States [27]. The second volume of its quarterly journal (*Technology Assessment*) is being distributed. ISTA also plans a documentation or book series to collect and make easily available the hard-to-get body of literature on TA. The Society held its First International Congress on TA in The Hague in late May of 1973, attended by 225 representatives of 21 countries. Many U.S. and other professional and trade associations have formed technology assessment committees or study groups, and more formal organizational structures are under consideration.

The Public

What of the public in all this? If Archie Bunker were its spokesman he would probably say, "Technology assessment, what the hell is that?" The public is much less aware of TA than the other groups discussed above. The public *is* keenly aware of technology, but its reactions are ambivalent. The presence of anti-technology and anti-rationalistic feelings was vividly demonstrated at the 1972 Washington meetings of the American Association for the Advancement of Science.

Technology pollutes the environment, provides instruments of war, causes social ills, and inflates the economy. But, simultaneously, how many consumers will reject TV, beer cans, air conditioning, the automobile, credit, or a host of other "essentials"? There are still strongly held and widespread convictions that only through more rational and more technically advanced means can we maintain and improve man's quality of life. "And survive," so-called technological optimists would add.

SOME ISSUES FOR PLANNERS

The above material should be sufficient to alert the planner and his institutions to the background and current status of what is sure to be an increasingly explicit element in his substantive and structural planning activities. But what about the planner professionally? The closing section of this chapter will suggest several areas in which planners can contribute their skills and knowledge to improving the total process of performing technology assessments. It will not dwell on the obvious point that planners, like many other professionals, can learn much from participation and observation of this broad interdisciplinary movement to improve policy-level decision-making. TA can be expected to cause planners to expand the scope of their models or systems. They must be more explicit and candid about the second-order consequences of their plans. Planning, like technology assessment, will become a less elitist and more participatory process. Planning theory and planning experience ought to assist in dealing with several of the following issues facing technology assessors.

Who Are the Assessors?

The first issue of concern to planners is the question, Who are the technology assessors? Are they the legislators and executives who pass the laws and make the action decisions—those *in* the power structure? Or are they the multidisciplinary professionals who perform the complex procedures of gathering and selecting the relevant information for analysis, synthesis, and presentation of options and their consequences? Or are the real assessors the public, the ones who are *affected* by the results of the decisions and analyses and who pay the ultimate bill? Or all of these?

Two dominant views appear on these questions which this author labels "sequential" and "participative." The sequentialists argue that the assessment practitioners should be permitted to perform their functions free from all political, organizational, and personal biases and *then* transmit or present the objective statement of options and impacts to the decision-maker. The participants argue that this procedure is neither practical nor desirable. Technology assessment is a process that explicitly involves more than objective factual elements. Values, judgments, choices, experience, and political, economic, social, and environmental forces are an integral part of TA. Those in the power structure, the affected party (public) and the practitioner must all interact for viable assessment. The issue is not which of these views are right or controlling but how to achieve an acceptable and workable balance between them in conducting real impact studies. Clearly technology assessment can benefit from the experiences in planning, as, for example, the "Fishbown Planning" [28] experiments by the Army Corps of Engineers in the Seattle, Washington, district.

Developing Methodology

While not yet crystallized as an issue, a second area of increasing tension exists among those interested and involved in TA. Three interrelated questions frame the area. What is *the* method of technology assessment? Is TA to become a formal academic discipline complete with theory, best procedure, and degrees? Who will be in charge of the interdisciplinary team?

In one search for methodology the President's Office of Science and Technology placed a contract to conceptually and empirically characterize the approach [29]. While performing a useful service by attempting to generalize and by furnishing a set of case histories, one observer cynically but to the point characterized the results in these words, "They *almost* reinvented the scientific method." Many assessors in the academic community, along with a large number of TA practitioners in government and industry, tacitly assume that, like systems engineering, operations research, and other interdisciplinary fields, technology assessment will also become a curriculum and degree area. It is this writer's hope that this does not occur.

As shown above, many disciplines and persons with multidisciplinary skills and knowledge are needed to conduct TA. On the other hand, TA is perhaps more substance-oriented than it is dependent on even the most powerful methodologies. The OTA authorization act indicates that a large portion of all technology assessment teams will be specially assembled for each task where specific subject knowledge and unique approaches are needed. The strongly felt but unvoiced answer as to who should lead the team is, "Me. Only my discipline and background are broad enough to integrate the works of all those other fellows." Does this sound familiar to planners?

The Role of Advocacy

Another issue is the role of advocacy in technology assessment. Many discussions of this subject have appeared in law journals and other professional publications, including a brief but thorough paper by Philip Bereano of Cornell [30]. Bereano concludes:

> The capability of the courts, as the prime example of the institutionalization of the adversary system, to handle technological issues appears somewhat mixed. In terms of three criteria—their competence, the acceptability of their product, and the personal qualities of the assessor—it can be said that they function adequately, although in a limited area. . . . The conclusion reached is that in spite of the fact that courts cannot handle the problems of modern technology by themselves they can play a role in the interstices of an assessment process conducted by other government organs or in situations where other agencies are not assessing or are assessing poorly. In addition to the task of designing adequate institutions to do technology assessment on a primary basis, it is to be hoped that judicial doctrines and procedures will continue to evolve so that the courts may function effectively as secondary institutions to deal with

the specific situations of hardship or injustice which appear, notwith-
standing the overall planning which will be done for guiding technological
change [31].

Distribution of Costs

A fourth issue in technology assessment is the one partially mentioned above by Bereano: how to assign the costs, benefits, and *risks*
and *responsibilities* among the many parties. The critical element of
this issue is "externalities"—a once obscure technical term of the
economists, now becoming one of those household words. When we
all own them and use them, how do we charge for and protect the
air, a view, quiet, water, the wilderness. . . .? And what about safety,
pursuit of a different life style, and those factors in the environment
and consumer products that are beyond a person's senses or his level
of technical sophistication?

Goals and Objectives

A fifth issue in technology assessment is very familiar to the planner: goals and objectives. Who sets them? How? Where do they come
from? Should they be specific and ordinal or vague and coexistent?
The list of questions is long and answers are scarce. Planners have
wrestled long and hard in this area, and the *least* of their contributions would be to prevent technology assessors from going over the
same ground and suffering the same frustrations as did the planners.

Scope of the System

One more illustrative problem from the many that could be cited
is that of choosing the appropriate level or scope of the "system" for
assessment. How do we select between the truisms that one can't do
everything at once and yet everything is related to everything else?
One hears calls for analysis of the 3rd and even the Nth order consequences! We are cautioned by the operations researchers not to
suboptimize. Professional planners and particularly the planning
decision-makers could offer much in dealing with these issues.

SO WHAT?

A technology assessment movement is under way. As the Senate
Staff study states:

> There is consensus that: (1) Sufficiently powerful concepts and method-
> ologies, and (2) sufficient qualified personnel are available to perform

meaningful Technology Assessments. If an appropriate policy and organizational framework backed with adequate resources is established, the Congress can have a new and valuable input to its deliberations and actions. This is not to claim too much. The blunt fact remains that in every policy decision there is and always will be incomplete information. The function of Technology Assessment is to bring to bear the maximum possible of information that is available [p. 5].

What applies above to the Congress can apply to other institutions as well. Other public and private organizations can take the initiative to use this approach in their own private or public interests, and they must be prepared to assimilate the results of technology assessment activities of the Congress and other institutions. The Report of the White House National Goals Research Staff states:

> Courses of action that do appear viable at this time are to: (1) continue for the immediate future to pursue our private and public affairs cautiously but without fear and pessimism—using existing market and government mechanisms; (2) simultaneously conduct pragmatic assessments with today's knowledge on subjectively selected areas or events to give answers to pressing problems and to learn by doing; and (3) initiate discussion, research and planning efforts to deal with the known inadequacies of our present ability to assess technology and build a basis for future improvements [p. 133].

Corporate, academic, and public planners need to inform themselves about this TA movement. They would do well to alert others in their institutions so that their colleagues may cooperatively take appropriate actions. TA is a new conceptual and information tool of government—at all levels. It is also a new element of corporate strategic or long-range planning. TA requires product, process, market, and research and development planners to take a longer and broader look at the impact or consequences of the implementation of their proposals. TA may present problems of delay for more study before action can raise costs. This type of planning may also require increased disclosure of information previously considered proprietary. Technology assessments are an effective tool for demonstrating corporate responsibility. For some organizations, TA is an opportunity to perform assessments under contract or to provide supplementary services to those groups who are doing the assessment study. Whether the planner is aware of it or not, TA *is* here, and its impacts will soon affect his organization.

NOTES TO CHAPTER 13

1. Raymond A. Bauer, Richard S. Rosenbloom and Laure Shape. *Second Order Consequences* (Cambridge: The M.I.T. Press, 1969).

2. U.S. Congress, House, Committee on Science and Astronautics, *Inquiries, Legislation, Policy Studies Re: Science and Technology: Review and Forecast*, Second Progress Report to Subcommittee on Science, Research, and Development, 89th Congress, 2nd sess. (Washington: U.S. Government Printing Office, 1966).

3. U.S. Gress, House, Committee on Science and Astronautics, Technology Assessment, Statement . . . of Subcommittee on Science, Research, and Development, 90th Congress, 1st sess. (Washington: U.S. Government Printing Office, 1967), pp. 12–13.

4. *Toward Balanced Growth: Quantity with Quality*, Report of the National Goals Research Staff (Wahington: U.S. Government Printing Office, July 4, 1970), Ch. 6.

5. U.S. Congress, Senate, Committee on Rules and Administration, *Technology Assessment for the Congress*, Staff Study of the Subcommittee on Computer Services, 92nd Congress, 2nd sess., November 1, 1972 (Washington: U.S. Government Printing Office, 1972).

6. U.S. Congress, Senate, Committee on Rules and Administration, *Technology Assessment Act of 1972*, S. Report 92–1123, 92nd Congress, 2nd sess., Sept. 13, 1972 (Washington: U.S. Government Printing Office, 1972).

7. U.S. Congress, House, Committee on Science and Astronautics, *Technology Assessment Seminar*, Proceedings of the Subcommittee on Science, Research, and Development, 90th Congress, 1st sess. (Washington: U.S. Government Printing Office, 1968).

8. U.S. Congress, House, Committee on Science and Astronautics, *Technical Information for Congress*, Report to the Subcommittee on Science, Research, and Development. Prepared by the Congressional Research Service, Library of Congress. 1st edition, 1969. Revised April 15, 1971, 92nd Congress, 1st sess. (Washington: U.S. Government Printing Office, 1971), p. 845.

9. U.S. Congress, House, Committee on Science and Astronautics, *Technology: Processes of Assessment And Choice*. Report of the National Academy of Sciences (Washington: U.S. Government Printing Office, 1969).

10. U.S. Congress, House, Committee on Science and Astronautics, *A Study of Technology Assessment*, Report of the Committee on Public Engineering Policy, National Academy of Engineering (Washington: U.S. Government Printing Office, 1969).

11. U.S. Congress, House, Committee on Science and Astronautics, "Establishing the Office of Technology Assessment and Amending the National Science Foundation Act of 1950," H. Report 92–469, 92nd Congress, 1st sess., August 16, 1971 (Washington: U.S. Government Printing Office, 1971), p. 22.

12. "Establishing the Office of Technology Assessment and Amending the National Science Foundation Act of 1950," Discussion and consideration of H.R. 10243 on the floor of the House. *Congressional Record* (February 8, 1972), pp. 11865–11887.

13. *Ibid.*, p. 11884.

14. U.S. Congress, Senate, Committee on Rules and Administration, "Office of Technology Assessment for the Congress," Hearings before the Subcommittee on Computer Services on S. 2302 and H.R. 10243, March 2, 1972, 92nd Congress, 2nd sess. (Washington: U.S. Government Printing Office, 1972), p. 120.

15. P.L. 92–484, Sec. 7, (a) (1).

16. P.L. 92–484, Sec. 10 (a).

17. P.L. 92–484, Sec. 3 (c).

18. *Technology Assessment for the Congress*, *op. cit.*, p. 10.

19. For a more detailed description see "The Future of Technology Assessment in Policy Formulation" by Walter A. Hahn in *Technology Assessment in a Dynamic Environment*, ed. M.J. Cetron, B. Bartocha, and C. Ralph (New York: Gordon and Breach, in press).

20. *Toward Balanced Growth*, *op. cit.*, p. 124.

21. U.S. Congress, House, Committee on Science and Astronautics. *Science Policy: A Working Glossary*, Prepared for the Subcommittee on Science, Research, and Development by the Science Policy Research Division, Congressional Research Service, Library of Congress, 92nd Congress, 2nd sess. (Washington: U.S. Government Printing Office, April 1972), p. 56. For more complete definitions of these and over 200 related terms, the reader is referred to this very useful document prepared by Dr. Franklin P. Huddle.

22. For a list of 137 substantive issues raised or referred to during discussion of technology assessment legislation by the Congress, see Appendix C of *Technology Assessment for the Congress*, *op. cit.*

23. P.L. 92–484, Sec. 4 (a).

24. Staff appointments included the Deputy Director of the Office (Daniel DeSimone) and the General Counsel (Timothy Atkeson.)

25. Vary T. Coates, "Technology and Public Policy: The Process of Technology Assessment in the Federal Government," Final report under NSF Grants GQ–r and GI–30422 (Washington: National Science Foundation, April 1972).

26. *Technology Assessment in State Government*, A Report on a Working Conference and Recommendations for Action (National Academy of Public Administration, September 1972).

27. For further information, write to: International Society for Technology Assessment, 1140 Connecticut Ave., N.W., Suite 305, Washington, D.C. 20036.

28. *Congressional Record*, (October 5, 1972), pp. 17059–61.

29. Martin V. Jones, "A Technology Assessment Methodology: Some Basic Propositions" (The Mitre Corporation, June 1971).

30. Philip L. Bereano, "Technological Planning Assessment and Adversarial Participation," Thesis in Comprehensive Health Planning, Center for Housing and Environmental Studies, Division of Urban Studies. See Ch. 5, "The Role of the Courts in Technology Assessment" (Ithaca, N.Y.: Cornell University, January 1971).

31. *Ibid.*, pp. 204–207. Bereano also has a fine chapter (3) on "The Relevance of Planning Theory to Technology Assessment."

Chapter 14

Technology Assessment: A New Tool for Public Policy Makers to Gauge Environmental Impacts

*Joseph F. Coates**

On the average of once a month since World War II, the United States public has been exposed to an incident of technological failure, alarm, concern, or major uncertainty sufficiently important to merit attention in the national press. Virtually every sector of our economy has contributed to this relentless flow of public concerns. Pesticide residues in Christmas cranberries, nerve gas stored on the flight path of the Denver Airport, mercury residue in tuna fish, regional electric power blackouts, chronic water pollution from petroleum with occasional major spills, faulty vehicles and faulty road design, toys that are unsafe, baby clothes that are highly combustible, convenience packages with inconvenient aesthetic side effects, and it goes on, and on, and on.

SCOPE AND CAUSES OF DYSFUNCTIONALISM

The incidents may be large or small. They may be of national or local scope. They may hit anyone, anywhere, randomly or systematically. What is the underlying situation that makes such incidents not only more frequent but of growing public concern? Basically I believe it is because we moved past a situation in which man was in constant struggle with a dominant natural environment. Until very recently nature could not only recover from man's intrusions

*Joseph F. Coates is with the Office of Technology Assessment of the U.S. Congress. The material in this paper is the author's sole responsibility and does not represent the position of any government agency or the U.S. Congress.

but could thwart the goals and intentions of most human endeavors. Within the last two generations, that situation has nearly reversed in the United States. The life of most Americans is within a fully man-made world. Most of the readers of this article are surrounded entirely by human artifacts and nothing else. We depend on them for food, shelter, clothing, work, entertainment, and leisure. Only on those special occasions when we purposely set aside the time, and go to the trouble, do we encounter something like nature in the raw. Even then, it is likely to be a simulated or man-sustained situation.

While our world has changed, the rules and regulations reflected in our institutional, personal, and organizational orientation toward the world have become obsolescent. They reflect catagories and approaches appropriate to a parochial gross struggle against a universally powerful nature. The enterprises of man have reached a stage where their scale, their scope, the size of investments, the speed with which technological change permeates society, the relative, irrevocability of big enterprises—all demand conceptually fresh approaches in the social management of technology. Crucial to that new approach are foresight, feedback, and flexibility. It is literally true that federal highway programs, be they good or bad, are set in concrete, and that concrete, except in rare instances, will remain set for 30 to 60 years. The building of a major power plant, whether conventional or nuclear, is an event which is likely to be functionally irreversible for a long time. The opening of a new waterway, the immigration of a new pest or predator, the construction of a new highrise building, all make more or less irrevocable commitments to the future. Even in the social area, the institution of a new social program, new benefits, new legislation, or new regulations tend to lack flexibility and responsiveness which permits timely compensation for error, mistake, or shortfall.

How did this come about? In my view, the technological economic planning in the United States has been overwhelmingly premised on an affirmative to very little more than three questions:

1. Is the technological objective feasible?
2. Will it sell? That may be via direct competition in a free market, or the competition may be for public funds and government programs.
3. Is it safe?

Reflection on any of the above illustrative shortfalls and failures of technology does not suggest that these criteria are not good, but rather that they are inadequate. Many of the most significant consequences in our highly technologized society do not happen immediately. They may be slow in building (such as the evil thoughts planted by a television program), they may be convergent (as when new contraceptive technology, increased levels of education, and prosperity promote the women's liberation movement), they may be incidental (as when the one in a few thousands of a broadly dispersed technological item fails) or they may be catastrophic (when an otherwise well-functioning system collapses as a result of an administrative or technological glitch (the crash of a giant passenger airplane).

The above criteria must be extended and expanded so that the range of considerations which enter into public and private decision-making are appropriate to our world.

TA CAN PLUG SOME OF THE GAPS IN FORESIGHT

Before any organizational, institutional, economic or technical remedies or controls are to be instituted, we must better understand the future implications of any particular technological development and the policies for its management. Technology assessment is one approach to providing this expanded foresight. It may be defined as a class of policy studies examining the fullest range of impact of the introduction of a new technology or the expansion of a present technology in new or different ways. It is an analysis of the total impact of a technology on society. Technology assessment, therefore, is much broader than the traditional technological planning, which is usually based on meeting some sort of potential or felt need, of satisfying or creating some new market.

Technology assessment does not deal only with the dark, the negative, the unfortunate consequences of technology. It is a tool for optimizing the benefits and penalties that technology may bring. Why is it, for example, that the widely touted benefits implicit in new approaches in education through computers and telecommunications have been such a disappointment? Why is it that cable television in the U.S. remains underdeveloped and relatively uninteresting? Why is it that the modern technological advances applicable to architecture, design, and building repeatedly end up in junky, malfunctioning, aesthetic insults? The answer, in part, has to do with the inadequacy of the three traditional technoeconomic planning criteria. With every actor in the drama optimizing in his own self-interest, with nobody in charge, with no one having a synoptic grasp of the matter, the yield must be less than the best.

A third class of activities that will also benefit from holistic evaluation are those situations in which there is a belief that physical, biological, or social technology offers some opportunity to alleviate or deal with a public issue. Problems of welfare, education, delinquency, crime, resource control, energy, conservation, and others in the limitless stream of issues are potential candidates for illumination by technology assessment.

Three major developments ought to be considered with regard to technology assessment, since the term was first coined and used by the Subcommittee on Science, Research and Development of the House of Representatives' Committee on Science and Astronautics.

First there is the development of a comprehensive, systematic, modestly funded program of technology assessment at the National Science Foundation (see Table 14–1). Second is the attempt at technology assessment by a number of federal agencies, most of which so far involve single attempts with little followthrough. There are, of course, the studies that qualify as more or less comprehensive or partial technology assessments, undertaken under other names by federal agencies for many years. These have been reviewed and analyzed through 1971 [1]. And finally there is the formation of the Office of Technology Assessment in November, 1973, as a new agency of government specifically dedicated to assisting Congress in meeting its study needs. Those needs relate to four Congressional functions; legislation, oversight, budget, and policy formulation.

HOW TO DO A TECHNOLOGY ASSESSMENT

It would be convenient were there a formula or prescription for technology assessment. Unfortunately it is unlikely that a general formula will ever be available, since the approach to and content of an assessment is determined by three primary considerations: the subject, the budget, and the primary user. Clearly, different factors are important in the technologies, consequences, and policies of genetic engineering, weather modification, and airport siting. Consequently different conceptual tools are certain to be appropriate in a holistic analysis of each of them. With regard to budget, a technology assessment may be done at a wide range of funding levels. One analyst or a panel of wise men working for a few months could do one kind of job for $20,000, while a major think tank study team with $500,000 and two years would do a quite different job. Different techniques would be appropriate for these different study efforts which might nevertheless be dealing with the same subject matter. The assessment of earthquake prediction technology, noted in Table 14–1, is being paralleled by an effort one-tenth as large by a single investigator. The third major determinant influencing the scope of the study is its principal user. The range of impacts and consequences of a drug considered by a drug company, a state agency, the Federal Drug Administration, the White House, and the Congress are increasingly wide in scope because of the increasing range of responsibility of each of those groups. Since experience and general principles preclude any common set of tools or techniques applicable to the examination of the impacts of all technologies, it is important to note that there are common features to all technology assessments. The organization of an effective work plan must take these common modules or elements into consideration if the goals of a technology assessment are to be met and it is to be more than a cost-benefit, marketing, feasibility, or systems study.

TEN MODULES OF A TECHNOLOGY ASSESSMENT

1. *Definition of the problem, the technology, issue or project to be assessed.* The client or user of a technology assessment is likely to be unclear as to what the problem is. Hence close examination and reworking is in order to put it in a proper form to permit a useful study with a decision-related output.

2. *Definition of alternative systems to be examined.*

3. *The unfolding of impacts.* The identification of impacts requires a combination of experience, skills, imagination, and creativity. There literally are no complete models, paradigms, or algorithms by which one can identify the consequences of a given technology. In some cases the technology itself may suggest where to look for impacts: for example, with geothermal energy, the physical system offers a logical path along which to look for effects. In some cases the technology may be so diffuse, as with the four-day workweek, that one must go to one or another "method of exhaustion" to identify impacts.

4. *Evaluation of the significance of impacts.* Many qualitative and quantitative tools may be brought to bear here, including tools of economic analysis, social surveys, scaling techniques, and others, but one can expect that the evaluation is likely to be a mixture of relatively hard and soft outputs. One must be on guard that the study team not limit its evaluation to what is easy to do, at the price of ignoring the crucial and difficult.

5. *The decision apparatus* relevant to the problem should be identified explicitly and the range of responsibilities of individual components defined as far as is feasible.

6. *Defining options and alternatives* open to the decision appa-

Table 14–1. NSF Completed and Current Technology Assessments

Agency	Title	Starting Date/ Duration	$ Amount
Completed Projects			
Stanford Research Institute Menlo Park, Calif.	Technology Assessment Study of Winter Orographic Snowpack Augmentation in the Upper Colorado River Basin	01/12/71 14 months	179,479
University of Oklahoma Norman, Okla.	A Technology Assessment of Offshore Oil Operations	07/01/71 28 months	288,600
Hittman Associates, Inc. Columbia, Md.	Evaluation of the Ecological, Resources and Socio-Economic Impacts of Advanced Automotive Propulsion Systems	07/01/71 34 months	326,129
Columbia University New York, N.Y.	The Automobile and the Regulation of its Impact on the Environment	09/01/71 24 months	310,000
Kansas State University Manhattan, Kan.	Political and Scientific Effectiveness in Nuclear Materials Control	06/01/70 24 months	254,000
Virginia Polytechnic Institute Blacksburg, Va.	Assessing the Implementation Aspects of Technology for the Disposal of Solid Waste	06/11/71 10 months	40,000
University of Michigan Ann Arbor, Mich.	Assessing the Impact of Remote Sensing of the Environment	06/01/72 15 months	141,500
Rensselaer Polytechnic Institute Troy, N.Y.	Technology Assessment for Cable Television	11/15/72 12 months	48,900

Current Projects

National Academy of Sciences Washington, D.C.	Assessment of Biomedical Technology	06/15/71 12 months	86,800
University of California Los Angeles, Calif.	A General Approach to Risk-Benefit Evaluation for Large Technological Systems	06/01/73 18 months	343,600
The Futures Group Glastonbury, Conn.	Technology Assessment of Geothermal Energy Resource Development	07/16/73 12 months	191,882
Arthur D. Little, Inc. Cambridge, Mass.	The Cashless-Checkless Society: An In-Depth Technology Assessment	09/28/73 18 months	220,706
Midwest Research Institute Kansas City, Mo.	A Technology Assessment of Biological Substitutes for Chemical Pesticides	01/02/74 12 months	113,700
Midwest Research Institute Kansas City, Mo.	An In-Depth Technology Assessment of Integrated Hog Farming	01/02/74 18 months	212,879
University of Minnesota Minneapolis, Minn.	Technology Assessment of Conversion from the English to Metric System in the United States	10/01/73 18 months	179,100
Haldi Associates, Inc. New York, N.Y.	Technology Assessment of Alternative Work Schedules	11/01/73 18 months	207,400
Braddock, Dunn and McDonald, Inc. Vienna, Va.	Technology Assessment of Alternative Strategies and Methods for Conserving Energy	11/15/73 18 months	238,638
Stanford Research Inst. Menlo Park, Calif.	A Technology Assessment of a Hydrogen Energy Economy	07/01/73 12 months	122,200
Arthur D. Little, Inc. Cambridge, Mass.	Technology Assessment of Terrestrial Solar Energy Resource Development	07/16/73 12 months	246,664
Stanford Research Inst. Menlo Park, Calif.	A Technology Assessment of Earthquake Prediction	06/01/74 12 months	283,500

ratus is something of a creative enterprise. One must attempt to innovate with regard to action options and alternatives and to relate to the apparatus at hand. The failure to do this often leads to vague, uncertain, or useless options and conclusions.

7. *Parties at interest with regard to a particular technology.* It is important to identify who, in fact or in principle, has a stake in the technology and in its possible impacts and consequences. This is important from an analytical view in helping to identify impacts and consequences. It is also important from a decision point of view by indicating who may influence the range and kind of action options which the decision maker has before him. The parties at interest after all are those who will or should have the strongest influence on the decision apparatus.

8. *It is important to recognize and analyze the impacts of variation on the technology under consideration.* However, there is another set of technological alternatives which must be considered and these are what one might call *macro alternatives.* For example, the various ways of removing oil from the north slope of Alaska would not comprise macro alternatives but rather systems alternatives. A macro alternative might be the development of geothermal resources, or the cutting down on the demand for energy.

9. *Exogenous factors should have a prominant place in any technology assessment.* By exogenous factors I mean those changes in society, its goals, its orientation, or its technology which could have an influence on the primary technology or factors interacting with it. These exogenous factors may vary anywhere from another new technology itself, to an economic upturn or downturn, change in the international situation or modification of legislation. Again, as with impacts, the identification of exogenous variables is a partially analytical and partially creative exercise. The shift in Arab oil policy is an example of the failure to anticipate a potential exogenous factor relating to energy policy and plans.

10. *One must examine all the above to come to some set of conclusions,* possibly to some recommendations. In general, it is best not to come to a precise and definitive single set of recommendations. A set of alternatives and an analysis of the consequences is most useful for the decision maker.

In general, a technology assessment cannot be conducted as a once-through exercise in filling out each of the categories mentioned above. Experience suggests that any particular assessment study should be done three times over: the first time to define and understand the problem, the second time to do it right, and the third to burnish the results, fill in the detail, and to bring the report to the best possible state within the available time, budget, and manpower. This recycling is important to keep in mind since many uninitiated schedule their work to do the study once and make no allowances for response, review, criticism, or their own learning process.

THE CONSEQUENCES OF TECHNOLOGY ASSESSMENT

The consequences of technology assessment are important to consider because the actions open to the decision maker may have a profound influence on the scope and depth of the examination and the very organization of a comprehensive technology assessment. Among the outcomes of a successful technology assessment may be the following:

1. Redefining the issue or restructuring the problem.
2. Modifying the project or technology to reduce disbenefits or to increase benefits.
3. Defining a monitoring or surveillance program with regard to the technology as it becomes operational.
4. Stimulating research and development, to define risks more reliably, forestall anticipated negative effects, identify alternative methods of achieving the goal of the technology, and identify feasible corrective measures for negative effects.
5. Identifying regulatory, legislative, or other control needs.
6. Identifying needed institutional changes or innovations.
7. Providing sound inputs to all parties at interest.
8. Preventing a technology from developing (an unusual but not impossible outcome).
9. Defining a set of intervention experiments or stepwise implementation of the technology.

TECHNOLOGY ASSESSMENT IN GOVERNMENT

Table 14-1 outlines the principal completed or ongoing technology assessment projects sponsored by the National Science Foundation. As the federal agency with lead responsibility in the field the principal goals of its program are:

1. To sponsor high-quality substantive assessments relevant to policy in order to demonstrate the value and practicality of the concept and to effect public policy in a useful way.
2. To promote the development of methodology and techniques for assessment.

3. To develop individual and institutional competence to undertake assessments for other agencies.

4. To support state-of-the-art review activities and to assist in organizing and consolidating this new field.

Needless to say, the full consequence of even the best technology assessment may be slow in developing, inasmuch as it is one input into the continuing policy process.

Other federal agencies, alert to the significance of technology assessment, have sponsored projects of direct interest to their missions. For example, the National Aeronautic and Space Administration (NASA) is currently sponsoring a technology assessment of intercity transportation and another one on fuels which could serve as alternatives to petroleum.

Several years ago, jointly with the Department of Transportation (DOT) it funded the Civil Aviation R&D Study which assessed a number of civil air systems. The Postal Service has sponsored a combination technological forecast and technology assessment. The Office of Coal Research has also been in the field.

DOT is about to receive the final report on a project stemming from the Congressional rejection of support for the SST. That study looks at the climatic implications of atmospheric pollution. The National Institutes of Health (NIH) has made some rudimentary movement into TA with studies of cardiac transplant and the artificial heart.

Municipal government has been indifferent to the concept, but several state agencies have become alert to TA. The State of Hawaii has sponsored an assessment of harvesting manganese modules from the ocean. The Western Interstate Nuclear Board has done an assessment of Project Plowshare. The Port of New York Authority sponsored an assessment by the National Academy of Sciences of a proposed extension of the Kennedy Jetport into Jamaica Bay. The West Virginia legislature sponsored an assessment of strip mining conducted by the Stanford Research Institute.

Of the international agencies, only the OECD (Organization for Economic Cooperation and Development) is significantly involved in technology assessment, although the UN and the EEC (European Economic Community) are taking the preliminary steps in this direction. Among foreign governments the Japanese are most conspicuously active. The Swedish, Canadian, British, and German governments directly or through associated institutions are active in technology assessment [23].

THE OFFICE OF TECHNOLOGY ASSESSMENT

Perhaps the most significant development in the United States in this field is the formation of the Office of Technology Assessment (OTA) established by the Technology Assessment Act of 1972 (Public Law 92—484). OTA's mission is to examine the many ways, expected and unexpected, in which technology affects people's lives. OTA consists of a non-partisan Congressional board, comprised of six Senators and six House members, which sets policy; a director, who also is a member of the board, a deputy director and other officers and employees, and a 12-member citizens advisory council, which includes as ex-officio members the Comptroller General of the United States and the Director of the Congressional Research Service of the Library of Congress (see Table 14—2 and Figure 14—1).

The chairmanship of OTA's Congressional board rotates between the Senate and the House in alternate Congresses. The first Board Chairman was Senator Edward M. Kennedy, Democrat of Massachusetts. The first Vice Chairman was Congressman Charles A. Mosher, Republican of Ohio.

The Director of OTA is Emilio Q. Daddario, a former Member of Congress who was instrumental in the development of the Technology Assessment Act. The Deputy Director is Daniel V. DeSimone, a former White House science policy assistant. The Chairman of the citizens advisory council is Dr. Harold Brown, President of the California Institute of Technology. The Vice Chairman is Dr. Edward Wenk, Jr., of the University of Washington.

Early in 1974, OTA began its work for Congress by launching assessments in six areas: food, energy, the oceanic materials resources, health, and urban mass transportation [4].

IMPLICATIONS OF TECHNOLOGY ASSESSMENT FOR BUSINESS

As part of the continuous tightly knit fabric of American society, business will be affected by technology assessment to its very core to the extent that government applies any new techniques of foresight, feedback, flexible control, policy analysis, and long-range planning. As a minimum, technology assessment will become another, and in my judgment, crucial long-range planning tool in business. The concept is central to the anticipation of new markets, future institutional and regulatory environments, and such elements of business as

Table 14-2.   Office of Technology Assessment

Emilio Q. Daddario, *Director, OFT*
Daniel De Simone, *Deputy Director, OFT*

Technology Assessment Board

Olin E. Teague, Texas, Chairman
Clifford P. Case, N.J., Vice Chairman

Edward M. Kennedy, Mass.	Morris K. Udall, Ariz.
Ernest F. Hollings, S.C.	George E. Brown, Jr., Calif.
Hubert H. Humphrey, Minn.	Charles A. Mosher, Ohio
Richard S. Schweiker, Pa.	Marvin L. Esch, Mich.
Ted Stevens, Alaska	Marjorie S. Holt, Md.

Emilio Q. Daddario

ADVISORY COUNCIL

Dr. Harold Brown, *Chairman*, President, California Institute of Technology.
Dr. Edward Wenk, Jr., *Vice Chairman*, Director, Program in the Social Management of Technology, University of Washington.
Mr. J. Fred Bucy, Executive Vice President, Texas Instruments, Inc.
Mrs. Hazel Henderson, author and lecturer on environmental and social issues, Princeton, New Jersey.
Mr. Lester S. Jayson, Director, Congressional Research Service, Library of Congress.
Mr. J.M. (Levi) Leathers, Executive Vice President, DOW Chemical Corporation.
Dr. John McAlister, Jr., Associate Professor, Department of Engineering-Economic Systems, Stanford University.
Dr. Eugene P. Odum, Director, Institute of Ecology, University of Georgia.
Dr. Frederick C. Robbins, Dean, Case Western Reserve University School of Medicine (Nobel Laureate).
Mr. Elmer B. Staats, Comptroller General of the United States.
Dr. Gilbert F. White, Director, Institute of Behavioral Science, University of Colorado.
Dr. Jerome B. Wiesner, President, Massachusetts Institute of Technology.

work force, resources, and public attitudes. Inasmuch as a large enterprise must have a long-time horizon (automotives, steel, resources, telecommunications, aircraft, chemicals, housing, transportation, marketing chains) they will need technology assessments of their own, for the very reason that government is using this tool, to set policy, plans, and programs.

By and large, industry to date has been indifferent, hostile, or confused about technology assessment. One study done by a management consulting firm revealed that large numbers of corporations claimed they were doing TA, but on closer examination virtually none was. They were confusing it with feasibility studies, market

Figure 14–1. Organizational Relationships of the Office of Technology Assessment

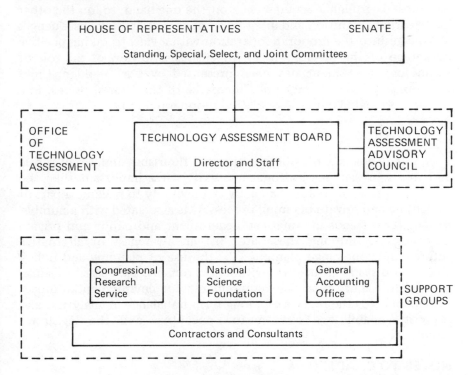

research, technological forecasting, product evaluation, and a variety of other well-established business tools.

On the other hand, many who have understood the goals and objectives of TA have highlighted a potential risk in excessive scrutiny and hyper-concern for potential risks in leading to a general ambience of technology arrestment. In general, I think one can anticipate that if any major bureaucracy with vast commitments of funds, labor, and investment in ongoing enterprises either willingly or unwillingly has its preconceptions and tacit assumptions laid bare and examined, trouble must result. One sees this to some extent in the environmental impact statement process, which attempts to get to the core of the environmental implications (a partial technology assessment) of many activities. I believe this turbulance is a necessary part of a transition process in which a systematic look to the future implications of technology will become integrated into earlier and earlier stages of public planning. As Ian Wilson of the General Electric Company has pointed out, any major corporation or large enterprise may exhibit a variety of responses to external and internal pressures for institutional change. These may vary from last ditch resistance and most begrudging acquiescence on the one hand, to, on the other hand, early recognition and integration of the inevitable consequences of change into the croporate operation with a view to taking positive advantage of the inevitabilities. An enthusiastic view of the role of technology assessment has been presented by Carl Madden, Chief Economist of the Chamber of Commerce of the United States, in a recent National Planning Association monograph [5].

CONCLUSION

Technology assessment, whether or not it flourishes under that rubric and in its present institutional context, is less important than the fact that it is a concept and an activity inevitably to become a part of the public and private planning process. It is associated with a number of long-term trends in American government and public and private bureaucracies. Among these are: (a) an awareness of alternative futures and long-range planning: (b) the use of planning and policy studies and study groups: (c) within government, the institutionalization of foresight, as in the requirements for environmental impact statements: (d) the redress of a long-term imbalance in analytical and support capabilities between the executive and the legislative branches.

NOTES TO CHAPTER 14

1. Vary Taylor Coates, *Technology and Public Policy: The Process of Technology Assessment in the Federal Government*, Program of Policy Studies in Science and Technology, The George Washington University, Washington, D. C., July 1972.

2. Marvin Cetron and Bodo Bartocha, eds., *Technology Assessment in a Dynamic Environment* (New York: Gordon and Breach, 1973). Contributors: American, European, and Japanese.

3. Francois Hetman, *Society and the Assessment of Technology: Premises, Concepts, Methodology, Experiments, Areas of Application* (Washington and Paris: 1974). Organization for Economic Cooperation & Development.

4. John F. Burby, "Science Report/Infant OTA Seeks to Alert Congress to Technological Impacts," *National Journal Reports* 5 (September 21, 1974): 1418–1429. Also: John F. Burby, "Technology Report/OTA Works to Produce Track Record with Six Major Projects," *National Journal Reports* 6 (September 28, 1974): 1454–1464.

5. Carl H. Madden, *Clash of Culture: Management in an Age of Changing Values*, Report No. 133 (Washington, D.C.: National Planning Association, October 1972).

ADDITIONAL READINGS

Technology Assessment, A Quarterly Journal of the International Society for Technology Assessment (ISTA) which contains general and in-depth articles on the methodology, organization, and activities involving technology assessment. The Society's Washington address is P.O. Box 4926, Cleveland Park Station, Washington, D. C. 20008.

Joseph F. Coates, "Technology Assessment," *McGraw-Hill Yearbook Science and Technology* (New York: McGraw-Hill Book Company, 1974).

Don E. Kash et at., *Energy Under the Oceans, A Technology Assessment of Outer Continental Shelf Oil and Gas Operations*, (Norman, Okla.: University of Oklahoma Press, 1973).

Leo W. Weisbecker, Stanford Research Institute, *The Impacts of Snow Enhancement: Technology Assessment of Winter Orographic Snowpack Augmentation in the Upper Colorado River Basin* (Norman, Okla.: University of Oklahoma Press, 1974).

Legislative Drafting Research Fund, Columbia University, New York, New York, *The Automobile and the Regulation of its Impact on the Environment* (Norman, Okla.: University of Oklahoma Press, in press).

A Technology Assessment of Geothermal Energy (Glastonbury, Conn.: The Futures Groups, in press).

Chapter 15

The Public's Role in
Technology Assessment

Byron Kennard*

In his new book, *Where the Wasteland Ends*, Theodore Rosak states, "Science is not merely another subject for discussion. It is *the* subject. It is the prime expression of the West's cultural uniqueness, the secret of our extraordinary dynamism, the keystone to technocratic politics, the curse and the gift we bring to history." It is now very clear that this "curse and gift" requires new and further examination, and technology assessment might just provide us that examination. (I, for one, am not sure yet whether or not it will, in fact, do so.)

I will not define technology assessment—for others have done so—except to point out that, although many persons who have been professionally or officially involved with the evolution of formal technology assessments approach it as a new academic "discipline," a look at how technology assessment (TA, for short) actually developed reveals its origins as a political tool, forged in the heat of public controversy and debate.

TECHNOLOGY ASSESSMENT—A
POLITICAL TOOL

Over the past decade, voluntary citizen advocacy groups concerned with the adverse impacts of technological developments have increasingly influenced decisions about science and technology. The influence of voluntary action was perhaps best symbolically represented

*Byron Kennard is Chairman of the National Council for the Public Assessment of Technology.

in the fight against the SST, but there are dozens of other, more significant examples of what amounts to a widespread civic revolt. Citizen opposition to highways, airports, power plants, and other forms of urban expansion has now flared up in virtually every American city. Ralph Nader and his colleagues have attracted vast public support for the reform of corporate and bureaucratic institutions producing or regulating consumer goods, including everything from food and water to clothing and shelter. Organizations devoted to racial and sexual equality have begun to zero in on inequities in the distribution of technology's benefits, such as jobs, income, and career opportunity. Industrial workers have grown restive about occupational health and safety and job satisfaction and security, all of which are increasingly determined by remote decisions about technology.

Some strong efforts have been made to portray the loud complaints about technology's ill effects as the work of a few know-nothing technophobes and hopelessly romantic fools, but several factors have prevented the derailment of citizen-initiated demands for more humane technology.

THE INTERESTS INVOLVED

First, it seems clear that the legitimate and vital interests of a great many people are involved: the young, the aged, the handicapped, the poor, minorities, women, workers, consumers, and taxpayers hardly constitute an insignificant portion of the population. (While all citizens fall into one or another of these categories, nevertheless, it is only a small percentage—those citizens who are also business executives, bankers, scientists, technologists, government policy makers, and foundation executives—that has a heavily weighted influence and special interest in the *generation* of technological change.)

Second, citizen leaders, whether representing large, well-organized voluntary groups or unorganized mass constituencies, have learned to promote their views and goals with growing skill and effectiveness. They have made vigorous and ingenious use of litigation, political pressure, public opinion, and community organization to force a perceptible widening of policy-making processes. Now, aided and abetted by expanding *pro bono publico* movements in various key disciplines—medicine, law, science, economics, design, accounting, etc.—citizen advocates are at last gaining access to the data, analysis, and professional representation they need to have any real chance of turning the scales.

Third, citizen groups in alliance with their new-found volunteer or

low-paid experts and technical advisors have now begun to consciously design and implement their own positive strategies for social
change. Far from being pipe-dreams, these strategies reflect experience tested under the harsh conditions of reality and are based upon
acute and highly accurate readings of social and political feasibility.
Thus, the frequently-heard charge that citizen organizations are
always against and never for something, is simply not true. The
citizen-initiated movement for clean air and water *has* already
created a multitude of new business opportunities and many thousands of jobs. The citizen-initiated movement for better public transportation *is* now creating a multitude of new business opportunities
and many thousands of jobs. The citizen-initiated demand for solar
energy *will* create a multitude of new business opportunities and
many thousands of jobs. And so on. Discerning and open-minded
leaders in govenment and in business and industry have begun to
detect the appeal of these and other citizen-generated technologies
that are socially desirable, environmentally benign, and economically
creative, at one and the same time.

Although the response of government and the private sector to the
thrusts of citizen organizations has been belated and small, one slight
indication that the message is getting through is the formal appearance of structured TA within established social institutions. TA, after
all, is supposed to anticipate and examine those very consequences of
technology that pop up unexpectedly to kill or harm people or to
destroy or threaten property or to otherwise provoke public opposition. Anyone acquainted with the sluggish pace with which technocratic bureaucracies greet change will doubt that true institutional
innovations, such as TA, will emerge or long survive without strong
outside pressure, in this case, from the public. (This is not to den-
igrate, however, the dedicated and sometimes brilliant work of some
scholars and theoreticians and of some political and business leaders
in giving substance and support to TA from within government, the
universities, and industry.)

It would be unfortunate if this incipient TA concept is given a
narrow definition and operated in a closed manner, for that would
deprive TA of its lusty origins. Decisions about technology nearly
always affect some group's health, jobs, taxes, housing, education, or
other vital concern. The constituencies thus impacted deserve a right
to some say in the decision.

If citizens are not consulted, their later opposition might flare up
and cause enormous problems for some proposed technology and
many headaches for administrators and other officials. Far more
important than possible delays and irritations, however, is the fact

that citizen groups often assert and defend ethical and social values which officials, experts, and technicans nearly always neglect. One may not always appreciate these interests and values, but they constitute very important social and political realities that any "objective" assessment would be foolish to ignore.

THE NEED FOR INSTITUTIONALIZED CHANNELS FOR TWO—WAY COMMUNICATION

If TA is to protect citizens and consumers impacted by technological change, there must be a vigorous institutionalized means of alerting and informing voluntary organizations of many kinds concerned with such impacts. These groups must be provided with lead time and *before-the-fact* information concerning new technologies and new applications of existing technologies. The National Council for the Public Assessment of Technology (NC/PAT), a new, non-profit organization, has been formed to meet these needs and to facilitate public participation in all aspects of technology assessment. NC/PAT, which views technology assessment as an essentially normative process involving issues of value preference and social choice, evolved over the last two years from an informal coalition of citizen and consumer groups concerned with such issues as housing, health, transportation, employment, social welfare, economic reform, energy, racial and sexual equality, consumer and environmental protection, etc. In addition, individuals involved in NC/PAT's formation include many highly qualified theorists and innovators in such fields as political science, economics, sociology, law, psychology, natural sciences, engineering, systems analysis, communications, design and planning, and technology forecasting. (See Appendix for a list of NC/PAT advisors.)

SOME GUIDELINES AS TO CONTENTS AND SCOPE

One of NC/PAT's first actions was to prepare criteria to aid governmental agencies in conducting technology assessment studies. These criteria were then widely circulated within the voluntary sector and endorsed by many groups and individual citizen leaders. Here is a summary of these criteria:

1. Assessment agencies should develop new concepts and methods for assessment, rather than merely gather new facts.

2. New ways of assessing private sector activities are needed, for these activities do much to shape our social and physical environment. The interactions between public and private sectors should also be assessed.

3. The agency should actively involve public participation in the assessment process by fully publicizing each assessment as soon as conceived and by full, quick, and easy disclosure of assessment data and reports. Active solicitation by the agency of citizen views on the technology being studied should be accomplished at a very early stage in the study's development.

4. Funds should be made available to enable non-profit citizen organizations to participate in assessment studies.

5. The agency should make use of an adversary approach to assessment when contrasting opinions exist. Separate assessments should be made by interests favoring the proposal as well as interests opposing the proposal. An assessment of the adverse effects of the technology should be carried out in detail. Views of experts and technicians outside the field of technology being assessed as well as views of competent generalists should also be included. Interaction should be promoted among those holding opposing viewpoints as well as those in the various disciplines involved.

6. Assessments should be comprehensive in scope and well defined in detail. The interdependence of related technologies should receive adequate consideration; to study one technology as isolated from all others can be misleading. The "do-nothing" alternative should always be considered.

7. Assessments should include a discussion of how economic costs and benefits are defined. Who will receive benefits and who will assume the risks and costs from a proposed technology? A discussion of the effect of the technology on minority and lower income groups should always be included.

8. Assumptions underlying assessment methods, and areas of ignorance or lack of data, should be clearly identified and discussed.

NC/PAT has been actively promoting these ideas and methods, and we have experienced some success in advancing these concepts. Should these criteria be adopted by the Congress and by the Executive Branch, the validity and usefulness of TA as a democratic planning tool may be established and, if so, TA's promise as a practical means of transition to a more rational and humane use of technology might be secured.

National Council for the Public Assessment of Technology

Advisors On Theory And Methodology

Professor Dean Abrahamson, Department of Public Affairs, University of Minnesota

Professor Kenneth J. Arrow, Department of Economics, Harvard University

Michael B. Barker, Administrator, Department of Environment and Design, The American Institute of Architects

Professor Philip L. Bereano, Program on Science, Technology and Society, Cornell University

Professor Kenneth Boulding, Department of Economics, University of Colorado

Robert Burco, Public Policy Analyst, Berkeley, California

Professor Charles Cicchetti, Department of Economics, University of Wisconsin

Theodore L. Cross, Editor, *Business and Society Review*, New York City

Nicholas DeMartino, Washington, D. C. Community Video Center

John Dixon, Washington, D. C.

Paul Bruce Dowling, Director, America the Beautiful Fund

Samuel Epstein, M.D., School of Medicine, Case Western Reserve University

Dr. Allen R. Ferguson, President, Public Interest Economics Center

Dr. Albert Fritsch, Co-Director, Center for Science in the Public Interest

Professor Edwin T. Haefele, Department of Political Science, University of Pennsylvania

Dr. Willis W. Harman, Director, Center for the Study of Social Policy, Stanford Research Institute

Dr. Robert Harris, Environmental Defense Fund

Dr. David B. Hertz, Chairman, Opportunity Funding Corporation, New York City

Karl Hess, Community Technology, Washington, D. C.

Barbara Marx Hubbard, Chairman, The Committee for the Future, Inc.

Dr. Michael Jacobson, Co-Director, Center for Science in the Public Interest

Gladys Kessler, Esq., Berlin, Roisman, Kessler & Kashdan

Professor Allen V. Kneese, Department of Economics, University of New Mexico

Morton Levy, Executive Director, National Association of Accountants for the Public Interest, San Francisco

Dr. Jennifer S. Macleod, former Chief Psychologist, Opinion Research Corporation, Princeton, New Jersey

Alice Tepper Marlin, Executive Director, Council on Economic Priorities, New York City

*Mary Ann Massey, Connecticut Department of Environmental Protection

Dr. John McHale, Director, Center for Integrative Studies, State University of New York

Professor Ian McHarg, Chairman of the Department of Landscape Architecture and Regional Planning, University of Pennsylvania

Dr. James McKenzie, Union of Concerned Scientists, Cambridge, Massachusetts

Dr. Margaret Mead, The American Museum of Natural History, New York City

Professor Jay S. Mendell, School of Technology, Florida International University, Miami

Dr. Xavier Mendoza, Director of Planning, East Los Angeles Community Union

Carl Nash, Washington, D. C.

Dr. Eugene P. Odum, Director, Institute of Ecology, University of Georgia

Professor Mancur Olson, Department of Economics, University of Maryland

*Dr. Glenn D. Paulson, Assistant Commissioner for Science, New Jersey Department of Environmental Protection, Trenton

Professor Charles R. Plott, Division of Humanities and Social Sciences, California Institute of Technology

*Member, NC/PAT Board of Directors

Richard Ridley, Architect/Planner, Washington, D. C.

Leonard Rodberg, Resident Fellow, Institute for Policy Studies

Ann Satterthwaite, A. I. P., Planning Consultant, Washington, D. C.

Professor Thomas R. Shworles, Assistant Research Professor of Medicine, George Washington University Medical School

Professor S. Prakash Sethi, School of Business Administration, University of California at Berkeley

Professor Robert Lewis Shayon, The Annenberg School of Communications, University of Pennsylvania

Professor Thomas Sheridan, School of Engineering, Massachusetts Institute of Technology

Theodora Sklover, Executive Director, Open Channel, Inc., New York City

Professor Ralph Smith, School of Communications, Howard University

Dr. Chandler H. Stevens, President, Participation Systems, Inc., Troy, New York

Martha Stuart, independent television producer, New York City

*Dr. James B. Sullivan, Co-Director, Center for Science in the Public Interest

Gene Sylvestre, Gene Sylvestre Associates, Minneapolis

Dr. Murray Turoff, Professor of Computer Science, New Jersey Institute of Technology

Stuart Umpleby, Engineering Research Laboratory, University of Illinois

Professor E. Robert Weiner, Department of Chemistry, University of Denver

Elliott J. Weiss, Executive Director, Investor Responsibility Research Center

Professor Carroll L. Wilson, Sloan School of Management, Massachusetts Institute of Technology

Advisors On Public Participation

John Adams, Executive Director, Natural Resources Defense Council

George Alderson, Director of Federal Affairs, The Wilderness Society

Barbara Reid Alexander, Bath, Maine

Herbert E. Alexander, Director, Citizens' Research Foundation, Princeton, New Jersey

Robert M. August, Concord, Massachusetts

Msgr. Geno Baroni, President, The National Center for Urban Ethnic Affairs

*Member, NC/PAT Board of Directors

Nancy Bartlit, New Mexico Citizens for Clean Air and Water, Los Alamos

Alice Beeman, Executive Director, American Association of University Women

Marcey Benstock, Clean Air Campaign, Inc., New York City

Walter J. Bierwagen, Director of Public Affairs, Amalgamated Transit Union, AFL–CIO

Mary Jane Boren, Secretary, North Carolina Conservation Council

Joseph Browder, Executive Vice President, Environmental Policy Center

Rod Cameron, Environmental Defense Fund

Robert J. Casey, News Director, National Association of Railroad Passengers

Wilson Clark, Energy Consultant, Washington, D. C.

Joan Claybrook, Director, Congress Watch

Lenore Cooley, Project Coordinator, Professionals in the Public Interest

Bert De Leeuw, Coordinator, Movement for Economic Justice

Robert Dennis, Executive Director, Zero Population Growth

Clarence Ditlow, Associate, Public Interest Research Group

Ira Einhorn, Poet, Philadelphia, Pennsylvania

Brock Evans, Director, Washington Office, Sierra Club

Carol Foreman, Executive Director, Consumer Federation of America

John Hampton, Executive Director, National Tenants Organization

Virginia Harbin, Program Director, The Georgia Conservancy, Inc.

Peter Harnik, Coordinator, Environmental Action

Ellen Stern Harris, Council for Planning and Conservation, Beverly Hills, California

Barbara Heller, Energy Policy Staff, Environmental Policy Center

Hazel Henderson, author and lecturer on environmental and social issues, Princeton, New Jersey

Nancy Ignatius, Immediate Past President, Concern, Inc.

Marcey Jaskulski, President, Milwaukee River Restoration Council, Hales Corners, Wisconsin

Douglas Kirkpatrick, Executive Director, National Intervenors

Grover C. Little, Southeast Representative, Izaak Walton League of America, West Virginia

Sam Love, Associate Director, Environmental Action Foundation

Davitt MacAteer, Solicitor for Safety Affairs, United Mine Workers

Jeanne Malchon, Chairman of the Florida Health Planning Council

Anthony Mazzocchi, Legislative Director, Oil, Chemical & Atomic Workers International Union, AFL–CIO

Alan McGowan, President, Scientists' Institute for Public Information

Mary Moss, WAVE–TV, Louisville, Kentucky

*Andrew Mott, Vice President, Center for Community Change

Albert Nunez Jr., Program Coordinator, Environmental Action of Colorado, Denver

David Paris, Washington, D. C. Ecology Center

Rafe Pomerance, Legislative Coordinator, National Clean Air Coalition

*Carl Pope, California Representative, League of Conservation Voters

Clem Rastatter, Senior Associate, Conservation Foundation

Wade Rathke, Chief Organizer, Arkansas Community Organization for Reform Now

Lola Redford, Consumer Action Now, New York City

Dr. Robert N. Rickles, Executive Director, Institute for Public Transportation, New York City

Angela Rooney, Executive Secretary, National Coalition on the Transportation Crisis

Ann Roosevelt, Legislative Director, Friends of the Earth

Donald K. Ross, Director, New York Public Interest Research Group, Inc.

*Peter Schuck, Director, Washington, D. C. Office, Consumers Union

Judith Senderowitz, Director of Organization Liaison Division, Population Institute

Marjorie Sharpe, Member, Board of Directors, Association of Junior Leagues, Chicago

John J. Sheehan, Legislative Director, United Steelworkers of America, AFL–CIO

Robert G. Smith, Executive Director, District of Columbia Lung Association

Shelby E. Southard, Director of Public Affairs, The Cooperative League of the USA, Washington, D. C.

Dr. Elvis Stahr, President, National Audubon Society

Stewart L. Udall, Chairman of the Board, Overview, Inc.

J. Ross Vincent, Director, Ecology Center of Louisiana

Tracy Westen, Director, Public Communications, Inc., Los Angeles

Josh C. Whetzel, Jr., President, Western Pennsylvania Conservancy, Pittsburgh

Char White, Chairman, Board of Directors, Texas Environmental Coalition

Barbara J. Williams, Executive Director, Congressional Black Caucus

Larry Williams, Executive Director, Oregon Environmental Council

John S. Winder, Jr., Esq., Director, Environmental Impact Assessment Project, The Institute of Ecology

*Member, NC/PAT Board of Directors

Part 6

Developing Coefficients for Measuring Economic/Ecological Efficiency

"You can't mix apples and pears" goes an old saying referring, obviously, to the taste differences between these
fruits. Strictly speaking, one cannot even add apples to
apples and count on a homogeneous basketful—unless one first sep-
arates the "Delicious" from the "McIntosh," and still other kinds.
The Greek philosopher who argued that no one could step into the
same river twice (what with the change of water and sediment, etc.,
due to the constant flow) was easily outdone at his own reasoning
by the other who held that no one could step into the "same" river
even once!

Yet, for all practical purposes, we tend to think in broad categories: we consider river or even fresh-water bathing as against ocean-
bathing; most of us are quite willing to substitute pears for apples,
and vice versa, or to consume some other fruit in season in place of
either of them. Two, probably most important, considerations for
our willingness to do so will be availability and price. So it is, essentially, a matter of tradeoffs between broadly comparable commodities or enjoyments.

Not so, however, when the choice lies between alternatives that
are difficult to compare, like mechanical conveniences or personal
comforts on the one hand, and clean air or attractive surroundings,
on the other. A recent cartoon showing two men on their way to
work on a busy, congested and presumably noisy and smelly city
street illustrates the predicament. Says one to the other: "The
trouble is that the moment the standard of living goes up, the quality
of life goes down!" The question is: how do we determine, measure,

and evaluate the tradeoffs? How can we be sure that the terms of
trade have to be necessarily those we encounter at a given time? And
how far can we actually go in either direction in our search for the
best of all possible worlds?

The three chapters in this final topical part of the book tackle
these several problems. Their authors start from very different vant-
age points and bring special knowledge to bear deriving in each case
from a different discipline or station in life.

Henry Peskin, an economist, attempts to adapt our national economic accounts and our established practices with regard to what we
include in, and exclude from these, respectively, in such a way as to
have them reflect environmental inputs to our social product. He is
careful to disavow any exhaustive intent in this regard. He is being
selective about what environmental phenomena are to be appraised
in this manner. Conversely, he is ambitious in allocating in broad
categories (geographically by Census areas, by economic sector, by
broadly defined income class, and by race) both the costs incurred
and the benefits derived from the unpaid use of environmental resources, notably air, in our economic processes. He is innovative in
that he attempts to isolate and quantify the negative inputs in the
form of pollution generated by nature itself.

Cautioning against firm conclusions to be drawn from very tentative estimates, Peskin no more than mentions *possible* doubts about
the cost effectiveness of our environmental policies. On the other
hand, he strongly suggests that an area so important in terms of
public concern and of public spending ought to rate more generous
research allocations from public funds in advance of any further government commitment to environmental controls.

Chester Kylstra, coming from the field of nuclear engineering,
attempts a grand feat, indeed, viz., to get away from dollar measures
altogether and substitute energy units as the common denominator
and measuring rod of both man's activities and nature's. Equally
interesting and important is his explanation of the changing characteristics of a (sub) system's survival optimizing behavior as an emana-
tion of the constraints deriving from the next higher system that
enfolds it. Kylstra's overall conclusions are best told in his own
words:

> If left alone, systems will optimize themselves to maximize the useful
> work possible under externally imposed constraints. If abundant energy is
> available, then rapid growth, low efficiencies are required to maximize
> power and to outcompete and outsurvive other systems. If energy is lim-
> ited, then survival requires minimizing waste, leading to high efficiencies

and complex inter-relationships between specialists or subsystems, to extract every bit of useful work out of the available energy. Unfortunately, it is possible to suffer traumatic, violent oscillations as a system is changing over from unlimited to limited energy rather than experiencing a smooth transition. The actual path followed by the system is under the control of the decision makers, whereas the eventual state reached by the system may not be.

The best system for man requires that both man's activities and other natural systems be considered as one system, so that balanced decisions can be made to maximize the survival of the combined system. Considering only man's activities results in a poorer economic condition for man than if the combined system is considered.

Concrete examples, supported by charts and tables, help the reader—even if he is a stranger to the physical and engineering sciences—to follow the writer in the development and demonstration of his all-inclusive energy-based accounting scheme.

Levi Leathers' paper represents a giant corporation's top manager's no-nonsense view concerning the practical prerequisites for, and limits on, any meaningful imposition of social responsibilities upon business. Interestingly, his "hard-line" approach is more explicit in all its brevity, about some social-ecology aspects, i.e., the grave potential for our social habitat of drastic economic measures, e.g., relocation of production facilities, than either of the other two economic-ecological conversion analyses.

✳ *Chapter 16*

Accounting for the Environment:
A Progress Report*

*Henry M. Peskin***

This chapter discusses a relatively recent research effort to measure and place in a national accounts framework the services of environmental assets such as air, water, and to a certain extent, land. This activity is part of a major project under way at the National Bureau of Economic Research.

The concern of this project is suggested by its title: "The Measurement of Economic and Social Performance." It is a concern shared by many who are searching for "social indicators" more meaningful than conventional indicators such as the Gross National Product (GNP) or the unemployment rate. However, the research effort is more modest in its objectives and more conservative in its approach than is, perhaps, suggested by the title.

The objectives are modest in that no attempt is being made to measure all aspects of economic and social performance. In the social sphere, we have no plans to measure, for example, changes in racial discrimination or the level of morality in government. Similarly, in the economic sphere, we will overlook the illegal gambling industry even though its balance sheet may dwarf many of the industries we shall consider. It is not that these areas of social activity are not worth measuring. It is only that we feel more confident if we direct our attention toward those areas for which we have analytical

*This paper has appeared in part in *Social Indicators* and in part in *The Distribution of Economic Well-Being*, ed. by F.R. Juster, NBER, 1976.

**Henry M. Peskin is Senior Research Associate at the National Bureau of Economic Research, and Fellow Resources for the Future. This chapter has not been subjected to the NBER review procedure. The views therein are the author's and not necessarily those of the National Bureau.

competence and for which we feel the data limitations are not overwhelming.

The approach is conservative in that it largely builds on our existing system of national economic accounts and the associated data base. The reason for this conservative approach, perhaps unsettling to some, considering the large amount of criticism directed against the GNP as a social indicator, is the belief that the accounting structure provides a framework that serves to discipline the data collection effort. It is conceivable that the project could have consisted of a large number of non-integrated efforts to measure activities that previously have not been measured. Or as another alternative, the project could have consisted of an effort to assemble in a single volume various sets of data in existence that are thought to be in some way useful as social indicators.

Yet we felt that these alternatives would probably cause us to flounder and eventually drown in a sea of numbers. There are simply too many things that could be measured and, indeed, too many things that have been measured. What is needed is a framework that sets data collection priorities, that reveals significant data omissions, and that provides useful and digestible summary statistics. It is not surprising that those of us affiliated with the NBER—the organization that fathered the national accounts—should look to the national accounting system as the appropriate framework.

Our use of the national accounts as a starting point has an additional justification. We should not overlook the fact that in spite of its well-known weaknesses, the accounts already measure activities, which constitute a large portion of what determines social well-being. Consumption, production, government activity are important elements of welfare even though the national accountant—as suggested recently by defenders of the GNP—may not have had any intentions of measuring these factors with a welfare objective in mind. Rather than ignore the role of the national accounts as a social indicator (or as a source of social indicators), we are focusing instead on two of its principal weaknesses: (a) its neglect of certain non-marketed services and (b) its neglect of distributional considerations.

The NBER project attacks these two weaknesses with two distinct but related research approaches. One group of researchers (Richard and Nancy Ruggles, Milton Moss, Thomas Juster, Robert Lipsey, Michael Gort, and John Quigley) is developing micro-data sets at the household, firm, and government level. One objective of their work is to provide a description of the economic and social behavior of these sectors in enough dissaggregated detail to allow for the analysis of welfare distributions. In addition, the micro-data sets provide inputs for a second group of researchers (John Kendrick, Robert Eisner, and myself) who are attempting to supplement the usual national economic accounts with imputations for non-marketed (but valuable) services such as the services of housewives (and other family members), volunteers, and certain forms of capital such as consumer durables and environmental assets. Certain non-marketed "costs" such as the time spent in commuting, the time spent in school by persons of working age, and the pollution damage that usually accompanies the consumption of environmental services will also be imputed. In addition, alternative treatments of currently accounted-for activities may be investigated in order to provide for more meaningful measures. Eisner, for example, is proposing less arbitrary measures of capital depreciation and alternative treatments of capital gains.

Eventually these two lines of research will be integrated in order that the micro-data sets and the macro accounts can be linked in a consistent manner. The responsibility for this coordination, as well as for the direction of the project in general, falls primarily on the shoulders of Richard and Nancy Ruggles.

NATIONAL ACCOUNTING AND THE ENVIRONMENT

The objective of the "National Accounting and the Environment" sub-project is to impute money values to two types of input and output flows that arise when any sector of the economy chooses to employ the services of the environment. When, for example, a producer discharges wastes into a river, he is in fact using the river's disposal services as a valuable input to his production process. He may not immediately recognize these services as productive inputs, but that is only because he usually enjoys them gratis. We assume that if these services were *not* valuable, in the sense that they did not contribute to profit maximization, he eventually would not see any need to continue dumping his wastes. Indeed, if everyone's uses of the disposal or other services of the environment were similarly "unproductive," environmental policy would be unnecessary.

In principle—the principle in question being derived from the theory of cost-benefit analysis—we attempt to set the value of this input flow equal to the least cost society would bear were the producer denied the use of the environmental service. Here, the concept of cost is far broader than the word usually conveys in common parlance. By "cost" we mean all losses suffered by society as the producer is denied access to the environmental asset and thus is forced to substitute other valuable resources for the free environmental services he had been receiving. The social cost of this resource shift may be reflected in the costs of pollution control equipment, changes in production process, reductions in the level of production (and corresponding reductions in the supply of goods), alterations in product characteristics, or a combination of all these factors.

In practice, however, we have to rely on cost data gathered by others, and these data may not reflect a cost concept as broad as the theory requires. For example, a large portion of our cost data is drawn from documents of the Environmental Protection Agency (EPA), which were developed to obtain the costs of meeting EPA standards. Unfortunately, many of these standards are expressed in terms of specific pollution control technologies, which may not be the least-cost strategy for all producers. Furthermore, the cost data are often developed by engineers who either do not consider product alteration as an acceptable strategy or, if they do, fail to account for any economic losses accompanying such alterations.

In addition to the input services the producer enjoys as he discharges his wastes and thus uses the disposal services of the river, he also creates an output flow equal to the damage or dis-benefit these discharges inflict on other sectors of the economy—including, of course, households. In principle, we would like to value this flow according to how much the damaged parties would be willing to pay in order to avoid these damages. However, in practice we have to use data on environmental damages that, like the cost data, have been developed by others. Unfortunately, the coverage and quality of these estimates are far worse than the coverage and quality of the available cost estimates. This fact is appreciated by EPA and probably explains why environmental damage estimates in dollar terms have not appeared in official EPA documents for the past several years [1].

Despite these data limitations, we are nonetheless attempting to develop flow accounts for all 2-digit SIC sectors including Governments and Households. In addition, because of its significant contribution to the generation of pollutants, we are also including "Nature" as a sector.

One might wonder why we are proceeding with empirical implementation of the accounts with admittedly poor data. Of course, as we have already noted, the accounts framework helps identify data omissions and priorities. Thus putting the available data in this framework gives us a basis of deciding just how poor various pieces of data are.

In addition there is, perhaps, a more tangible benefit from the implementation effort. In order to make our account imputations in 2-digit SIC detail, it has been necessary to assemble data on emissions, pollution control technology, and on costs. The data we have gathered on these factors are often far more comprehensive and detailed than similar data available from EPA and other published sources. This information, while ancillary to our principal objective, has provided the basis for several interesting investigations, one of which is described below.

SOME PROJECT FINDINGS

First, however, I shall report on some of our preliminary accounting of the values of environmental asset services (the "inputs") and related damages (the "outputs"). So far, we have not completed sector-by-sector estimates of costs and damages for water pollution. Therefore, the data in Table 16–1 refer only to the value of air as a disposal medium and the values of the associated damages from air pollution. In addition, Table 16–1 shows the relative contribution of the various sectors to the national totals of these input and output values.

The damage estimates were based on a procedure that distributed published estimates of national damages by pollutant according to the sector's generation of pollutants, the location of the sector's establishments, and the location's population density.

The cost estimates do not refer to the cost facing a sector were it denied total access to the air as a disposal medium, but only to the cost associated with the pollution reduction necessary to assure no damage according to EPA standards. Presumably, even if all sectors met EPA standards, there still would be some use of the air for disposal purposes. Indeed, the total cost of complete denial to the air would be astronomical.*

Table 16–1 shows clearly that the sector enjoying the largest input services from the air is Households. In 1968 this sector enjoyed input services from the air greatly in excess of the damages it caused. This is largely explained by the demands placed on the environment from the automobile and homeheating. Even if all the damages caused by Households were inflicted on Households (which is, for the most part, the case), compliance with the 1977 EPA standards (greatly reducing the discharge of residuals from autos and home heating) would not "pay." The $4 billion relief from damages would be more than offset by an $11 billion loss of disposal services.

*This is one reason why, for the final version of the accounts, we will not calculate the total input value and damages associated with the level of environmental asset used (as in the case of Table 16–1), but rather a marginal valuation, e.g., the number of units of asset service used times the value of the marginal unit. A procedure for estimating marginal valuations given the total input or output value of a finite change in asset use has been developed.

Table 16–1. Air Pollution Damage and Value of Disposal Service (1968), Preliminary Estimates *(Millions of 1970 Dollars)*

	Sector	Damage	% of Total Damage	Annual Cost to Meet EPA Standards[a]	% of Total Control Cost
01	Agriculture	241	1.2	1,137[b]	5.4
07	Agricultural services	202	1.0	107	0.5
08	Forestry	835	4.1	160[b]	0.8
10	Metal mining	15	0.1	19[b]	0.1
11–12	Coal mining	92	0.4	161	0.8
13	Oil & gas drilling	25	0.1	8	—
14	Nonmetal mining	13	0.1	7	—
15–17	Construction	95	0.5	169[c]	0.8
19	Ordnance	3	—[d]	3	—
20	Food products	133	0.7	55	0.3
21	Tobacco products	4	—	2	—
22	Textiles	56	0.3	19	0.1
23	Apparel	11	0.1	2	—
24	Wood products	36	0.2	63	0.3
25	Furniture	10	—	3	—
26	Pulp & paper	274	1.4	90	0.4
27	Printing, publishing	7	—	2	—
28	Chemicals	1,009	5.0	199	0.9
29	Petroleum products	1,474	7.3	207	1.0
30	Rubber products	88	0.4	11	0.1
31	Leather products	15	0.1	6	—
32	Stone, clay, glass	1,072	5.3	254	1.2
33	Primary metals	2,377	11.8	858	4.1
34	Fabricated metals	61	0.3	32	0.2
35	Machinery except electrical	55	0.3	16	0.1
36	Electrical machinery	45	0.2	10	—
37	Transportation equipment	96	0.5	27	0.1
38	Instruments	16	0.1	3	—
39	Miscellaneous manufacturing	21	0.1	3	—
40	Railroads	146	0.7	66[b]	0.3

41	Local & suburban transit	139	0.7	165[b]	0.8
42	Motor freight	121	0.6	133[c]	0.6
44	Water transportation	198	1.0	49[b]	0.2
45	Air transportation	42	0.2	274[b]	1.3
46	Pipelines	16	0.1	34	0.2
49	Utilities	4,596	22.8	1,634	7.7
55	Gas stations	79	0.4	540[b]	2.6
50–81	Trades and services	894	4.4	1,405[c]	6.7
82	Education	18	0.1	67[c]	0.3
88	Households	4,098	20.3	10,800[c]	51.2
91–93	Governments	153	0.8	2,303[c]	10.9
	Natural	1,266	6.3	NA	NA
	Total	20,147	100.0	21,103	100.0

Note: N.A. = not applicable.

[a]The primary data source was *The Economics of Clean Air*, Annual Report of the Administrator of the Environmental Protection Agency, March 1972. Many EPA cost numbers have since been revised upward. Many other sources (e.g., journal articles, contractors' reports, industry studies, etc.) were used to obtain the two-digit SIC breakdowns. Complete documentation on these sources and estimating methods is available from the project investigators.

EPA does not provide estimates of the costs to meet standards for fuel combustion from stationary sources broken down by sector. Therefore, aggregate EPA cost estimates are distributed by estimated fuel usage. EPA cost estimates, reflecting emission levels in 1977–1978, were adjusted to the 1968 base year by assuming a fixed proportion between a sector's activity level and its emissions.

[b]EPA standards not established. Cost estimates are based on industry estimates of clean-up costs and EPA contractors' reports.

[c]Estimate assumes all gasoline vehicles in 1968 are fitted with pollution control equipment necessary to meet 1977 standards.

[d]Less than 0.1 percent.

Table 16-1 also shows that there is an approximate balance between the total value of disposal services enjoyed and the total damages caused by the economy (even though there is a lack of balance sector by sector). If these numbers could be taken seriously (admittedly a difficult feat), this balance implies that a "cleanup" of the air would have been of neutral benefit to the economy as a whole.* Of course the social cost of such a policy would be borne by some sectors far more than others. Furthermore, each sector's contribution of this cost would not, in general, be balanced by the resulting reduction in damage.

We note finally that about $1.2 billion in damage is due to natural generation of pollutants. Natural pollutants, especially particulates, account for a major portion of total generation. While this fact is well established in the technical literature, to our knowledge no one has attempted previously to measure nature's relative and absolute contribution to the nation's total pollution damage.

I shall now briefly report on an investigation that relied on data that were ancillary to our principal accounting objective. This study is of interest because it also relied on a micro-data set (the U.S. Census Public Use Sample) and serves to illustrate how micro-data development and national accounts development can serve common research goals.

The purpose of this study was to estimate the distributional implications of air pollution damage—the value of damage to persons according to where they reside, according to their income class, and according to their race. The formula shown was implemented with data from the Public Use Sample and from our own data bank of emissions by economic sector.

The following tables are from an earlier paper co-authored by the writer [2]. Here I shall briefly mention some of the highlights. Table 16-2 shows some per capita damages for selected SMSA's[†] and for groups of counties that are not designated as SMSA's. The key feature of this table is the large variation in per capita damages depending on where one resides. In fact, the 20 "worst" SMSA's account for 58 percent of national damage, even though they contain only 25 percent of the U.S. population. Table 16-3, which displays total damage by census regions, also suggests wide regional variation and

---

*This result does *not* indicate that there is an optimal utilization of the disposal services. However, if these valuations were the *marginal* valuations discussed in the previous footnote, the balance of the input and output total would indicate optimality. This is another reason for computing the marginal valuations.

[†]SMSA is the abbreviation used by the Census Bureau for standard metropolitan statistical areas.

Table 16-2. Ranking of Selected SMSA's and Non-SMSA's by Per Capita Damage in Dollars

20 "Worst" SMSA's		20 "Best" SMSA's		20 "Best" Non-SMSA's	
1. Jersey City, N.J.	$1,435.40	1. Binghamton, N.Y.-Pa.	$15.21	1. Montana	$1.05
2. New York City, N.Y.	504.16	2. Bakersfield, Calif.	16.75	2. W.N. Dak.	1.97
3. Erie, Pa.	489.75	3. Santa Barbara, Calif.	17.98	3. NW Minn.-E.N. Dak.	3.15
4. Newark, N.J.	347.68	4. San Bernardino, Calif.	19.36	4. N Kan.	3.34
5. Paterson-Clifton, N.J.	320.15	5. Duluth, Minn.-Wisc.	20.88	5. NW Tex.	3.40
6. Detroit, Mich.	287.08	6. W. Palm Beach, Fla.	22.54	6. EC Calif.	3.95
7. Philadelphia, Pa.	255.37	7. Salines Monterey-Calif.	22.90	7. SE S. Dak.-SE Minn.	4.15
8. Chicago, Ill.	255.11	8. Utica-Rome, N.Y.	24.68	8. SW Tex.	4.16
9. Cleveland, Ohio	254.56	9. Flint, Mich.	24.77	9. SE Neb.	4.56
10. Providence, R.I.	238.16	10. Sacramento, Calif.	25.05	10. SE Col.	4.63
11. Gary-Hammond, Ind.	234.96	11. Fresno, Calif.	27.11	11. S. Dak.	4.84
12. Salt Lake City, Utah	220.63	12. Oklahoma City, Okla.	27.71	12. S. Tex.	5.42
13. Pittsburgh, Pa.	220.12	13. Tucson, Ariz.	27.72	13. NW Fla.	6.67
14. Los Angeles, Calif.	208.70	14. Austin, Tex.	29.54	14. SC Tex.	6.88
15. New Haven, Conn.	208.10	15. Rochester, N.Y.	29.61	15. SW Okla.-NC Tex.	7.86
16. Milwaukee, Wisc.	207.38	16. Stockton, Calif.	30.57	16. W Ga.-E Ala.	7.95
17. Boston, Mass.	185.82	17. Las Vegas, Nev.	30.93	17. NE Col.	8.00
18. Beaumont-Orange, Tex.	182.57	18. Greenville, S.C.	31.74	18. Alaska	8.78
19. Bridgeport, Conn.	170.36	19. Honolulu, Ha.	32.46	19. E Iowa-SW Wisc.	8.82
20. Trenton, N.J.	163.81	20. San Diego, Calif.	32.81	20. NW Ohio	8.86

shows the importance of Nature as a polluter especially in more rural areas of the nation.

Damages by income class are shown in Table 16—4. The most notable aspect of this table is the suggestion that, on the average, the rich suffer more absolute damage than the poor. This result, which may seem surprising, is most likely due to the fact that our study covered persons living in relatively clean rural areas (as well as persons living in urban areas) and that incomes in these rural areas are among the lowest in the nation. Unfortunately, we were unable to investigate this question within an urbanized area since our data base forced us to assume uniform air qualities throughout each SMSA.

Finally, Table 16—5 shows that non-whites suffer greater absolute damage than whites, a result which is not inconsistent with the results in Table 16—4. It simply reflects the fact that a disproportionate percentage of non-whites live in urbanized areas.

Table 16—3.   Total Pollution Damage (in Millions of Dollars) to Regions by Source

Region	*1* *Total*	*2* *Industry*	*3* *Household*	*4* *Nature*
New England	1,051.4	821.7	217.9	11.9
Middle Atlantic	10,209.6	7,379.2	2,794.7	35.6
South Atlantic	1,744.9	1,277.7	275.9	191.2
East South Central	687.7	495.8	47.0	144.9
West South Central	751.2	532.3	85.4	133.5
East North Central	3,210.9	2,598.2	409.8	202.8
West North Central	657.3	394.2	54.7	208.5
Mountain States	364.2	192.8	25.0	146.3
Pacific States	1,420.1	1,057.9	174.1	188.2
Total[a]	20.097.2	14,749.7	4,084.7	1,262.8

[a] Less Alaska and Hawaii (accounting for approximately $27 million of damage).

Table 16—4.   Mean Per Capita Pollution Damage (in Dollars) Incurred by Income Class

Income Class	Mean Pollution Damage	Percent of Persons in Income Class
$1,000 or less	76.96	19.0
$1,001–$3,000	92.98	47.7
$3,001–$5,000	113.42	20.0
$5,001–$7,000	128.68	7.2
$7,001–$10,000	137.32	4.0
$10,001–$15,000	128.12	0.8
$15,000 and above	146.29	1.2
Overall	99.29	100.00

Table 16–5. Mean Per Capita Pollution Damage (in Dollars) Incurred by Whites and Non-Whites

Race	Mean Pollution Damage	Mean Income	Percent of Persons
Whites	96.55	3,080.97	88.6
Non-whites	121.61	1,823.22	11.4
Total	99.29	2,937.62	100.00

POLICY AND RESEARCH IMPLICATIONS

What do the above tables and supporting analyses say about environmental policy? The answer to this question depends on how much faith one is willing to place in admittedly poor data. Some may feel that the numbers are so bad that they should be treated as purely hypothetical and that they should have no more policy implications than other sets of equally "arbitrary" numbers.

On the other hand, if one believes that policymakers should use such numbers, regardless of their poor quality, since they are the best available (which, I believe, is the case), then our data have a lot of implications about policy—mostly negative. This is especially true of Table 16–1. To those with appetites sufficient to digest some very raw statistics, the message of Table 16–1 is clear: environmental policy may not pay. Indeed, the enemies of EPA may find these numbers quite tasty.*

My attitude toward the data falls somewhere between these two extreme positions. I feel the absolute values of the estimates are too imprecise to draw any firm conclusions about whether the present policies designed to reduce air pollution are worth their social cost. Yet, I doubt that the *relative* magnitudes of the numbers—especially where these relative magnitudes are large—will change very much as our data are refined. The apparent differences in the severity of air pollution damages between, say, Jersey City, New Jersey, and Bakersfield, California, will most likely remain regardless of how refined the data become. A policy conclusion based on these differences—for example, that uniform national emission standards are inappropriate—will similarly be unaltered.

---

*It should be emphasized that the "environmental policy" referred to is the assumed EPA policy behind the numbers in Table 16–1. These policies dictate a given incremental reduction in pollution. One could suggest other policies that would dictate a different reduction and it could be that the benefits of these alternatives would exceed their costs. Since Table 16–1 does not compare *marginal* benefits and costs, it indicates nothing about these possible alternatives.

Regardless of one's judgment about the data—whether one takes an extreme position or not—the fact remains that the data are very poor. Policies involving millions of dollars in tangible and intangible social costs are being acted upon without a substantial factual base. Of course, given the *possibility* that dire consequences may result in the absence of some effort to control our use of the environment, acting in the absence of hard information may be justified.

Yet a need for positive action in the name of prudence should not free the policymaker from devoting a significant portion of resources toward the development of information—even if this information should show that earlier policies were unjustified. Considering the large social costs involved, to do otherwise is, in my view, irresponsible.

The U.S. government plans to spend in fiscal year 1976 about $7 billion on environmental programs, of which $1.3 billion will be directed toward outlays for research and development. These figures alone suggest that the government is acting quite responsibly in its allocations of resources for the development of information. However, upon closer inspection, the picture is not as impressive. Of the $1.3 billion, will be spent on the development of control technology. Such an outlay *assumes*, rightly or wrongly, the validity of control in the first place without providing significant information on the costs and benefits of control.

Thus only $0.6 billion remains for the development of the type of data described in this chapter. Of this figure, over half is being directed toward descriptive studies of natural environments, including weather forecasting research. As a result, the government plans to spend less than $0.4 billion on the development of information necessary to establish whether the full environmental outlay of $7 billion is worth it.*

While $240 million may seem quite generous, it must cover the costs of studying the physical and health impacts of changes in environmental quality (as well as the analyses necessary to convert these impacts into common dollar terms) and the costs of technical, engineering, and economic analyses necessary to determine the full opportunity costs of control strategies. This is a tall order. Considering the importance of this research effort and the implications that the research might have regarding a $7 billion budget, a review of spending priorities is in order. It should not be considered self-evident that the government's environmental budget outlays and their allocation are in the best public interest.

*All these figures are from the *Special Analyses of the Budget of the United States Government, Fiscal Year 1976* (Washington, D.C.: U.S. Government Printing Office), pp. 268–281.

NOTES TO CHAPTER 16

1. Estimates have appeared in unofficial EPA research reports, notably Thomas E. Waddell, *The Economic Damages of Air Pollution*, EPA–600/5–74–012, May 1974.

2. L.P. Gianessi, H.M. Peskin, and E. Wolff, "The Distributional Implications of National Air Pollution Damage Estimates," paper prepared for the Conference on Research in Income and Wealth, on the *Distribution of Economic Well-Being*, at the University of Michigan, May 15–17, 1974.

3. All these figures are from the *Special Analyses of the Budget of the United States Government, Fiscal Year 1975* (Washington, D.C.: U.S. Government Printing Office), pp. 235–249.

4. L.R. Babock and M.L. Nagda, "Cost Effectiveness of Emission Control," *Journal of the Air Pollution Control Association* (March 1973):1973–1979.

5. L.B. Barrett and T.E. Waddell, "The Cost of Air Pollution Damages: A Status Report," Appendix I–J in the *Final Report of the Ad Hoc Committee on the Cumulative Regulatory Effects on the Cost of Automotive Transportation*, Office of Science and Technology, February 28, 1972.

Chapter 17

Energy Analysis as a Common Basis for Optimally Combining Man's Activities and Nature's

*Chester D. Kylstra**

What is our main purpose? What are all of us trying to do as individuals, as decision makers in various organizations, as members of our communities, and citizens of the United States and the world?

The basic need seems to be to survive. We would prefer to survive in high style, with luxuries and abundance, but we will do our best to survive in whatever situation or environment we find ourselves. Probably a lot of our fears and hopes that we all wrestle with each day involve survival, ranging from fears due to losing our job and the resulting consequences on our income, to the hopes of advancement or significant achievement that will not only get us richly rewarded in the here and now but will perpetuate our names into the future (a very abstract form of survival).

If we accept the notion that survival is basic, then we must take an interest in the laws of survival—the guiding principles that help to tip the dice our way. Using the principles of survival does not insure success, since there are still random, chance happenings that can upset our best-laid plans, but we can at least maximize our likelihood of surviving. Also, let us realize that to a large extent our survival depends on the free contributions from nature, such as water, rain,

*Chester D. Kylstra is in the Department of Nuclear Engineering Sciences at the University of Florida.

The author wishes to acknowledge with appreciation the stimulating and creative atmosphere provided by many associates working on various aspects of General Energy Systems Theory at the University of Florida as well as his debt in drawing on their work. He is especially appreciative of interchanges with H. T. Odum and of joint efforts with J. Boyles.

sewage treatment, flood control, clean air, microclimates, recreation, etc. Thus, we must be aware of these potential contributions as we analyze actions we might take that would cause us to lose them.

This chapter addresses the problem of survival at the organization, community, and regional levels, although the principles and procedures described are directly applicable to all levels, from the individual to the world. Before getting into the step-by-step process and the special areas of knowledge we must draw from, let us recall the general principles underlying survival and the various supporting laws.

PRINCIPLES OF SURVIVAL

The principles of survival draw upon the energy conservation law and the entropy law of thermodynamics, with the main contribution coming from Lotka's principle [1]. This principle provides the guidance or objective function for decision makers and planners everywhere. It comprises all desired outcomes, whether they be higher profits, lower capital investments, increased efficiency, significant social goods, etc.

While statements such as "natural selection," "may the best man win," and "survival of the fittest" tell us after-the-fact who would survive, Lotka's principle gives before-the-fact criteria that determine survival. Simply stated:

> Those systems will survive and will outcompete other systems that obtain the largest number of energy sources and that maximize the flow of useful energy through themselves.

What does this mean? The first part means that we as individuals and organizations should try to have available as many sources of necessary fossil fuel energies, natural* energies, materials, information, labor pools, machinery, structure or buildings, etc., as we can obtain and are likely to need.

We must at least have a water energy source, or our survival time is very short. We also must have a food energy source, or we don't last much longer. If these two basic energy sources are available to us, we can look for others, perhaps the skins from other animals to keep us warm. The energy source of information† can greatly increase our

---

*Throughout this chapter, the word natural is used to mean all natural systems other than man and his activities. Of course, everything is "natural," including man. Natural energies include the sun, directly and indirectly, as wind, rain, waves, biomass, rivers, etc.

†Information is the most concentrated form of energy. While information in pure form has no substance or material structure, the amount of human energy

survival likelihood, as demonstrated by our learning to plant and grow crops, inventing better weapons, and discovering how to use fossil fuels to greatly supplement the natural energy sources that support us. Having more than one supplier for item X, being able to substitute one input ingredient for another, are common business practices designed to improve business' capacity to survive.

The second part of Lotka's principle involves the system itself, and the things it must do internally to maximize its survival potential. Essentially, a system must draw energy from the sources available to it at a rate that will permit the greatest amount of useful work to be done per unit time. Useful work is defined as those activities that enhance survival, by improving efficiency of wasteful processes, by creating output, or by deriving more energy from given sources.

One of the corollaries of Lotka's principle requires that some energy be directed into generating new possibilities or choices, so that the system may evolve as external conditions change. Research teams in companies looking for new products, the creation of new companies by entrepreneurs, and the laying of thousands of eggs by a fish, all supply choices to the next bigger system. Since the next bigger system imposes the external energy sources (which are usually in continual change) on the system generating the choices, availability of many more choices than can be supported by the available energy sources allows continuous adaptation of the system. Only those choices best fitted to the conditions of the bigger system will survive. This is the selection of the fittest. The products that make it to market, the companies that make it past the startup difficulties, the baby fish that reach adulthood, have all done the best in applying Lotka's principle to their environment. They may be, and probably are, different from their predecessors, because external influences or environment most likely will have changed since their time. Thus, to survive, a continual evolving of the system to match changing conditions is necessary. This constitutes natural selection at the systems level.

Lotka's principle also extends over time. Systems sometimes must store energy to overcome seasonal or unexpected interruptions in the flow from or to energy sources. Saving money for a rainy day, storing seed for the spring, and stockpiling nuts for the winter are examples.

(perhaps lives), natural energies, and fossil fuel energies that has gone into organizations such as research teams, education institutions, and libraries, etc., for obtaining knowledge is very high relative to the heat value of information. However, since information can unlock new energy sources or improve the use of old energy sources, it is the highest quality form of energy and a most important feedback to all parts of a system.

The application of Lotka's principle falls under the constraints of the thermodynamic laws. The first is the conservation-of-energy law. It states that we cannot use more energy than we have and that we cannot create or destroy energy. We can only change its form. If 1,000 kilowatt hours (kwhr) of electricity comes into a factory to run motors, etc., 1,000 kilowatt hours of energy will leave the factory either as stored energy in the product or as low grade heat warming the environment. Balancing the corporate asset-liability statement and the income statement are examples of the conservation of energy.

The second law of thermodynamics states that energy must be degraded in any process. High grade (concentrated) energy in the form of fossil fuels, electricity, food, etc., is degraded into low concentration energy as part of creating a product, moving goods, or just letting a structure depreciate. Any shaping, refining, or moving materials requires energy, which is converted into low-temperature, diluted heat that cannot do any further useful work. Thus, there is "no free lunch." Energy is always expended somewhere, by someone, for every good and service we consume.

The evolution of a company illustrates the working of Lotka's principle and energy constraints. A new company may start with a new idea (information) that allows the founders to tap an energy source called money. While money is not actually energy, it can be exchanged for energy in the forms of labor, materials, structure, etc. The money lenders, of course, lend the money because they expect to be able to increase their own energy sources when they are paid back. The emerging company, with the unique idea (a superior energy source) may outcompete its established competitors if its energies are not drained by excessive harassment or stresses from the existing systems. Once accepted by the customers, the new company continues to grow, taking energy sources away from competitors, with the growth rate limited or controlled by the ability of the company itself to handle more customers, build facilities (structure), a larger workforce, etc. This is definitely a maximum energy flow (power) phase, where efficiency is not important, just the production of output any way possible. This phase is referred to as the succession or "weed" stage, since energy sources are not limiting and the system expands as fast as it can to create more structure to tap more energy. If it does not, its competitors will, and the system will stop growing and lose out to its competitors.

As the company begins to achieve market saturation, or supply shortages affect one or more of its inputs, it enters the phase of limiting energy sources. Of course, its competitors will be experiencing similar external (to the company) events. Further growth of the company may become unwise because the additional structure cannot be used, yet there is an energy drain required to maintain it. Improved efficiency becomes the key phase, with everyone looking for ways to eliminate waste, i.e., stop energy expenditures that do not promote survival. The maximum power (flow of energy through the company) strategy, however, still applies. The company creates more specialists, interconnections between subparts, etc., to get maximum use out of all energies that the company can still get.

Note that maximum efficiency is not really desirable even though everyone talks about efficiency and not throughput. The highest efficiency (100 percent) is obtained only if the company grinds to a halt, if it is stalled. No output, of course, but also no input, no friction, no maintenance, none of the necessary costs of running a process. Since the lowest efficiency is zero percent, which corresponds to the process running too fast, with all of the input energies going into friction, disorder, waste, etc., and to no final production, the optimum speed to run the company and the resulting efficiency is somewhere between the two extremes. The optimum speed is still the maximum power point, but the energy sources are now the limiting factors.

As the company stabilizes and matures, its growth slows and then stops. For natural systems, this is referred to as the "climax" stage. If the limiting energy sources remain constant (constant flow rate of input energies and materials), the size of the company will also remain essentially constant. Climax natural systems include coral reefs, tropical rain forests, deserts, etc. All are characterized by a large diversity of species (specialists?), stability in total structure and in the productivity (output created). Essentially all of the output, however, is used within the natural system to support the internal populations, structures, etc., so that no net output to other systems occurs. While companies, as subsystems of our larger societal system, must have both input and output, the other characteristics of climax systems are found. Our society is the system level comparable to climax natural systems.

The company starts the declining phase when it begins losing its energy sources. Either the company has not changed (evolved) its internal structure and organization to match a continuing changing external environment of energy sources and customer desires, or another company with a better idea has come along. Declining energy sources lead to a disassembly of the company in the reverse order of its assembly. First, the high technology specialists, the research functions, the advisors, and the staff positions begin to go, then excess administrative personnel, and some of the less profitable product lines. The company may stabilize at a lower level or continue into bankruptcy, another casuality of the natural selection process, a non-survivor.

At all times the company was trying to satisfy Lotka's principle, either knowingly or unknowingly. Conscious application of the survival principles can improve an organization's chances for continued survival.

TRADITIONAL PLANNING

If Lotka's principle is to be used for planning and decision-making, we should be aware of the advantages and disadvantages of other planning methods. Let us briefly look at the main features of three general classes of methods, discuss the effect on them of price disequilibria, and the inability to plug into the natural systems.

Methods

Perhaps the easiest (and maybe the most common) technique for predicting the future is to extrapolate from the past, the trendline approach. The advantages are obvious: no specialized skill or knowledge is needed, and it frequently works. The technique, of course, takes no account of causal forces, or changing external influences. It assumes a continuation of all related processes, which is a fine assumption until something changes.

The economic feasibility study, perhaps as a cost/benefit study or just an ordinary rate of return analysis, is also widely used. While equations for the process or system of interest may be used, giving a realistic internal dependence and tradeoff, the external forces or driving functions represent a problem. They may be assumed constant, or the trendline method may be applied.

The input/output (I/O) models allow for great complexity between many inputs and outputs, but the linear nature of the I/O matrix or exchange coefficients and the additive feature (all inputs added to get output) limits the distance into the future one dares to go. Also, the external driving functions are usually neglected. The I/O models are very valuable for studying what has happened in the past, but they lack the theoretical basis needed for models that are to be used for long-range forecasting and planning.

Prices

Prices are always a problem in economic models, and usually receive the majority of the study effort to determine current and future exchange ratios between energy and material flows and dollars. If we remember that one of the functions of money is to serve as a third party value exchange for goods and of our system, it is important that comparable (equilibrium) prices be established for the economic feasibility study. Since our U.S. system is seldom in equilibrium (steady state or slow, steady growth rates in all parts of the system), prices throughout our economy are also rarely in equilibrium.

For example, economic feasibility studies performed in the past, when prices were in near equilibrium, for the extraction of oil from shale rock, concluded that it was economically unsound: the expenses would exceed the revenue, or, in terms I prefer, the studies implied that the energies of all types required to extract and process the shale oil exceeded the energy content of the resulting oil. If we define the difference between the energy income and the energy expenses as net energy, the net energy content of most of the shale oil was negative. Today, however, economic studies using the current prices of oil and estimated current and future prices for labor, materials, capital structure, operating necessities, reach the opposite conclusion—that the extraction of shale oil is economically feasible. Why the difference? What has changed? While there has been some improvement in technology, the technology itself requires more energy. It is hard to believe that the energy flows associated with the process have changed sufficiently for the process to suddenly yield positive net energy.

The main difference between the past and now is that the price of imported oil has gone up, approximately four times. This has made shale oil now appear profitable. But can this really be true over the long-term since we do have such a large disequilibrium of prices, particularly since the net energy yield is unlikely to have changed?*

The large, sudden increase in the exchange ratio for one of our country's important energy sources is still just beginning to reverberate throughout our economy. Our society's functioning is so intertwined with oil and its products that every other price must also increase. As the prices of input materials increase, all industries will increase the prices of their products. This will force consumers (labor) to remain militant and demand continuing wage increases. With both material and labor costs increasing, industries will raise the prices of their products. This vicious cycle will continue until all prices have increased approximately three times due to the one oil price increase of four times. Of course, any further oil price increases

*Current studies are underway at the University of Florida to determine the net energy of the various grades of shale oil.

or continued changing of the money supply will alter the eventual outcome. Also short-term supply-demand imbalances will cause short-term price oscillations about the long-term, upward trend. Thus, disequilibrium of prices and rapid inflation seem likely to remain with us for some time, until either we or the Arabs change policies.

The main points to be drawn from the above discussion is that economic feasibility studies are hard to perform, particularly in changing times, such as now, since the time delays or lags within our system prevent equilibrium prices most of the time. This makes predicting future prices even more difficult than it might otherwise be.

Environmental Contributions

Another difficulty with the above economic methods arises because of our current environmental concern. In general, the models work with dollars only, and thus are representative only for man's activities. Now, however, the natural systems that contribute so much to our survival are being stressed by man's release of energy and the accompanying wastes and pollutants. Yet, because they have no dollars flowing through them, the contributions of natural systems to our society and our stresses on nature are being left out of the decisions, or inadequately considered. Dollars only go where man must pay man. It is usually considered too difficult to try to include the environmental aspects of the economic analysis in an objective way, so environmental costs or benefits are "externalized" and thus become part of the system beyond the control of the decision maker. This approach is usually unsatisfactory, at least from the point of view of society at large, since its survival potential may be damaged by one of its subsystems. This may only become apparent later, after damage has been done to, say, a local region.

These difficulties of disequilibrium or lagging prices, leaving out of decisions the free work of nature, and the inherent lack in most economic models of the energy sources and their effects, must be eliminated if comprehensive decision-making by planners at all levels is to be achieved.

COMBINING MAN'S ACTIVITIES
AND NATURE'S

There has to be a better way that organization decision makers can discharge their responsibility to their organization to maximize its survival and, at the same time, objectively understand the effects of their decisions on the larger system. The larger system includes our community and the natural systems that provide our support, i.e., water, air, sewage processing, flood control, recreation, etc. If the survival principles are understood and applied at both levels by the organization and by the community or regional leaders, it soon becomes obvious that the best long-term survival of the organization results when its actions also contribute to long-term survival of the higher-level system.

All of us want long-term survival for ourselves, our families, our organizations, our communities, our country, and our world. I do not mean that we want an unchanging world, since it will change. We want the ability to adapt to, and to survive, the changes. We have not had the tools before to objectively apply the survival principles. We have had to do the best we could with the tools at hand. Let us look at the various pieces we need to put together in an objective decision-making process that comprises ourselves as well as the system we are a part of—including man's activities, nature, and the resulting interactions.

This task involves the application of general energy systems theory to the analysis and modeling of systems, and the combining of systems in a realistic manner—reflecting the way many systems of man and nature are tightly intertwined. Without getting into details of dynamic modeling theory, use of the basic concepts will help us take account of all interrelated systems that affect the application of Lotka's principle to our planning decisions, and thus our survival. Since these tools are also evolving and improving as we learn more about the application of general energy systems to real problems, the information in this chapter represents only part of our rapidly changing capability.

Various Useful Tools

From a variety of useful tools in developing a system's view of the results of any organization/community planning, we must choose whichever alternative contributes most to the survival of the organization/community. To this end, we need to know how to include the effects of natural systems, how to convert between dollars and energy flow, and what are the costs (energy and dollars) of various developments.

Since dollars only flow within man's system, we have to switch to another measure that is common to all systems that we are familiar with or are apt to come in contact with. However, after an analysis is completed, it is possible to convert the results back into dollars, a more familiar unit for most of us.

Energy, or more correctly, potential energy or the ability to do work, and the flow of energy are common to all thermodynamic systems. There appear to be no exceptions to the requirements that potential energy be available to run any type of system we know, and that part of that potential energy must be degraded into ambient heat with no more ability to do useful work. The exploiting, extraction, conversion, transportation, distribution, and yes, the consumption of materials, goods and services all require the use of energy, whether it is a natural system or part of man's activities.

Energy Concentration Ratios

Energy can be used as the common thread through all systems. However, not all forms of energy are the same. Some forms of energy such as nuclear fission, electricity, or gasoline are quite concentrated or of high quality. These forms can perform a lot of useful work per pound or cubic foot of material. Other forms, such as sunshine, tides, wind, low temperature heat, are somewhat dilute and spread out over a large surface or volume. These forms do not have much useful work to offer, even though the total amount of energy might be the same as for a more concentrated form. Thus, in combining and evaluating the contributions of various systems, it is important that equivalent forms of energy be used. This is analogous to the old saying that we cannot add apples and pears. Likewise, we cannot add sunshine Btu's or kilocalories to gasoline Btu's or kilocalories and expect the total to accurately reflect the amount of work that can be done by that energy. Fortunately, the ratios of the energy concentration or energy quality have been approximately determined for some forms of energy. Table 17-1 shows the current values being used at the University of Florida. These values were obtained by examining the energy costs of the processes necessary to convert one form of energy into another, where the processes were satisfying Lotka's principle for maximum survival. It is expected that these values will change as improved energy cost/benefit studies are completed.

We see that the fossil fuel (coal) equivalent of sunshine is .0005 or the sunshine equivalent of coal is 2000. This means that 2000 energy units of sunshine can do the same work as 1 unit of coal. Thus, if we want to compare a solar collector for heating water with a coal-fired water heater, without diagramming and modeling the details of the two energy source systems, we can make the energy sources equivalent by the use of Table 17-1.

Energy-Dollar Conversions

The dollar equivalents shown in Table 17-1 are used to convert dollars of final demand, as measured by the Gross National Product

Table 17—1. Chain Conversion Factors Between Energy Concentration (Quality Factors[a])

(Read Across for Equivalence)	Sun	Gross Sugar	Wood	Coal	Electrical	Dollar Flow[b]
Solar equivalents	1	0.01	.001	.0005	.00014	2.0×10^{-8}
Sugar equivalents	100	1	.01	.005	.0014	2.0×10^{-6}
Wood equivalents	1000	10	1	.5	.14	2.0×10^{-5}
Coal equivalents	2000	20	2	1	.28	4.0×10^{-5}
Electrical equivalents[b]	7200	72	7.2	3.6	1	1.437×10^{-4}
Dollar equivalents[b]	50×10^6 (33m^2)	500,000	50,000	25,000	6,960	1

[a]Preliminary values currently in use; expected to change.
[b]Energy to dollar equivalents are based on 25,000 KC of fossil fuel equivalent to $1 of GNP.
Source: Note 2.

(GNP) into the amount of energy used by the U.S. in generating the goods and services purchased by the final demand. The ratio used in Table 17–1 is 25,000 kilocalories (KC) of fossil fuel work equivalents (FFWE) per dollar of GNP. Table 17–2 shows how this conversion factor was obtained. Twenty-five years of history of fossil fuel use and the GNP are shown. The fifth column shows the simple ratio of fossil fuel use per dollar of GNP. Another important energy input into our society consists of the natural energies of sun, wind, rain, plants and animals, etc. To calculate all of these directly would be very difficult. Considering, however, that potential energy cannot be thrown away (application of Lotka's principle), we make the assumption that some type of useful work will be done with it; hence we can simply add up all of the solar energy falling on the U.S. and, using the conversion ratio in Table 17–1 of 2000 solar units per fossil fuel unit, obtain the fossil fuel work equivalent of all the sunshine as 6.74×10^{15} (quadrillion) KC_{FFWE} per year. Adding this to the fossil fuel use rate for the U.S. gives us column 3, the total fossil fuel equivalent energy used each year in the U.S. Dividing this work by the GNP yields the last column, which is total energy input into the U.S. per dollar of GNP. For the 1968 to 1970 period, approximately 25,000 KC_{FFWE} were used to generate \$1 of GNP. This is the value used in Table 17–1. Table 17–2 will have further use when we come to convert dollar flows occurring in different years for a wide mixture of goods and services into equivalent energy units.

If the dollar cost of a flow of goods and services from a particular sector of our economy is known, e.g., the purchase of primary metals for input into a metal fabrication process, the energy equivalent of the flow can be estimated from tables similar to Table 17–3. This type of data helps minimize the effect of disequilibrium of prices. Table 17–3 contains an estimate (in column 7) of the total fossil fuel energy consumed by a sector of our economy per dollar of sale from that sector for 1963. The total energy consumed includes the direct energy (oil, gasoline, etc.) into each sector plus the fossil fuel energy expended elsewhere on all materials used by that sector. No natural energy is included. Following the above example, the primary metals sector uses 28,665 KC of fossil fuel per dollar of sale, versus 21,050 KC per dollar of GNP for 1963. This table is considered preliminary. An improved (more accurate) version for the years 1947, 1951, 1958, 1963, 1967, and perhaps 1971 is currently being prepared by Boyles at the University of Florida [3].

Natural Systems Work

One aspect of land use planning involves the proposed replacement of one land use by another. When these are two man-related activi-

Table 17–2. Ratio of Energy Flows in U.S. Society to GNP

Year	Fossil Fuels 10^{15} KC/yr	Fossil Fuels Plus Natural 10^{15} KC/yr[a]	GNP 10^9 \$	Fossil Fuel Per GNP 10^3 KC_{FF}/\$	Fossil Fuel Plus Natural per GNP 10^3 KC_{FFWE}/\$
1947	8.28	15.02	231.3	35.8	64.9
1948	8.57	15.31	257.6	33.3	59.4
1949	7.96	14.70	256.5	31.0	57.3
1950	8.60	15.34	284.8	30.2	53.9
1951	9.30	16.04	328.4	28.3	48.8
1952	9.22	15.96	345.5	26.7	46.2
1953	9.50	16.24	364.6	26.1	44.5
1954	9.16	15.9	364.8	25.1	43.6
1955	10.07	16.81	398.0	25.3	42.2
1956	10.58	17.32	419.2	25.2	41.3
1957	10.56	17.30	441.1	23.9	39.2
1958	10.46	17.20	447.3	23.4	38.4
1959	10.94	17.68	483.7	22.6	36.6
1960	11.33	18.07	503.7	22.5	35.9
1961	11.52	18.26	520.1	22.1	35.1
1962	12.06	18.80	560.3	21.5	33.6
1963	12.51	19.25	590.5	21.2	32.6
1964	12.98	19.72	632.4	20.5	31.2
1965	13.60	20.34	684.9	19.9	29.7
1966	14.40	21.14	749.9	19.2	28.2
1967	14.68	21.42	793.9	18.5	27.0
1968	15.56	22.30	864.2	18.0	25.8
1969	16.37	23.11	930.3	17.6	24.8
1970	16.94	23.68	976.4	17.3	24.3
1971	17.33	24.07	1050.4	16.5	22.9
1972	18.17	24.91	1151.8	15.8	21.6

[a]Solar energy contribution to the U.S. is estimated at 6.74 x 10^{15} KC_{FFWE} /yr.

Table 17−3. U.S. Energy and Economic Ratios for 1963

SIC Codes	Sector	Direct Energy[a]	Total Energy[b]
1–9	Ag., forestry, fish	326,305.7	410,193.4
10–14	Mining	493,501.66	493,501.66
20, 22, 23, 31, 21	Food, clothing, textiles, Leather, tobacco	413,738.58	936,102.6
24, 26, 27	Lumber, paper, printing	419,349.18	490,139.5
28, 30, 30	Chemicals, plastics, rubber	828,384.72	903,278.2
29	Petroleum refining	369,738.93	620,931.3
32	Stone, clay, glass	345,161.34	369,342.9
33	Primary metals	867,624.22	963,460.6
25, 34, 85, 35–39, 19	Furniture; fixtures fabricated metal prod; mach., except elect; elect. equip. & supplies; transportation equip; instruments & related prod; ordnance	428,030.39	1,367,909.3
	Total U.S. economy	14,451,350	14,451,350

[a]Direct Energy Consumed (millions of kwht) in fossil fuel equivalents.
[b]Direct Energy plus Energy consumed Indirectly as materials (fossil fuel energy only, no natural energy).
[c]Numbers in ( ) are kilocalories per dollar.
Source: Note 4.

ties, each with its own dollar flows, the problem can be easily solved. However, even here the effect on natural systems elsewhere through imports should be considered. When the displaced land use involves a natural system, we immediately run into the problem of the worth of the natural system and its contribution or effect on other parts of our society.

As in pricing any asset, there are several ways to determine the worth of the assets of a natural system. We can use the replacement cost (amount of work required per year times the number of years necessary to regrow the equivalent natural system), the service or contribution-of-output worth (the increase in the amount of work that can be done by other systems because of the services provided by the system under reference), and the scarcity or rarity worth (valuable because of its short supply, making its service essential to

Table 17—3. continued

Dollar Sales (Millions of Dollars)	Dollar[c] Sales ÷ Direct Energy	Dollar[c] Sales ÷ Total Energy	Total Number of Employees	Total Earnings (Millions of Dollars)
36,191	.1109(7754)	.088(9775)	3,597,000	3189.2
19,465	.039(22,050)	.039(22,050)	635,000	2838.6
90,717	.219(3930)	.097(8865)	4,358,000	13,454.9
31,145	.074(11,620)	.064(13,440)	2,141,700	8140.7
32,087	.039(22,050)	.036(23,890)	1,283,800	4812.6
20,033	.054(15,925)	.032(26,875)	188,700	833.3
10,910	.032(26,875)	.030(28,665)	600,800	2413.2
28,223	.033(26,060)	.030(28,665)	1,172,200	5733.3
118,248	.276(3115)	.086(10,000)	7,250,000	28,314.2
590,500	.0419(21,050)			

the performance of other systems). All of these aspects occur as part of a general-energy-system analysis, but if we are attempting a preliminary or simplified assessment, just knowing the value of the (free) work being accomplished by a particular natural system is adequate. Column 2 of Table 17—4 shows some typical gross productivity values for natural systems in South Florida, as reported by Odum et al [4]. Gross productivity in this case is the amount of energy (in kilocalories) in the form of sugar (chemical energy) produced per square meter of area per average day (averaged over one year). This energy is used by the natural systems to maintain themselves (self-maintaining systems), and to add new growth, if possible. Using the fossil fuel work equivalent factor of 20 from Table 17—1, we can obtain column 4 as the gross productivity in kilocalories of fossil fuel work equivalents (FFWE) per acre per year. In other words, replacing the natural system by an optimum system using fossil fuel (coal) at the indicated power density would result in the same amount of useful work being accomplished. The useful work can be converted into dollar equivalents of GNP using the 25,000

Table 17-4. Gross Productivity for Typical Natural Systems in South Florida

Natural System	Gross Productivity			
	KC_{GP}^a m^2/day	$10^6\,KC_{GP}$ acres/year	$10^6\,KC_{FFEW}^b$ acre/year	$\$^c$ acre/year
1. Pinelands	75	110	5.5	220
2. Cypress	40	60	3.0	120
3. Scrub cypress	80	115	5.75	230
4. Mesic hammocks	40	60	3.0	120
5. Hydric hammocks	105	155	7.75	310
6. Mangroves	135	200	10.0	405
7. Lakes and ponds	20	30	1.5	60
8. Fresh H_2O marshes	200	295	14.75	590
9. Wet prairie	72	105	5.25	210
10. Dry prairie	10.7	16	0.8	74
11. Irrigated pasture	90	135	6.75	270
12. Truck crops	75	110	5.5	220
13. Sugar cane	300	440	22.0	880
14. Beaches and dunes	0.55	.8	.04	1.6
15. Dune transition	1.0	1.5	.08	3
16. Coastal marsh	70.0	105	5.25	210
17. Estuary (turbid to clear water)	75(2-250)	110(3-370)	5.5(0.15-18.5)	220(6-740)

[a] Primary values from "South Florida Environmental Study," Center for Wetlands, University of Florida, September 1974. (See Note 3).
[b] Concentration ratio between Gross Productivity of biomass and fossil fuel is taken as 20.
[c] 1970 units of fossil fuel equivalent work flowing (both man-released and natural) for each dollar of GNP generated is approximately 25,000.

$KC_{FFWE}/\$$ ratio applicable to the 1968–1970 period. The proper dollar flow for other years can be obtained by using the correct ratio from Table 17–1. Thus, the contribution to our yearly GNP by the natural systems of South Florida varies from \$1.60 to \$590 per acre. As a comparison, the natural contribution of energy for the entire U.S. used in Table 17–2 (6.74×10^{15} KC_{FFWE}/yr) converts to an average contribution to the GNP of \$116 per acre per year, whereas the total GNP per acre is \$402. Most of the South Florida values are higher than \$116 per acre, as they should be compared to the national average. Since the \$116 value is obtained by considering the solar input to the U.S. only, while the gross productivity values in Table 17–4 come from actual measurements on real systems, the good correlation between the values is encouraging.

City Metabolic Rates

The last table (Table 17–5) included in this section presents the consumption rates in Orlando, Florida, as determined by the Interface-4 Urban Design Studio as part of a study of the impact of Disney World on Central Florida, and of the best long-term land use patterns [5]. For the various manned systems shown, the gross productivity in mean income is shown in column 8, with electric and water consumption rates shown in columns 2 and 3. The average population, structure, and paving densities are also given. Unfortunately, the income for non-residential areas was not determined. Also not determined was the consumption of other goods and services, such as direct use of fossil fuels, and nondurable consumer goods. The more detailed analysis of the "metabolic rate" of typical subsectors of Florida will be carried out as part of the carrying capacity projects for various parts of Florida [6].

ENERGY COST/BENEFIT
DECISION-MAKING

The best approach to planning with the use of Lotka's principle is to model the system of interest and the next larger system, using general energy systems theory [7]. Developing a model that shows the important internal relationships or interactions among subsystems, and the important external energy sources, or driving functions, help insure that all of the factors are considered that affect the decision.

If the model can be dynamically simulated, then the effects of the various alternatives over time can be observed to obtain both the short-term and long-term consequences of the possible decisions.

If the external energy sources eventually become constant, how-

Table 17—5.   Gross Productivity and Consumption Values for Manned Systems in Orlando, Florida

Land Use	Electric Power Density (10^3 kwh/acre/yr)	Water Consumption (10^3 gal/acre/yr)	Population Density (People/ Acre)
1. Stable housing	39.61	339.4	13.06
2. Senescent housing	45.49	430.8	17.13
3. Mature housing	34.96	302.1	8.90
4. High maintenance housing	54.34	560.0	5.95
5. Apartment housing	52.54	487.0	45.25
6. Mobile housing	44.50	313.0	40.50
7. Central business district	507.80	2138.25	
8. Commercial strip	138.02	551.4	
9. Transportation terminals	2.88	14.31	
10. Governmental installations	10.06	550.0	
11. Industrial	146.24	666.7	
12. Public recreational	35.63	243.9	
13. Private recreational	13.99	98.44	
14. Cultural institutional	36.36	147.6	
15. Schools	66.64	439.0	

Source: Note 5.

ever, then the case of limiting energy sources will develop, as discussed earlier, and the energy flows and the storages of structure within the systems will also become constant. The climax phase will have developed.

All long-range planning should include a strategy for the climax or steady-state future. While the growth phase has characterized our country's past, the likelihood is that a slower growth rate or an approach to the leveling or climax stage will occur in the future.

This leads to a much simpler approach than dynamic modeling for long-range decision-making. For many problems, the required insight and understanding of the system can be obtained by just analyzing the climax or steady-state results of a decision, avoiding the often difficult and expensive dynamic modeling effort. This simpler approach to planning can be summarized in energy cost/benefit tables, showing the long-range costs or benefits associated with each affect-

Table 17-5. continued

Structure Density Units (Structure/ Unit Land)	Structure Value ($/ft²) Structure)	Paved Surface Area Index Units (Paving/ Unit Land)	Mean Income ($/per- son/yr)	Edge Index (Edges/ Acre)	Affluence Index
.227	6.13	.2035	2750	15.64	48.23
.217	5.04	.2550	1213	10.49	32.74
.134	6.77	.1578	3237	17.54	61.73
.123	7.95	.2617	20860	13.86	98.80
.354	8.52	.1106	4620	13.71	51.89
.254	3.54	.3010	2919	25.80	41.82
1.18	15.00	.4147		10.54	
.133	9.00	.3979		1.00	
.070		.6001		0.37	
.128		.3611		.250	
.188	6.64	.2031		2.97	
.018		.0710		2.09	
.029		.0510		1.61	
.790		.2600		2.90	
.300		.3619		13.70	

ed part of the system. Some simple examples are probably the best way to explain the construction and use of such tables (see Tables 17–6 and 17–7).

Example 1: Thermal Pollution Control Versus Local Natural System [8] (Figure 17–1)

The management of an accepted and approved electrical power plant is trying to decide whether to add a thermal pollution control cooling tower to eliminate the environmental stress and potentially lethal effect on the estuary that will otherwise receive the waste heat from the power plant. The obvious choices seem to be:

1. Use once through cooling with estuary water and maybe cause complete destruction of up to one square mile of estuary, but have no expense for a cooling tower or its negative effect on the performance of the power plant.

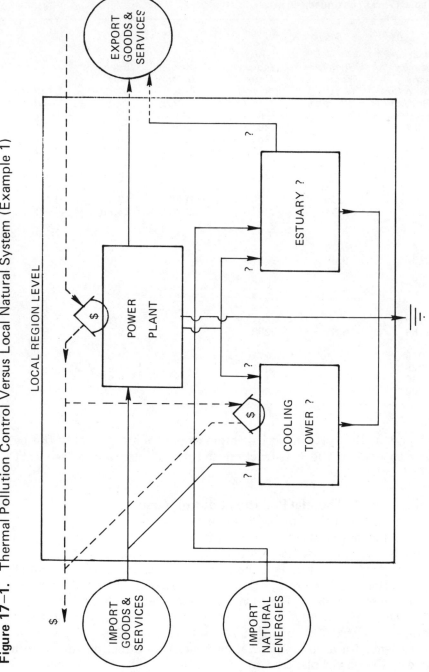

Figure 17–1. Thermal Pollution Control Versus Local Natural System (Example 1)

2. Use a cooling tower, releasing the waste heat directly into the atmosphere, using some additional land area, but having essentially no effect on the estuary.

This example is very simple, and leaves out all interactions between the power plant and the estuary except for the effect of the cooling waters and all interactions with other industries, communities, etc. However, this very problem is being faced by managers of all new power plants, with the Environmental Protection Agency insisting on cooling towers at essentially all new power plants. Detailed energy cost/benefit studies are underway at Crystal River, Florida, to objectively evaluate the best cooling alternative [9].

The Energy Cost/Benefit results are given in Table 17–6. The values are arrived at as follows: for the cooling tower alternative, the estimated annual cost for operation, repair, maintenance, amortization of the construction cost, reduction in operating efficiency of the power plant, etc., totals approximately $5 million in 1974 dollars. From Table 17–2, we can estimate that 1974 dollars of final demand will represent approximately 19,000 KC_{FFWE} of work expended somewhere in our economy to deliver the goods and services necessary to the operation of the cooling tower per dollar of cost, or a total of 95 billion KC_{FFWE} a year. These energy and dollar costs are entered in the table as negative, or cost values. The disruption of the estuary is negligible under this alternative, so the energy and dollar cost is zero. Approximately 5 acres of coastal land must be altered from its natural state to a cooling tower land use. If we assume a natural system of something like pinelands or scrub cypress and use Table 17–4, the cooling tower will disrupt approximately 5.5 million KC of fossil fuel equivalent work per acre per year or 27.5 million KC/year for the five acres. The dollar column in Table 17–4 is in 1969 dollars, so we can convert the above energy value into 1974 dollars by using the 19,000 KC/$ value obtained above from Table 17–1. This yields $1,450/year, or a small cost compared to the cooling tower. Thus, the total cost for the cooling tower alternative is $5.001 million or 95.03 billion KC_{FFWE}.

The estuary cooling alternative involves zero cost for the cooling tower and for the additional land area. The disruption of the estuary, in the worst case, is the complete loss of the productivity of one square mile (640 acres). From Table 17–4, the average estuary has a gross productivity of 5.5 million KC per acre per year of fossil fuel equivalent work, or 3.52 billion KC_{FFWE} per year for the entire endangered area. This converts into $185,000.

Comparing the two alternatives, we see that estuary cooling approach is approximately $4.81 million and 91.51 billion KC_{FFWE} a

Table 17–6. Energy Cost/Benefit Results for Example 1 (Local Region Level)

Cost/Benefit	Estuary Cooling		Cooling Tower	
	10^9 KC/year	10^6 \$/year	10^9 KC/year	10^6 \$/year
Cost of cooling tower	0	0	−95	−5
Disruption of natural system productivity				
Estuary	−3.52	−.185	0	0
Land	0	0	−0.0275	−.00145
Total cost/benefit	−3.52	−.185	−95.03	−5.001
Net waste for cooling tower			−91.51	−4.81

Source: Note 8.

year cheaper than the cooling tower, even with complete disruption of the estuary (an unlikely event). If estuaries are not in short supply, and thus very valuable to other parts of the larger system, spending the additional fossil fuel energy and dollars on a cooling tower is a waste to our local and national economies, since the energy and money could be used for productive purposes, to add to our survival potential rather than detract from it.

Example 2: Tertiary Sewage Plant Versus Wetlands System (Figure 17–2)

A town has grown to the point where the discharge of its secondary treated sewage into the local lake is causing excessive organic levels and eutrophication of the lake. The town has about decided on the expense of a tertiary treatment plant to further lower the organic concentration of the discharge into the lake. However, someone suggests that a current research program at the University of Florida investigate whether the effects of secondary sewage on the productivity and water quality of various wetlands, such as cypress domes and marshes, might constitute a cheaper alternative, since—if this is done right—nature might still absorb the sewage cost-free. While the lake, which naturally is low in productivity and thus does not normally need additional nutrients, can no longer absorb increasing concentrations of sewage, some nearby swampy areas with cypress domes might be capable of absorbing it, since swampy areas are normally highly productive and often use most of the available nutrients.

While the results of the research are not yet available, some indication of what might be accomplished can be obtained if we make a few assumptions. Table 17–7 summarizes the results. Assuming that each acre of wetlands can process the secondary sewage of three people, assume that 30,000 acres of wetlands are needed. Also, assume that the gross and net productivity of the natural systems are both increased 10 percent. From Table 17–4, assume that a mixture of marsh and cypress results in a gross productivity of 100 KC_{GP}/m^2 day. A 10 percent increase leads to an additional benefit from the swamp of 0.74 million KC_{FFWE} per acre per year, or 22,200 million KC_{FFWE} per year for the entire 30,000 acres. Using the 1974 conversion factor of 19,000 KC_{FFWE} per dollar, this benefit becomes $1.18 million per year. Much of this additional benefit can be directly used by man's system by harvesting cypress trees and by using portions of the area for recreation. Additional piping and pumps are needed to distribute the sewage throughout the swamp. The yearly operating, maintenance, and amortization cost for this system is estimated at $300,000 per year or 5.7×10^9 KC_{FFWE} per year, using 19,000 KC_{FFWE} per dollar.

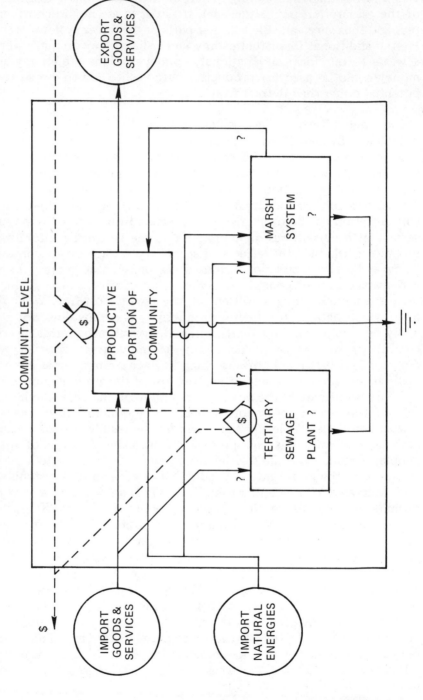

Figure 17–2.   Tertiary Sewage Plant Versus Wetlands System (Example 2)

Table 17–7. Energy Cost/Benefit Results for Example 2 *(Community Level)*

	Alternatives			
	Marsh Sewage Treatment		Tertiary Sewage Plant	
Cost/Benefits	$10^9\ KC_{FFWE}/year$	10^6 $/year$	$10^9\ KC/year$	10^6 $/year$
Cost of sewage plant	0	0	−25.65	−1.35
Additional productivity of marsh system	+22.2	+1.18	0	0
Cost of marsh system facility	−5.7	− .3	0	0
Recreation benefit	+.114	+.006		
Total	+16.614	+.886	−25.65	−1.35
Net waste for sewage plant			−42.26	−2.24
Available for leasing marsh			45 $/acre year	

Since the sewage will be cycled to different parts of the swamp at different times, portions of the area (the higher parts) can be used for recreation. The town was going to buy some land and create some parks, but using the swamp will save the land costs and tax loss of other land. This savings is estimated at $6,000 per year.

The construction and operation of a tertiary sewage plant will cost about $1.35 million per year, in 1974 dollars. This converts into 25.65 billion KC_{FFWE} per year.

In this example, the tertiary sewage plant is a poor alternative. Unfortunately, the numbers used are all estimated, and thus, while the example shows the method, the conclusion is not defensible at this point. Note that some of the money not spent on the sewage plant can be justifiably spent on leasing the swamp land (up to $45/acre per year), even though the land owner is already receiving an additional benefit from the sewage.

In general, any time that the free work of nature can be used to perform a function for man rather than using man's costly machinery and fossil fuels, the best approach is to use the natural system. However, if the function stresses the natural system to the point that it cannot do its job in a steady manner or it causes other bad (contrasurvival) effects on man's systems, the function should be accomplished by man.

Example 3: Pollution Control Equipment
Versus River System (Figure 17–3)

The management of a new factory is considering pollution control equipment to minimize the heavy metal and chemical pollutant concentrations in their waste stream. They would prefer to just dump the waste directly into the nearby river and save the money (and energy) involved with the equipment, but, since they intend to be a part of the local community for some time, they are concerned about the long-range survival of the community. An energy cost/benefit analysis of the entire community system affected by their decision is proposed (Table 17–3), since the main affect on the community will occur by way of the natural systems rather than directly by economics.

The use of the pollution control equipment will mean essentially no effect on the river system, but will require disposal of the collected waste at a land site. Total yearly costs in 1972 dollars (for amortization, operating, maintenance, disposal, etc.) is estimated at $2.83 million per year. From Table 17–2 we use 21,600 KC_{FFWE} per dollar to get an energy equivalence of 61.1 billion KC_{FFWE} per

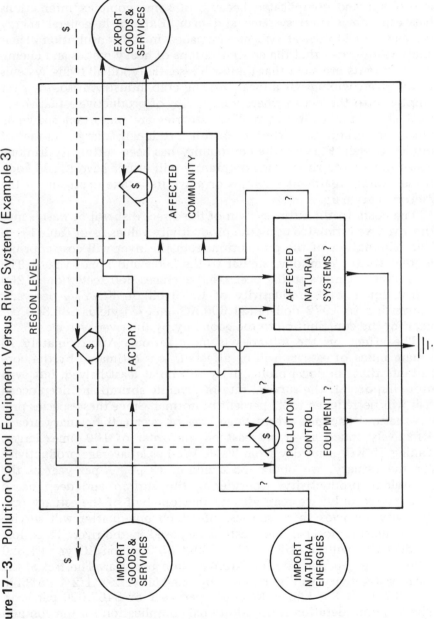

Figure 17–3. Pollution Control Equipment Versus River System (Example 3)

year that is being expended somewhere (both fossil fuel and natural energies) that support the pollution control costs.

The analysis of the direct disposal of the wastes into the river is difficult and complicated because of some complex interactions between the natural systems and man. Experts in general energy systems and biological systems are called in for consultation. Their analysis indicates that the concentrations of heavy metals and chemical pollutants are such that they will essentially kill all living systems in the river, wiping out a local thriving crab industry. Also, the river empties into the ocean where many acres of productive estuaries are flushed by the river water. The estuaries are important spawning areas for shrimp and deep ocean fish, producing a large number of mullet as well. Further, the community has been getting its drinking water out of the river. The community will either have to add additional water treatment facilities or move its intake upstream of the factory's discharge.

The costs to the entire system of the direct disposal of wastes into the river are estimated using the productivity values from Table 17–4. The elimination of the production from the river will cost approximately 20 KC_{GP}/m^2 day (similar to the lakes and ponds value). The river runs 10 miles to the ocean and averages 250 feet wide (1,250 acres), for a total productivity of 1.875 billion KC_{FFWE} per year. Converting to 1972 dollars (21,600 $KC_{FFWE}/\$$) yields \$86,800 per year for the contribution to the economy by the river system.

The effect on the estuaries is more serious. Approximately 10 square miles of estuary will be affected. It is estimated by the consultants that the local productivity will be at least halved, but even more important, the survival rate of juvenile shrimp and deep ocean fish will be reduced to 25 percent of normal. Since these species process natural energies over a huge area of ocean, the estuary area is effectively much larger, at least on the order of 100 times larger. Taking 75 KC_{GP}/m^2 day from Table 17–4 as an average productivity for the estuary, we obtain 35.2 billion KC_{FFWE} per year as the equivalent productivity. Considering the shrimp and deep ocean fish species only, we may assume that one-half of the estuary productivity involves these species, of which one-quarter will survive (three-quarters lost) if the waste is disposed in the river. Thus, lost productivity will be (1/2 × 3/4 × 100 × 35.2 billion KC/yr =) 1,320 billion KC_{FFWE} per year, or \$60.9 million per year. The rest of the local productivity will be reduced by one-half (1/2 × 1/2 × 35.3 billion KC/yr =) 8.8 billion KC_{FFWE} per year or \$407,000 per year. The last consideration is the additional complication for the community to obtain adequate quality drinking water. The cost of moving the intake is not too high; it is estimated at \$2,000 per year.

Table 17–8. Energy Cost/Benefit Results for Example 3 *(Regional Level)*

Cost/Benefits	River and Ocean Disposal		Pollution Control	
	$10^9\ KC_{FFWE}$/year	10^6 $/year	$10^9\ KC_{FFWE}$	10^6 $/year
Cost of pollution control	0	0	−61.1	−2.83
Disruption of natural system productivity				
River	−1.88	−.087	0	0
Estuary				
Deep ocean	−1,320	−60.9	0	0
Local	−8.8	−.407	0	0
Cost of additional water treatment	−.043	−.002	0	0
Total cost	−1330.7	−61.4	−61.1	−2.83
Net benefit for pollution control equipment			+1,269.6	+58.57

The total in Table 17–8 reveal that the pollution control equipment alternative will cost the community (and the even larger system that also benefits from the shrimp and fish production) less by $58.57 million than just dumping the waste into the river. Note that if just the local dollars were considered, the river dumping would be cheaper and would appear to be the correct alternative.

This example illustrates the point that whenever our actions affect either a significant portion of the natural systems or natural systems that feed back into several parts of our manned system, it is usually better survival tactics to minimize our disruption of the natural systems because they truly are our life support systems.

NOTES TO CHAPTER 17

1. A.J. Lotka, "Contribution to the Energetics of Evolution," *Proceedings of the National Academy of Sciences* 8 (1922):147–188.

2. H.T. Odum, "Energy Quality Concentration Factors for Estimating Equivalent Abilities of Energies of Various Types to Support Work," Chapter D, of June 1974 Process Report to Atomic Energy Commission on *Simulation of Macroenergetic Models of Environment, Power and Society*, University of Florida.

3. J. Boyles, Private communication, University of Florida.

4. H.T. Odum et al. "The System of Man and Nature in South Florida," Center for Wetlands, University of Florida, September 1974.

5. J. Shadix, ed. "Report #4, 'Interface 4' Urban Design Studio," University of Florida, March 1974.

6. C. Kylstra, ed. "Carrying Capacity Project for the State of Florida and Its Major Regions, Plus Natural System Inventory and Comprehensive Planning," State Carrying Capacity Committee, University of Florida, June 1974.

7. H.T. Odum, *Environment, Power and Society* (New York: John Wiley, 1970).

8. H.T. Odum, "Energy Cost Benefit Approach to Evaluating Power Plant Alternatives," Unpublished paper, University of Florida, August 1974.

9. H.T. Odum et al. "Simulation of Models of Estuarine Ecosystems at Crystal River," Process Report to Florida Power Corporation. University of Florida, April 1974.

Chapter 18

A Comprehensive View of
Corporate Management's Role
Within Its Social Environment

J.M. Levi Leathers*

I'd like to talk about what corporate social policy means to my company, and what we have been and are doing to fulfill our corporate social responsibilities.

When the term corporate social responsibility is mentioned, it may bring to mind support of day-care centers, fine arts facilities, minority groups, playground and park areas, etc. These are good things and we are involved in them, too. But, really, they are only the outcroppings, the offshoots, made possible when a corporation does a far more basic job of meeting its social obligations.

Now, the corporation with which I have been associated for better than 30 years is engaged in the manufacture of chemicals, plastics, and metals.

FIRST THINGS FIRST

Broadly, only three things are required to manufacture these products: (a) people, (b) natural resources, and (c) tools—that is, manufacturing plants with their related equipment, hardware, etc.

These are the things, then, which my company must deal with, about which it must be concerned, and which it must manage well if it is to meet its social responsibilities. And these are the things I want to talk about.

*J.M. Levi Leathers is Executive Vice President and Director of Operations at Dow Chemical Company.

PEOPLE MANAGEMENT

There is nothing mysterious about a corporation. A corporation is people. Really—I promise you—even those at the top—the hierarchy—the chairman of the board or the president of Carbide, of DuPont, of my own company—are all just people. Granted, they are important people to a corporation because the success or failure of the enterprise depends on them. They set policies and make decisions that form the "atmosphere," if you will, under which business operates. And believe me, if that atmosphere is not (a) people-oriented, and (b) profit-oriented, the business is in trouble.

We have realized for a long time at Dow, from top management down, that people—good people—are our most valuable asset. They are absolutely essential. But we believe that it is our responsibility to manage these good people so that they become even better—the best they can be.

We have a specific program going now; we call it "whole jobbing." Its object is to stretch people, to give them breathing room, to give them not just more work, but new tasks that challenge them to grow. We have sought to improve the quality of the job. We have pushed decision-making responsibility down to the lowest possible level. We believe that no set of psychological tests, no computer printout will ever replace the individual employee who has been trained to make good decisions and who is not afraid to make them.

We are seeking new ways to permit people to identify personally with a particular plant or product or service. We believe it is important that a person be able to measure his own contribution in terms that are meaningful to him.

We believe it is important to provide our employees with tasks that allow them to work effectively, not just efficiently. And believe me, it is possible to do one without the other. In my own company, I have seen people work very efficiently at projects that were never going to amount to a hill of beans insofar as the growth and economic health of the company are concerned, and so they were not working effectively.

We encourage a simple organization structure, a flat organization. We are trying to minimize the continued growth of front office bureaucracy and the red tape which begins to feed on itself.

We encourage our supervisors to know their employees personally and to treat them as individuals. (I am, of course, referring here to our salaried employees. Union contracts preclude our treatment of bargained-for employees' needs as individuals.)

Our newer plants being built in new locations, are, without exception, salaried operations. The freedom to achieve and the teamwork between supervisor and employee which is possible and which usually develops under these circumstances has been very gratifying to us. It just reinforces my belief that people, basically, want to be treated as individuals. And we are trying to do just that.

We feel strongly, too, that our salaried people are entitled to all the "accessories" that go along with employment at Dow—health and life insurance at substantially reduced rates, a good retirement program, a profit-sharing program, opportunities to buy our company's stock at reduced prices.

I would not want you to think that in all of this, our motives are purely altruistic. Good people management is good business. It pays off. People achieve for themselves and for their company when their work is rewarding and stimulating—when they enjoy what they are doing.

NATURAL RESOURCES MANAGEMENT

Let me move on now to my second topic, social responsibility for the management of our natural resources.

About seven years ago before most of us had given any real thought to the threat of an energy shortage, we at Dow declared what we call the "War on Btu's." (Btu stands for British thermal unit and is the quantity of heat required to raise the temperature of one pound of water one degree Fahrenheit at or near $39.2°F$.)

At the time we instituted our War on Btu's it was for economic reasons. We could see pounds of our raw materials going down plant sewers, into our waste ditches, out our stacks. Those wasted pounds were dollars, gone and irrecoverable. We began to try to do something about it. Our policy was to stop those wasted pounds before they got into the sewers, the ditches, the stacks. Recycle them. Use them.

To do this required, in some cases, that our processes be redesigned. In other cases, we have replaced and are replacing existing facilities with facilities having new and better technology. We are modernizing other facilities. The efficiency of our electricity and steam production plants is being improved. (I might explain that my company produces most of the power used in its production plants.)

Our goal is a 10 percent reduction per year in consumption of Btu's. For the past two years that goal has been reached. Realistically, we have to admit that a 10 percent reduction every year from from now isn't possible so our goals will have to be readjusted.

An audit system has been devised so that the results of our efforts can be measured. The energy content of a large number of our end products has been determined. That information is programmed into a computer which can tell me at any time of the day or night, the amount of energy going into those products. I say day or night because I have a portable machine in my home which gives me access to this information when I am not in my office. With this system, it is possible to tell instantly where our energy use problems lie.

In addition, before any new capital installation is approved, it must be shown that the technology included will reduce the number of Btu's previously used to make a pound of the product to be produced in the new facility. Incidentally, our environmental control efforts are interwoven without War on Btu's so that the same goals are achieved.

There are two other points I feel compelled to make about energy use although they do not relate directly to our corporate responsibility in that area. One is this: many government regulations and rules are forcing industry and consumers alike to utilize energy supplies extravagantly. I mean, for example, automobile emission control equipment. However good the intent, the effect has been that mileage per gallon has decreased, and that we must use more gallons of gas, at higher cost, to make up the mileage we've lost. Another example is that with the precipitous government move on sulfur dioxide emissions, we cannot burn high-sulfur fuel or coal. We are forced to use more fossil fuels that normally would go either into the transportation industry or home heating. That's extravagance, in my opinion. And we need to do something about it; we need to move in a more orderly, thoughtful way and give our developing technology time to catch up with the problems it seeks to solve.

The other point I wished to make concerns something I believe we should do and it is this: we must take steps to estimate the total amount of energy left in this country in terms of Btu's. Then we must learn to calculate the total amount of energy required to construct a given project—a home, an office building, a production facility. By this I mean that we need to know how much energy is represented in that project's components—in a compressor, for instance; in 100 square feet of concrete foundation; in its structural steel members.

Then we must allocate. We must decide whether it will be "this" or "that"—whether we will spend our energy on transient or long-lasting things. We must learn to remember that the same energy used to drive an air compressor or power a vacuum cleaner can also be used to build a highway or a hydro-electric dam.

I see the coming years as an age of choice insofar as raw material usage is concerned, and I believe we ought to prepare ourselves, through the steps I've outlined, to make wise choices.

By the way, if you read into this idea that I think we are going to need 20 new government bureaus employing another 100,000 people to oversee this "allocation," you are wrong. There has to be a better way than that!

THE MANAGEMENT OF TOOLS

I come now to the last part of my discussion—corporate social responsibility concerning our "tools"—our production facilities. Let me draw an analogy for you between a chemical production facility, which is called a "plant," and a pot of English ivy which is a plant of another kind. That ivy plant lives on natural resources. It takes earth and air and water and sunlight; from them, through a very wonderful process, makes green leaves. Its well-being depends on getting the right amounts of the needed natural resources. Sometimes it may need a shot in the arm, some fertilizer perhaps. Occasionally, for good health, it may need something more drastic—surgery, pruning.

The circumstances are exactly the same for a chemical plant. It, too, takes natural resources and upgrades them into higher value products needed by its customers. It, too, may need an occasional shot in the arm or a bit of surgery. And so enters our social responsibility. Management must be the resource provider, the shot-giver, the pruner.

In the really basic sense, a manufacturing plant has to be healthy and competitive or nothing else is possible. Therefore, keeping it that way is our most important social responsibility.

Our marketplace today is not one country but the whole world. And the competition is fierce—not just between companies but in many cases between different production locations within a single company. In my own company, for instance, there are some 45 production sites within the United States. The majority of these are in relatively small towns; we are a small town company. We tend very much to be a major economic factor, if not the biggest economic factor in these locations. This in itself almost dictates what our first and greatest social responsibility is to that town where we have a plant, and that is to keep that plant healthy and prosperous and competitive.

For each Dow employee in these smaller towns, there are four other non-Dow employees who derive their income indirectly from the same source—the barbers, haberdashers, grocerymen, plumbers. This means that if we have 100 Dow employees in a town, Dow actually supports 500 jobs in that town. And so our sphere of social responsibility widens.

PROFITS, FAIR DEALING, AND RECOGNITION

I read often in the newspapers and trade magazines that a company is shutting down its plant at some geographical location and moving its operations elsewhere, leaving former employees and the community in economic hardship.

We are dedicated to seeing that this doesn't happen to us. This determination necessitates that at times we take a very firm stand against external pressures. I mean by that such things as demands of employee groups that translate into unreasonably higher manpower costs; construction cost increases, tax increases; higher raw materials costs.

My point is that it is management's social responsibility to see to it that a company, or a location within a company, doesn't put itself at a cost disadvantage compared to another company or another location, just to solve a short-term problem.

Now you are aware, no doubt, that one continuous thread has woven itself through all of this chapter. It is this: although a corporation should be socially responsible in a number of ways, the first, the most important, the very basis of these responsibilities, is to be successful—to make a profit.

I make this statement realizing that it will not be well accepted by a great many people. Nevertheless, it is true.

It is useless to talk of corporate social obligations if the wherewithal to fulfill them does not exist, just as it is useless for the United Fund or the Salvation Army or the Red Cross, or any other really worthwhile cause, to approach you for your "fair share" if your "fair share" has already been allocated for food and rent. What is true for you personally is also true for the corporation.

As a reader, you are probably business-oriented. Therefore, I hope you will appreciate that it is the proper business of business to operate so that dependable, satisfying work at fair compensation can be offered to those who seek it. This can be done only if business meets its social obligations in the three areas I have talked about. This is our corporate responsibility.

On the other hand, it is the proper business of government to provide a climate in which legitimate business can flourish so that good jobs are possible for all our people—and to do this with as few controls as are possible.

Now in all candor, business is not omnipotent or faultless or without its shortcomings. But, in all fairness, who or what is? Lately in this country, we have been prone sometimes to penalize the achievers along with the do-nothings. Many corporations, and that means many people, are working hard to fulfill their social responsibilities—in employee and community relations, in the preservation of our environment, and in the wise use of natural resources. For those individuals and companies who are—how about a pat on the shoulder instead of a kick in the hindquarters?

Epilogue

George F. Rohrlich

There are different ways of conceptualizing our environment. In this volume, by and large, we have addressed ourselves to various problems arising from man's impact upon the good earth, with its physical resources, flora, fauna, water, and air—nearly all of them in jeopardy because of man's ever more massive intervention into nature's ecological balance. Within this context, the problems of pollution and exhaustion of some vital physical resources dominated the attention and concern of virtually all our authors. Most of the discussion has dealt with man's impact upon nature—both as despoiler and as potential steward and trustee.

Another way of viewing the environment was epitomized, well over half a century ago, in a terse observation by John Maurice Clark, this most far-sighted of American social economists of an earlier generation: ". . . the environment of each of us," said Clark, "consists chiefly of the rest of us" [1]. The problems and concerns ensuing from this conceptualization of the environment center around our *social habitat*, as contrasted with our *physical habitat*. Seen in this perspective, certain environmental concepts, e.g., "pollution," may take on a different meaning, as in Robert S. McNamara's recent reference to human habitations as "an expression of man's attempt to achieve his potential" and to *"poverty"* as the syndrome *"that pollutes that promise"* [2].

In this latter purview, another facet of our environment, the social ambiance, is stressed. All too long it has been taken for granted and left to itself, as one takes account of the weather across the change of seasons. This, until fairly recently, had been precisely our attitude toward our natural surroundings: their supposedly unlimited capacity for self-renewal was commonly assumed as a matter of course—up until the rude awakening.

In this concluding section of the book, it may not be amiss to indulge in some observations—in part, mere conjectures—as regards the social ecology [3], so to speak, of our environmental predicament and the jeopardy in which our social fabric finds itself, not so much as a result of pollution that threatens our physical habitat, as it is a result of some of our reactions to certain "remedial actions," present and proposed. Three aspects will be touched on: the relationship between man and the products of his inventiveness; the limits to the enforcement of official mandates; and the residual task of cultivating a better and wider understanding of the interconnection between individual and common welfare.

MAN AND TECHNOLOGY—WHICH IS MASTER?

Few of us in this country, and a minority in all of the Western world, are Marxists. Yet, much of what is being said about the supposedly inevitable thrust of technology has a Marxist ring to it—as if Marx's dictum encapsulating his materialist faith, whereby it is allegedly our mode of production that determined our mode of thought, rather than the other way around, was being widely believed! At any rate, it seems to form at least the inarticulate premise of many current assessments of our environmental predicament and outlook.

Dissident voices are not lacking, but they are few and far between. H.G. Rickover went on record, some years back protesting against the uncritical acceptance of this idea, even if, and perhaps especially if, it manifests itself in the acceptance of the inevitability of "technological progress." Said Rickover:

> It troubles me that we are so easily pressured by purveyors of technology into permitting so-called "progress" to alter our lives without attempting to control it—as if technology were an irrepressible force of nature to which we must meekly submit.

He went on to add:

> It is important to maintain a humanistic attitude toward technology: to recognize clearly that since it is the product of human effort, technology can have no legitimate purpose but to serve man—man in general, not merely some men; future generations, not merely those who currently wish to gain advantage for themselves; man in the totality of his humanity,

encompassing all his manifold interests and needs, not merely some one particular concern of his. When viewed humanistically, technology is seen not as an end in itself but a means to an end, the end being determined by man himself in accordance with the laws prevailing in his society [4].

This point of view has been reiterated more recently with considerable force in an international confab on Technology Assessment and Quality of Life (1972) [5].

Of course, it would be silly to deny or doubt that a system functions pursuant to its motive force and its ground rules. In capitalism, presumably, the profit motive consitutes a prime criterion in decision-making. It must, for without profits a business cannot long survive. But how often does profit *maximization* give way to other objectives deemed equally or more important, and how have free enterprise and free competition been transformed in the transition from a "purely competitive" market to monopolistic competition with price leadership, on the one hand, and the growing admixture of a public sector with government intervention, on the other! These were, after all, accommodations of a system to changing needs and interests.

The important question is, whose needs and interests? Gunnar Myrdal has observed with great severity that the disregard of the distributional issue makes what he terms "the now common brave and broad pronouncements (concerning the environmental problem, particularly in regard to. . . depletion of irreplacable resources) utterly superficial and misleading, indeed meaningless" [6]. And he concludes, accordingly, that "any discussion of threatening depletion of resources in global terms. . . must define a stand on the distributional issue" [7].

Economics used to be called "the dismal science," because of its supposedly immutable laws, primarily as expounded by Robert Malthus and later popularized by LaSalle's and other socialists' frequent reference to the "iron law of wages"—whereby workers' wages were "proved" always and of necessity to hover around a level just above the starvation point. History has disposed of this contention. Economics may be an underdeveloped science. But it is anything but dismal in what it has done and probably can do to promote human betterment.

Today's runnerup for the title of new dismal science appears to be ecology [8]. Basically, the argument is the same: the alleged incapacity or unwillingness of man to avert his own doom, even if clearly foreseeable. This, essentially, rests on man's seemingly innate limitation to perceive of his self-interest in any but narrow and proximate terms, and to regard any attempt at sharing as robbing Peter (namely, him— or herself) to pay Paul (the other). This view of man is "proved" to hold true even if the sharing would be incontestably for the common good [9].

Protection of the environment is a good case in point, viz:

> The protection of the environment is... what the economist calls a "public good," one that normally benefits a large group. It can be logically proven that rational, self-interested individuals do not make voluntary sacrifices, even through support of public interest lobbies, to provide themselves with public goods, or with a sufficient supply of them. So, characteristically, the minority that particularly benefits from a given policy or industry is organized, whereas the public at large with a significant but diffuse interest in the matter is not. As a result, we can expect that societies will sometimes persist in policies that are clearly pernicious. A policy that was initially chosen out of ignorance and innocence may be maintained by organized vested interests long after its ill effects have been recognized [10].

Reduced to its roots, this theory or model of man rests on two premises about his nature: (a) crass selfishness and (b) utter distrust of his fellow human beings. These, then, account (a) for the exclusively self-regarding nature of individual satisfactions that underlies economic reasoning about human choices where separate interests are clearly discernible, and (b) for the "free rider" problem where common interests are at stake.*

But this model of human behavior falls far short of doing justice to the majesty and sovereignty of the human spirit. This is a point to which we shall return at the end.

LIMITS TO REGULATION AND ITS HEAVY-HANDEDNESS

"None of the broad pollution problems are simple," says Myrdal [11]. In making this point, however, Myrdal focuses his critical examination on the other horn of the dilemma, pointing out the limitations inherent in the alternative generic solution, viz., government intervention and regulatory action. He reminds us of "the very narrow limits for effective planning and plan implementation in our type of national communities," the common desire of people for a

---

*In other words, the problem that, given a large number of individuals, none will engage in any voluntary sacrifice or self-restraining action for the common good because (a) he can't be sure that other will do likewise, and (b) his own near-infinitely small contribution to the common effort won't make any difference to the overall outcome, whether most of the others do or don't comply with the joint-action imperative.

higher quality of life, but "without any infringement on all their other desires" while, unhappily, "policy measures. . . to preserve and improve our environment will regularly restrain people's freedom to do what they please." Hence the ensuing necessity for "huge policing and controlling administration which would be. . . too expensive and also too obnoxious to the people": in short, the very limited "practicability of exerting authority to discipline the behavior of masses of people" which Myrdal feels is already now (in 1972) severly hampering policy" [12].

Yet, Myrdal concludes, even though people be ignorant, short-sighted and narrowminded, *"to some extent they can be brought to act against what they have become accustomed to feel to be in their own short-term interests"* [emphasis supplied]. For, as Myrdal reminds us in his conclusion, "Economics itself is a moral science [13].

This may yet turn out to be the clue to finding almost any solution to environmental problems: to make people understand and care.

THE ETHICAL IMPERATIVE—A MATTER OF SELF-INTEREST

In 1975, a well known photographer-journalist couple, W. Eugene and Aileen M. Smith, published a full-length picture story, observed firsthand over several years, of a severe case of local water pollution and its long-drawn out and tragic aftermath, *Minamata* [14]. It spans a nearly 25-year history of the success and growth of a chemical corporation in a southern Japanese fishing town, the appearance of a "strange disease" crippling and killing townspeople, the gradual discovery and growing certainty of its cause: the plant's poisonous industrial waste consumed by local fish, caught and eaten by the town's inhabitants. It relates the initial attempts at suppression of the evidence, the grudging and niggardly concession of compensation to a limited number of victims, the ugly attempts at stilling voices of conscience, the internecine struggles between workers fearful for their livelihood and others determined to seek recognition of and compensation for their own and their families' deprivation, suffering, and premature death; the cowardly evasiveness of officialdom; and the personal valor and sacrifice of some private citizens leading to ultimate victory in the courts. The legal judgment in the Minamate case may be deemed quite out of the ordinary because of the verdict's reference to social ethics, rather than to statutory or customary gauges of liability:

... No plant can be permitted to infringe on and run at the sacrifice of the lives and health of regional residents .... The defendant's plant discharged acetaldehyde waste water with negligence at all times, and even though the quality and content of the waste water of the defendant's plant satisfied statutory limitations and administrative standards, and even if the treatment methods it employed were superior to those taken at the work yards of other companies in the same industry, these are not enough ... the defendant cannot escape from the liability of negligence [15].

The Smiths would go even further: "The morality that pollution is criminal only after legal conviction is the morality that causes pollution" [16].

One of several recent collections of essays on environmental problems stands out by addressing, among others, the problem of "environmental ethics." The author, Roderick Nash, tends to view "*mind* pollution" as the worst of all types of pollution on the ground that "the root problem in man-environment relations does not involve what man *does* so much as what he *thinks* and, more precisely, what he *values* [17]. Nash holds that a perception of community based on a sense of oneness with the universe is a prerequisite for environmental ethics, and that "ethics must underlie the environmental movement .... Conservation must become a matter of morality, not merely a matter of economics or aesthetics or even of law. We must be concerned ... because it is right" [18].

How does this concern for the "right" and for the welfare of the whole community relate to the much vaunted instinct of narrowly conceived self-interest that has been said earlier to stand in the way of even the most all-around beneficial collective action? At least two among many prominent answers to this question are worth citing. They were given about 130 years apart, would appear to start from opposite assumptions, and yet produce not only compatibility between individual and community interest (or "the right") but imply the necessity of their complementarity. Cf. Kenneth Boulding (1966):

... the welfare of the individual depends on the extent to which he can identify himself with others and ... the most satisfactory individual identifies not only with a community in space but also with a community extending over time from the past into the future ... a society which loses its identity with posterity and which loses its positive image of the future loses also its capacity to deal with present problems, and soon falls apart.

And Alexis de Tocqueville (1835):

If you do not succeed in connecting the notion of right with that of personal interest, which is the only immutable point in the human heart, what means will you have of governing the world except by fear? [20]

Exactly 20 years before the Smiths published their photographic documentary, another distinguished pair of photographer-writer collaborators had brought us the unforgettable worldwide exhibit, *The Family of Man*. Carl Sandburg wrote in his prologue: "There is only one man in the world and his name is All Men. . . ." Its cover and ever-recurrent theme-photograph of the roguish young piper carried as its subscript the Pueblo Indian saying, "We shall be one person." [21] In subscribing to this proposition, one might add, by way of explanation: We shall be one person either in deference to the ethical imperative, or out of the most crass self-interest, once we understand where it lies.

NOTES TO THE EPILOGUE

1. John Maurice Clark, *A Preface to Social Economics—Essays on Economic Theory and Social Problems* (New York: Augustus M. Kelly Reprint, 1967), p. 76.

2. Robert S. McNamara, Annual Address to the World Bank's Board of Governors, quoted in "The UN at 30," *New York Times Supplement* (October 26, 1975), p. 20.

3. Cf. George F. Rohrlich, "The Potential of *Social* Ecology for Economic Science," *Review of Social Economy* 31 (April 1973): 31–39.

4. H. G. Rickover (1969), as quoted by Lewis W. Montcrief, "The Cultural Basis for Our Environmental Crisis," in *Science* 170, p. 511.

5. *Technology Assessment and Quality of Life*, Proceedings of the Fourth General Conference of SAINT, September 1972, Gerhard J. Stöber and Dieter Schumacher, eds. (Amsterdam, London, New York: Elsevier Scientific Publishing Company, 1973). *Passim*, but especially, Francois Hetman, "Social Objectives and New Desirable Technologies," pp. 42 ff.

6. Gunnar Myrdal, "Economics of an Improved Environment," Lecture delivered in the Distinguished Lecture Series, sponsored by the International Institute for Environmental Affairs with the support of the Population Institute, held in connection with the United Nations Conference on the Human Environment, Stockholm, June 8, 1972, Processed, pp. 15–16.

7. *Ibid.*, p. 17.

8. Cf. Mancur Olson and H. H. Landsberg, eds., *The No-Growth Society* (New York: Norton & Co., 1973), p. 230.

9. Cf., e.g., Mancur Olson, *The Logic of Collective Action* (Cambridge: Harvard University Press, 1965), and James M. Buchanan and Gordon Tullock, *The Calculus of Consent* (Ann Arbor: University of Michigan Press, 1962), *Passim*.

10. *The No-Growth Society*, *op. cit.*, p. 238.

11. Myrdal, *loc. cit.*, p. 29.

12. *Ibid.*, pp. 25, 21, 9, and again 21.

13. *Ibid*, p. 30.

14. W. Eugene Smith and Aileen M. Smith, *Minamata: The Story of the Poisoning of a City and of the People Who Chose to Carry the Burden of Courage.* (New York: Holt, Rinehart and Winston, 1975).

15. Minamata, *op. cit.*, p. 129.

16. *Ibid*, p. 171.

17. Roderic Nash, "Environmental Ethics," Ch. 10 (p. 142), in *Environmental Spectrum: Social and Economic Views on the Quality of Life*, ed. Ronald O. Clarke and Peter C. List (New York: D. Van Nostrand Co., 1974).

18. *Ibid.*, p. 155.

19. Kenneth Boulding, *"The Economics of the Coming Spaceship Earth,"* orginally published in *Environmental Quality in a Growing Economy*, ed. Henry Jarret (Baltimore: Johns Hopkins Press, 1966). The present quotation is taken from a reprint in *The Environmental Handbook*, ed. Garrett de Bell (New York: Ballentine Books, 1970), pp. 99–100.

20. Alexis de Tocquiville, *Democracy in America*, as quoted by Allen V. Kneese in "Strategies for Environmental Management," *Public Policy* 19 (Winter 1971): 39.

21. Edward Steichen, *The Family of Man* (New York: Museum of Modern Art, 1955), pp. 3 and 15.

Index

About the Editor

George F. Rohrlich is a social economist. Born in Austria, and a graduate of the University of Vienna, Dr. Rohrlich emigrated to the U.S. in 1939, and received his Ph.D. from Harvard. He has spent many years in national and international public service in socioeconomic planning and programming positions. During World War II Dr. Rohrlich served with the Office of Strategic Services and, later, the Department of State, and following the war was on General MacArthur's staff in Japan. He has also been a senior staff member of the International Labour Office in Geneva, Switzerland, and has held high level positions with the U.S. Social Security Administration, the Department of Labor and the President's Commission on Veterans Pensions. In recent years he has taught social economics and policy at the University of Chicago, Columbia University and Temple University. During the academic year 1975–1976, while on leave from Temple, he has been serving as director of research of a socioeconomic planning commission established by the Puerto Rican legislature in San Juan, Puerto Rico. Dr. Rohrlich's publications include *Social Economics—Concepts and Perspectives*, Monograph No. 2, International Institute of Social Economics (Hull, U.K.: Emmasglen, Academic Publishers, 1974); *Social Economics for the 1970's*: Programs for Social Security, Health and Manpower (Cambridge, Mass.: University Press, 1970); *Veterans' Non-Service-Connected Pensions* (Washington, D.C.: U.S. Government Printing Office, 1956); and *Pensions in the United States* (Washington, D.C.: U.S. Government Printing Office, 1952); as well as many other monographs and journal articles.

About the Contributors

R. Lisle Baker, a specialist in environmental law and land use control, received his A.B. degree cum laude from Williams College and his LL.B. cum laude from Harvard Law School. From 1968 to 1973 he was an associate with the Boston firm of Hill & Barlow, except for a leave of absence in 1969—1970 when he was an Advocate on the public television program "The Advocates." He is presently an associate professor of law at Suffolk University Law School, and is chairman of the Environment Committee of the Boston Bar Association.

Carolyn Shaw Bell, who received her Ph.D. from London University, holds the Katharine Coman Chair of Economics at Wellesley College. Her studies of income and its disposition have included marketing (*Consumer Choice in the American Economy* [New York: Random House, 1967]); specific groups within the economy (*The Economics of the Ghetto* [New York Press: Pegasus, 1971]); "Working Women's Contribution to Family Income" (*Eastern Economic Journal* I:2—3 [1974]); and the relevant unit, "Should Every Job Support A Family?" (*The Public Interest*, Summer 1975). Aside from lecturing, radio and television commentary, and writing, her professional commitments include chairing the Federal Advisory Council on Unemployment Insurance, and serving on the Executive Committee of the American Economic Association, the Board of Overseers of the Amos Tuck Graduate School of Business Administration at Dartmouth College, the Board of Trustees of the Joint Council on Economic Education, and other bodies.

Joseph F. Coates, who holds degrees from the Brooklyn Polytechnic Institute, Pennsylvania State University, and the University of Pennsylvania, is assistant to the director of the Office of Technology Assessment of the U.S. Congress. He began his career as a chemist, but has developed major professional and avocational interests in planning for the future. The impact of technology on society is one of his principal concerns. He has also served as program manager for technology assessment at the National Science Foundation, senior staff member of the Institute of Defense Analyses, and secretary of the General Section of the American Association for the Advancement of Science.

Steven Ebbin's varied professional life has encompassed academics, government, business, research, administration consulting and writing, most recently as chairman of the interdisciplinary team that wrote the *Logan Airport Master Plan Study*, published in late 1975. His government experience includes assignments with the Department of State and the U.S.I.A., as assistant to the majority leader in the U.S. Senate and as staff director of the Senate Subcommittee on Research and Development of the Government Operations Committee. He has served as a consultant to state and regional governments, to the New York Stock Exchange, and to several federal agencies, including the Environmental Protection Agency and the Department of Health, Education and Welfare, on science policy, population and environmental education, energy policy, international affairs and other matters.

Mason Gaffney is presently executive director of the British Columbia Institute for Analysis of Economic Policy. He has published extensively and is a frequent participant and contributor to the National Tax Association and the American Real Estate and Urban Economics Association. His major books and articles include *Concepts of Financial Maturity of Timber and Other Assets*, Agricultural Economics Information Series No. 62 (Raleigh: North Carolina State College, 1957; 2nd printing, 1960); *Extractive Resources and Taxation* (Madison: University of Wisconsin Press, 1967); "What Kind of Cities Do We Want?" *The Nation's Cities*, April 1967, entire issue; "Better Assessments for Better Cities," *The Nation's Cities*, May 1970, entire issue; "When to Build What: The Timing and Sizing of Public Works," in Paul Downing, ed., *The Pricing of Local Services and Effects on Urban Spatial Structure* (Vancouver: U.B.C. Press, 1975); "An Agenda for Strengthening the Property Tax," in George Peterson, ed., *Property Tax Reform* (Washington, D.C.: The Urban

Institute, 1973); and "More Jobs With Less Land, No More Capital, and No Inflation," in Arthur Lynn, Jr., ed., *Property Taxation, Land Use, and Public Policy* (Madison: University of Wisconsin Press, 1975).

Walter A. Hahn has attended New York, American and Syracuse universities and holds degrees in physical science and public administration. Positions with the National Academy of Sciences–National Research Council, the General Electric Company and the National Aeronautics and Space Administration preceded his appointment in 1969 as deputy assistant secretary of commerce for science and technology, a position he held until selected as senior research associate on the White House National Goals Research Staff. Presently he is senior specialist in Science and Technology with the Congressional Research Service of the Library of Congress. In 1975 Hahn, on a "reverse sabbatical" leave, was visiting professor of public technology policy and engineering in the Program for the Social Management of Technology at the University of Washington.

Edwin T. Haefele, a native of Illinois, was educated at Illinois Wesleyan University and the University of Chicago. He has held appointments with the Public Administration Clearing House, Northwestern University, The Brookings Institution, Resources for the Future, and is now professor of Political Science, University of Pennsylvania. He is author of *Representative Government and Environmental Management, Government Controls on Transport; an African Case*, and editor of *The Governance of Common Property Resources* and *Transport and National Goals*.

Hazel Henderson is an author, social critic and activist. She is codirector of the Princeton Center for Alternative Futures, Inc., of Princeton, New Jersey, a member of the advisory council to the U.S. Congress Office of Technology Assessment; the National Research Council Committee on Public Engineering Policy, National Academy of Sciences; and a director of the Council on Economic Priorities of New York, as well as advisor to other public interest organizations. Her articles have appeared in such journals as *Harvard Business Review, The Annals of the American Academy of Political and Social Science, Saturday Review, Financial Analysts Journal, Columbia Journal of World Business, Business Economics* and *The Futurist*.

Byron Kennard is a community organizer with ten years experience in helping civic and consumer groups involve themselves in public policy debates. Mr. Kennard is now chairman of the National

Council for the Public Assessment of Technology, a nonprofit research and education organization devoted to securing greater public participation in science policy and technological development.

Chester D. Kylstra is currently technical director of the Carrying Capacity Project, developing a holistic, general energy systems land use planning tool. He is an associate professor of Nuclear Engineering Sciences at the University of Florida, and is affiliated with the Environmental Engineering Sciences Department via a courtesy appointment. Past efforts include various preliminary feasibility and systems studies on the U.S. nuclear power system, offshore nuclear power plants, waste heat disposal, plus other energy and economic problems.

J. M. (Levi) Leathers is executive vice president and director of Operations for Dow Chemical U.S.A. and a vice president and member of the board of directors of The Dow Chemical Company. He also serves as a member of the board of directors of Dow Chemical Investment and Finance Company, a wholly owned Dow subsidiary involved in venture capital investments; Dow Badische Company, Williamsburg, Virginia, a Dow-associated company; and the Missouri Pacific Railroad Company. He is a graduate of Sam Houston State College, Huntsville, Texas, and was presented an honorary doctor of engineering degree in 1972 by Michigan Technological University, Houghton, Michigan. He is a member of the American Chemical Society and the American Institute of Chemical Engineers.

Morton Levy, a graduate of Northeastern University, has been a certified public accountant since 1954. He is founder and executive director of Accountants for the Public Interest. A member of the American Institute of CPAs and California Society of CPAs, and partner in the firm of Harb, Levy & Weiland, San Francisco, he is a former instructor at Golden Gate University. He currently is a member of the advisory board of National Council for the Public Assessment of Technology, and on the board of trustees of the San Francisco Mental Health Association.

Sam Love is a writer and activist in the environmental field. In 1970 he served as one of the coordinators of Earth Day. From 1970 until 1974 he worked with Environmental Action, a national political action organization, as coordinator and editor of its magazine. His articles on energy and environmental topics have appeared in such magazines as *The Futurist, Progressive, Smithsonian, Washingtonian,*

Business and Society Review and *Skeptic.* He serves as a visiting professor at Goddard College's Social Ecology Institute.

Carl H. Madden, chief economist of the Chamber of Commerce of the United States since 1964, earlier served as dean of the College of Business Administration of Lehigh University in Bethlehem, Pennsylvania, and at the Federal Reserve Bank of New York in its public information function. Dr. Madden was educated at the University of Virginia, attended the Harvard Law School, and is a graduate of the Stonier Graduate School of Banking. He has been president of the National Association of Business Economists, is a director of the World Future Society, and is a trustee of the Joint Council on Economic Education.

William L. Mobraaten is vice president and treasurer of the American Telephone and Telegraph Company, responsible for the financial program of the nationwide Bell System. In this capacity, he oversees the annual external financing program. In addition, he administers the decisionmaking process that determines the type of financing the various Bell units will undertake and directs the financial operations of the AT&T company, including its vast stock and bond division, which acts as transfer agent for all Bell System securities. He is a native of Wendell, Minnesota, and a graduate of Harvard. Before assuming his present duties in July 1973, he was vice president–administration of the Pacific Telephone and Telegraph Company.

Henry M. Peskin is a fellow with Resources for the Future, Inc., and was formerly senior research associate of the National Bureau of Economic Research and on the staffs of the Central Bureau of Statistics of Norway, the Institute for Defense Analyses, Mathematics, Inc., the U.S. Office of Emergency Preparedness, and the Urban Institute. He also taught at Princeton University and the George Washington University. He studied chemical engineering at the Massachusetts Institute of Technology and received a B.A. in Political Science from Wesleyan University. He did postgraduate work at Princeton University and received his Ph.D. in economics. His research and publications are in the areas of cost-benefit analysis, econometrics and environmental economics.

Sheldon W. Samuels is director, Health, Safety and Environment Affairs, for the Industrial Union Department, AFL–CIO. He is a founding member of the Society for Occupational and Environmental Health, serves on the faculty of the Mount Sinai School of

Medicine, and represents the labor movement on the National Advisory Committee of the Blue Cross Association and the U.S. Department of Commerce Technical Advisory Board, and as a consultant to the National Institute for Environmental Health Sciences and the National Cancer Institute. He has served as an advisor to the Ohio OSHA program, the National Academy of Sciences, the National Health Council, and other academic and governmental institutions. Formerly chief of field services for the Air Pollution Control Office of the Environmental Protection Agency, and a pioneer in the area of federal, state and citizen roles in environmental action, he has also developed and taught courses at the State University of New York at Cortland and at Fulton-Montgomery Community College, and founded and was director of the Institute on Environment and Health conducted by the State University at Whiteface Mountain.

Thomas F. Williams is currently serving as director, Technical Information Staff, Office of Solid Waste Management Programs, U.S. Environmental Protection Agency. Mr. Williams has been working to involve the public in environmental decisionmaking since 1957. Prior to creation of the EPA, he served as director of public affairs of the Consumer Protection and Environmental Health Service and as director of public information for the Federal Air Pollution Program in the Department of HEW. In 1967, he received the Silver Anvil Award of the Public Relations Society of America for outstanding public service; in 1968, the Superior Service Award of the Department of HEW for creating broad public awareness of the threat of air pollution; in 1969, a Distinguished Service Award from Southern Illinois University for his contributions to environmental improvement; and, in 1974, EPA's Bronze Medal for promoting greater participation between citizen groups and the scientific community of solid waste management.